The M.E. Sharpe Library of
Franklin D. Roosevelt Studies

Volume Two

The M.E. Sharpe Library of
Franklin D. Roosevelt Studies

Franklin D. Roosevelt and Congress
The New Deal and Its Aftermath

Volume Two

Thomas P. Wolf,
William D. Pederson,
and Byron W. Daynes
Editors

M.E. Sharpe
Armonk, New York
London, England

Library of Congress Cataloging-in-Publication Data

Franklin D. Roosevelt and Congress : the New Deal and its aftermath / edited by Thomas
Phillip Wolf, William D. Pederson, and Byron W. Daynes.
    p.cm.
  Based on presentation made at a conference at Louisiana State University at
Shreveport in September 1995.
  Includes bibliographical references (p.) and index.
  ISBN 0-7656-0622-4 (alk. paper)
    1. Roosevelt, Franklin D. (Franklin Delano), 1882–1945—Congresses. 2. United
States—Politics and government—1933–1945—Congresses. 3. United States—
Congress—History—20th century—Congresses. 4. Legislators—United
States—History—20th century—Congresses. 5. New Deal, 1933–1939—Congresses. I.
Wolf, Thomas Phillip, 1933– II. Pederson, William D., 1946– III. Daynes, Byron W.

E806 .F6915 2000
973.917—dc21   99-087719

CONTENTS

Section III: Looking at the Record Fifty Years Later

ACKNOWLEDGEMENTS

The editors wish to express their gratitude to those responsible for sponsoring and funding the 1995 conference, "FDR After 50 Years," at Louisiana State University at Shreveport. Without that support this volume would not have appeared.

Portions of Matthew Coulter's chapter have been published in *Senate Munitions Inquiry of the 1930s: Beyond the Merchants of Death* (Greenwood Press, 1997). Permission has been given by Coulter and Greenwood Press to publish those portions in this volume.

Thomas P. Wolf takes this opportunity to indicate his professional debt to three persons who were instrumental to his career: the late Marvin "Mike" Harder, who inspired Wolf to become a political scientist and sparked his initial fascination with Franklin D. Roosevelt; Heinz Eulau, who judiciously and with prompt attention served as dissertation chairperson many years ago; and John Bunzel, who rendered most helpful advice at a critical stage in Wolf's early career.

Secretarial assistance from the School of Social Sciences at Indiana University Southeast was crucial to this work, especially that of Ms. Brigette Colligan. She had a persistent hand in the completion of this work, implementing numerous revisions that the editors made and noting flaws that they missed.

Indiana University Southeast provided a grant that facilitated preparation of this book. With those funds, we had the assistance of Virginia Lee Bruce and Patrick Smith, who provided valuable service on this project.

Many questions of fact were resolved by the efforts of the Indiana University Southeast Library's reference staff: Nancy Totten, Martin Rosen, Jacqueline Johnson, Gabrielle Carr and Dennis Kreps.

We are grateful for the contributions of each of these persons at Indiana University Southeast, as well as those of the institution.

The M.E. Sharpe Library of
Franklin D. Roosevelt Studies

Volume Two

INTRODUCTION

THOMAS PHILLIP WOLF

The studies in this volume were originally presented at a conference at Louisiana State University at Shreveport in September 1995. One of the Shreveport campus's conferences on American presidents, it commemorated the passage of a half century since Franklin Delano Roosevelt's death at Warm Springs, Georgia in April 1945.

FDR's presidency remains one of the most significant, not just in the twentieth century, but in our nation's history. Although lacking a grand scheme or single plan to transform the role of the national government, the incremental measures adopted during the New Deal administration changed the federal government's role to a degree unmatched in American history.

President Roosevelt was both revered and despised. He was castigated by his critics for actions they deemed dictatorial. The more radical sector of the political spectrum on the left was often disenchanted that he did not use his presidency vigorously to undermine the power of the upper classes. But most Americans found his approach on the mark. He introduced his programs to the public in a speaking voice that reassured vast numbers of the electorate.

Probably the most realistic approach to assessing a leader is to compare him with others of similar stature and historical period. In the second quarter of the century, Roosevelt was joined on the world stage by a coterie of national leaders who were international figures, perhaps without parallel in any other era: Germany's Adolf Hitler, the Soviet Union's Josef Stalin, Britain's Winston Churchill, and Italy's Benito Mussolini. FDR's presidency ran parallel to Hitler's reign—both gained national office in early 1933 and died within days of each other in April 1945. Their styles and the consequences of their leadership could hardly have been more different: Hitler did achieve short-term economic resurgence for Germany, followed by territorial expansion, but led his nation to ultimate defeat and destruction accompanied by the loss of tens of millions of lives.

In contrast, although there were actions today considered to be inexcusable, such as the unconstitutional internment of Japanese Americans, Franklin Roosevelt left the United States as the most militarily powerful and prosperous nation on the globe. It is worth noting as well that he did this while maintaining the basic mechanism of a democratic society: elections. Presidential and congressional elections were held in 1940 and 1944, as well as congressional elections in 1942. That may not seem remarkable, but the other major democratic nation and one that is often considered a model of representative government, Great Britain, suspended elections during World War II. There were no parliamentary elections in Britain from 1935 until 1945, although by statute one should have been held no later than 1940.

None of the substantive chapters present the range of programs and the overall impact of the New Deal. Many governmental initiatives that became commonplace in the following decades were ground-shaking when first enacted in the 1930s. Among those were Social Security; the construction and operation of massive reclamation and hydroelectric projects, perhaps the most notable of which are the Tennessee Valley Authority, Hoover (originally Boulder) Dam, and Grand Coulee Dam; programs to provide assistance to the poor, especially children; and government agencies to assist the unemployed in finding jobs. In the 1940s, a massive buildup of American military power was launched; despite occasional cutbacks, the United States maintained a military presence far beyond that in the years before FDR became president. Of course, the continuation of this military prominence was dictated by events after his death: the cold war. For numerous reasons, life in the United States was markedly altered by FDR's presidency.

To many readers, FDR's presidency is in the distant past. It is likely that even those who experienced the Great Depression and World War II will not recall several of the individuals mentioned in subsequent chapters. Therefore, appendices have been compiled to assist readers.

This anthology with ten substantive chapters, plus supplementary materials, examines the reactions of particular groups both within Congress and beyond, as well as those of individual congressmen. In addition, three retrospective pieces examine facets of the New Deal era from longitudinal perspectives.

Richard Lowitt's chapter about Roosevelt and the Progressive Republicans alludes to the political cross currents that have been examined in numerous doctoral dissertations and published works over the last half-century. The Progressives, whose membership transcended party lines, were ideological allies of Franklin Roosevelt, but Republicans among Progressive ranks often found it difficult to support the president. Lowitt explores this problem with a few brief cases: the controversy over the 1934 election contest between Bronson Cutting and Dennis Chavez,[1] FDR's apparent support for the reelection of Republicans Hiram Johnson and Robert LaFollette Jr.,[2] the president's "court-packing" proposal, and his foreign policy. Only George Norris stood by Roosevelt consistently. The other Progressive Republicans, although in sympathy with his domestic policy, gradually split with him.

In chapter 2, Dennis N. Mihelich addresses the efforts of another group, the "Mavericks," that sought to work with and influence New Deal policy. They differed from the Lowitt's Progressive Republicans on key traits: (1) They were congressmen, not senators; (2) they were more radical; (3) they were less experienced in congressional politics, having been elected in 1934. Although their numbers were fewer, the agenda they produced can be characterized as a mirror image of that of the Republican freshmen elected sixty years later. Just as those Republicans considered their senior party members to be overly cautious and insufficiently conservative, the "Congressional Mavericks" entering the House in 1935 thought their seniors were insufficiently liberal. Perhaps ironically, since most were Democrats, the Mavericks proved less successful than did the Progressive Republicans in achieving their goals and maintaining durable ties with the White House. The generic meaning of the word "maverick" is a range calf that has lost its mother. If Mihelich's Mavericks expected Franklin Roosevelt to offer parentage, they were disappointed: They remained orphans.

While the Lowitt and Mihelich chapters focus on informal groups in Congress, Matthew Coulter scrutinizes a formal one, the controversial Senate Special Committee on Investigations of the Munitions Industry, better known as the Nye Committee for its chairman, Senator Gerald P. Nye, Republican of North Dakota. Coulter assesses contrasting interpretations, both contemporary and subsequent, of President Roosevelt's relations with the Nye Committee. As Lewis Carroll might describe it, the situation became "curiouser and curiouser," beginning with a major Senate committee chaired by a member of the minority party in that chamber. The president's posture toward the investigation of World War I profiteering by the American munitions industry was contradictory and no doubt influenced by the turbulent international climate his presidency endured. Parallels with American temperament during early years of the cold war are evident both in actions of the 1930s and in analyses of that behavior.

Marc Dollinger's chapter moves beyond the confines of Congress as he chronicles the response of the American Jewish community to the New Deal. From the 1650s until the 1930s, this community was dedicated to rejecting government assistance. Instead, American Jews would take care of the needs of their people through their own efforts. They created an impressive array of philanthropic organizations to serve the welfare needs of their ethnic brethren and sisters. Dollinger traces the eventual about-face on this issue, along with rejection of the Stuyvesant Pledge that committed Jews to refusing public welfare. The Great Depression overwhelmed noble private efforts, and New Deal programs were eventually accepted by American Jewry as an appropriate solution. Although Dollinger does not explore it, this change of mind had another significant consequence: The shift in policy orientation was concomitant with one in voting behavior, as two groups, Jews and blacks, that until the New Deal were not aligned with the Democratic Party, became firm supporters of that party.

In the opening chapter of Part II, Anthony Champagne demonstrates how Sam Rayburn, a recognized giant among congressional leaders, skillfully pursued a career that enabled him to serve his district well, rise to a position of leadership, and maintain friendly relations with often bitter foes. Rayburn achieved all this while serving throughout his congressional career—except when he was Speaker—on only one committee, the seemingly unimportant one of Interstate and Foreign Commerce. Although Rayburn's ties to the White House were strained by his support of his close friend, John Nance Garner, for president in 1940, and, more important, by his staunch belief in congressional independence from the executive branch, Rayburn was influential in achieving New Deal goals. Usually those reflected his own preferences. Champagne reveals the complexity confronting Rayburn in weighing the factors that influenced his actions during the New Deal portion of his near half century in Congress.

Nancy Beck Young's chapter is about another legendary Texas congressman, Wright Patman. His legislative style could hardly have been more different from Rayburn's. The latter pursued his well-known advice that in order to "get along" (achieve positions of significance and power in the House) one had to "go along" (not create controversy or challenge the customary ways of the House). Patman, instead, sharply challenged the expectation that junior members of Congress quietly wait their turn in power. In a pattern that would recur in the 1970s and again in the 1990s, Patman promptly gained national attention with his skillful public relations in advocating passage of the veterans bonus and restructuring of the Federal Reserve system.

His program was not as expansive as that of Newt Gingrich, but it was at least as visible. In the congressional minority during the Hoover years, Patman was unable to advance his proposals. Once Democrats controlled Capitol Hill and the White House, he moved quickly. In pursuit of his goals, he received the support of controversial allies, such as Father Charles E. Coughlin. Patman's efforts were effective with the veterans bonus bill but not in reform of the Federal Reserve.

During the first decade of his congressional service, his career illustrates the impact of one individual who, by writing books and speaking widely, supplements the customary techniques of marshaling support for new public policies. Well before there was a receptive Congress, he put his proposals before the public. Eventually he got them on the national agenda, where he was partially successful in getting them enacted into law.

The subject of Joseph Edward Lee's chapter is a far less well-known member of Congress. Yet, James P. Richards' vote on revision of the Neutrality Act in 1941 may be more characteristic of the factors that influence the typical congressman than are the careers of prominent figures such as Sam Rayburn and Wright Patman. Although a loyal supporter of President Roosevelt and not a pacifist, Richards abandoned his president, his party, and fellow members of the South Carolina congressional delegation in opposing amendment of the Neutrality Act. In Lee's analysis, one also has clues to the factors that would lead to the growing estrangement of Southern Democrats from their party's national agenda.

In Part III, three legacies of the New Deal are explored. Two studies are about electoral patterns; the final one is about the effort to achieve full employment by legislative mandate, an implicit and eventually explicit goal of the New Deal. The three studies also question scholarly interpretations of matters arising from the New Deal era.

"The 1938 Purge: A Reexamination" takes on what has become part of the conventional wisdom of American politics: Franklin Roosevelt's efforts to "purge" his party of uncooperative incumbents was a failure. The analysis in the chapter contends that this conclusion is based on a faulty expectation of success in politics and that the criteria used to reach this conclusion are contrary to those customarily employed by scholars in evaluating congressional elections. Moreover, if this issue is examined from a broader perspective—that of presidential intervention, rather than purging—the 1938 effort was at least moderately successful.

Stefano Luconi traces a scholarly examination of partisan realignment, a concept that is often applied to the origins of the New Deal electoral mandate. Luconi documents the academic and journalistic disagreement about whether a subsequent realignment has occurred, an event that, according to some realignment theories, should have happened by the 1970s. Luconi shows that even in the 1990s there is no clear electoral pattern that conclusively confirms a realignment.

The lengthiest chapter in this book is by Arthur R. Williams, Karl F. Johnson, and Michael P. Barrett, who seek to understand why the Employment Act of 1946 did not, in fact, include a requirement for full employment. Although this is not the first scholarly effort to analyze this omission from the act, the authors find the interpretations thus far to be unpersuasive. In what they term a preliminary examination of this issue, they reject a handful of previously postulated explanations, most notably that President Truman provided inadequate legislative leadership and that full employment was impractical in 1946. Instead, they suggest, in 1946 and earlier attempts to enact full employment, racism was the primary determinant of legislative failure.

Luconi's conclusion will not surprise students of American elections. Indeed, he documents the numerous scholarly efforts to explain realignment or, as some have concluded, dealignment. In contrast, the other chapters of Part III offer fresh interpretations of matters for which standard explanations have been long accepted. To paraphrase a slogan from the 1992 presidential election campaign, Wolf says "It's the criteria, stupid!" Whether Roosevelt's 1938 purge was a success or not rests on the standards by which it is evaluated.

The ten substantive chapters in this volume constitute a fresh set of perspectives about a key period in modern American politics. They illuminate the impact of individuals and of groups, as well as long-term trends.

NOTES

1. On the Cutting and Chavez contest, see T.P. Wolf, "Cutting versus Chavez Re-Examined: A Commentary on Pickens' Analysis," *New Mexico Historical Review* 47, no. 4 (October 1972), 317–336, and T.P. Wolf, "Bronson Cutting and Franklin Roosevelt: Factors in Presidential Endorsement," ibid., 52, no. 4 (October 1977), 317–334.

2. Wolf, "Bronson Cutting," pp. 324–328.

I

FDR and Groups

CHAPTER ONE

Roosevelt and Progressive Republicans:
Friends and Foes

RICHARD LOWITT

At 10:00 A.M. on March 11, 1931, Senator George W. Norris, Republican of Nebraska, called to order a Conference of Progressives at the Carlton Hotel in Washington, D.C. The conference was to outline a program of constructive legislation dealing with economic and political conditions to be presented to the first session of the seventy-second Congress. It was called by Norris and four other progressive senators: Edward P. Costigan, Colorado; Bronson M. Cutting, New Mexico; Robert M. LaFollette Jr., Wisconsin; and Burton K. Wheeler, Montana. Wheeler and Costigan were Democrats. All but LaFollette were from the West. In a brief statement Wheeler outlined the conference objective in part as follows.

> In the midst of depression, the nation is without effective political or economic leadership.
>
> The session now drawing to a close has revealed the imperative need for formulating a constructive legislative program. Months of misery in the industrial centers and on the farms have disclosed lack of any proposals for the solution of one of the greatest economic crises ever confronting the nation.
>
> The signers of this call believe that there are certain economic and political problems affecting the welfare of every citizen which must be solved if this Republic is to endure.[1]

Also speaking at the conference were John J. Blaine, Wisconsin; William E. Borah, Idaho; Smith W. Bookhart, Iowa; and Gerald P. Nye, North Dakota; all Republicans. Two Democratic congressmen—David J. Lewis, Maryland, and George Huddleston, Alabama—also participated. Others wired their regrets, including Governor Franklin Roosevelt. He expressed interest, but owing to New York's legislative situation, could not attend.

In one way or another, all who attended this two-day conference agreed that governmental bungling had brought misery and ruin to many Americans and that the only way to restore the economy was through a complete change of government policy. In the course of his remarks, Norris commented that even with a progressive Congress, little could be achieved while "the engineer is in the White House." He added that "what we do need in order to bring prosperity and happiness to the common individual is another [Theodore] Roosevelt in the White House." But, he believed, there was "little hope of electing a President of the United States who is progressive."[2]

In 1932 when FDR received his party's nomination, progressives in general flocked to his candidacy. A Progressive League headed by Charles A. Beard, with Norris serving as honorary chairman, championed his cause and did so again in both 1936 and 1940. Four prominent Republican senators broke ranks in 1932 and campaigned for Roosevelt. Three—Norris, Cutting, and LaFollette—had helped organize the 1931 Conference of Progressives. The fourth, Hiram Johnson of California, was Theodore Roosevelt's running mate on the 1912 Progressive Party ticket. What I propose to do in this chapter primarily is to examine the relationship of these four senators with Roosevelt, in order to understand the attraction of progressive senators, most of whom were from the West, to FDR and the New Deal.

In the case of George W. Norris, the relationship was a reciprocal one. Both men admired and genuinely liked one another. Norris quite enthusiastically supported most New Deal domestic measures, less so those in foreign policy, but he broke only in 1941 when he voted against extending the draft to include eighteen-year-olds. When he criticized—usually in the case of appointments—he blamed James A. Farley, Postmaster General and Democratic National Committee chairman, for placing patronage and partisanship above principle and the national interest. In 1932 Norris engaged in an extensive campaign tour on behalf of the Democratic candidate. He started in Philadelphia and concluded in Los Angeles. On his way home to McCook, he stopped briefly in Denver to join Senator Edward Costigan in again endorsing Roosevelt's candidacy.

Meanwhile, FDR, returning home from his extensive campaign tour of the Pacific Coast, stopped off in McCook. To the best of my knowledge Roosevelt never spoke as glowingly about another living individual as he did about Norris on a late September afternoon before the largest crowd that ever assembled in that small Nebraska community. Let me quote from Roosevelt's remarks:

> We should remember that the ultimate analysis of history asks the answer to questions which are not concerned so much with what you and I, in these modern days, call ballyhoo, or headlines, as they are with much simpler fundamentals.
> History asks "Did the man have integrity?"
> "Did the man have unselfishness?"
> "Did the man have courage?"
> "Did the man have consistency?"
> And if the individual under the scrutiny of the historic microscope measured up to an affirmative answer to these questions, then history has set him down as great indeed in the pages of all the years to come.
> There are few statesmen in America today who so definitely and clearly measure up to an affirmative answer to the four questions

as does the senior Senator from Nebraska, George W. Norris.
In his rare case, history has already written the verdict.[3]

What bound Norris to Roosevelt was the fact that, as Governor of New York and as the Democratic candidate, FDR championed the cause of public power in his own state and at Muscle Shoals, Alabama. He endorsed Norris's lonely fight to preserve the power potential of the Tennessee River for public ownership as part of the multiple-purpose development of the seven states encompassing the draining area of one of the most poverty-stricken and underdeveloped areas in the United States. For Norris, Roosevelt became the instrument that would allow his dreams to come true. Five times he had tried and five times he had failed. During the first hundred days of the New Deal, the legislation creating the Tennessee Valley Authority (TVA) was the only measure enacted that did not relate directly to the depression crisis.

In 1936 both Roosevelt and Norris were seeking reelection. Norris was much too busy with his own fight for a fifth term in the Senate to campaign for Roosevelt. But the president, violating his self-imposed restraint from taking part in elections in states other than New York, made what he called "one magnificently justified exception." Norris's candidacy, Roosevelt explained, transcended both party and state lines. And as in 1932, he lauded Norris as "one of the major prophets of America" in his October campaign speech in Omaha.[4]

In the late 1930s as hostility to Roosevelt mounted in Congress, when many Republicans and Southern Democrats joined forces to curb and even eliminate several domestic New Deal programs, Norris, now serving as an Independent (probably the only senator ever elected as an Independent) remained steadfast. In 1940 he again proved of enormous help to the president. Campaigning in the Northwest and in California, he stressed public power, and lambasted Republican candidate Wendell Willkie as the very embodiment of the "power trust." So effective was Norris that Senator Charles McNary, a strong advocate of public power and Willkie's running mate, was unable to carry his home state, Oregon, into the Republican fold. Roosevelt carried the entire Northwest and California as well.

Norris was defeated in 1942 and returned to McCook where he continued to support the president. In 1944 he served as honorary chair of a citizens' political action committee endorsing Roosevelt for a fourth term. He died in McCook before the national election.

Roosevelt's relations with the other Republican progressives was not nearly so satisfactory. All became increasingly critical and even hostile to the New Deal, although on domestic issues they generally, albeit at times reluctantly, supported measures they considered inadequate, largely because they were not broader in scope. Bronson Cutting and Robert M. LaFollette Jr., the youngest members of the Senate, were possibly the keenest intellectuals in the chamber. They were interested in getting at fundamental causes of the Great Depression. In the case of Bronson Cutting, the outcome was tragic.

Cutting had criticized the Hoover administration on two counts: its shabby treatment of veterans, particularly disabled veterans, and its failure to suggest a program to cope with the economic crisis. Briefly, as he and LaFollette saw it, what was needed was a broad program to diffuse purchasing power. Assisting corporations to produce more would be of no help in a mass-production–mass-consumption economy that was badly out of balance. A massive public works program to put people to work would be a sensible first step; promoting broad access to credit, something that banks without substantial federal assistance could not do, would be another. To Cutting, LaFollette, and most of the other participants in the Conference of Progressives, the Hoover administration had no notion of how to balance the mass-production–mass-consumption American economy. The same criticisms that Cutting levelled against Hoover, he later levelled against Roosevelt prior to his death in a 1935 airplane crash.

In the beginning, however, all was sweetness and light. Cutting spoke twice over a national network on behalf of FDR in 1932. James A. Farley said Cutting's speeches were most effective in Roosevelt's winning of the West. And the president-elect thought so too. He offered first Hiram Johnson and then Cutting the post of Secretary of the Interior. While Cutting declined the invitation, he did recommend John Collier for the post of Commissioner of Indian Affairs.

One might have expected Roosevelt and Cutting to hit it off well. Their families were on a first-name basis, both had overcome serious health problems, and Cutting had trailed Roosevelt by several years at both Groton and Harvard. But Cutting, as already noted, found the early New Deal inadequate. The only New Deal programs he could say something positive about were the Civil Works Administration (CWA) which put four and a half million people to work in the winter of 1933 before it—as a temporary agency—was slowly dismantled. The agricultural program, in what he considered a perverted approach, also put purchasing power into the hands of millions of farm families.

In criticizing the early New Deal, particularly its treatment of veterans, Cutting aroused the ire of the president in a way that few of his other critics did. The implication of Cutting's remarks about the impact of the Economy Act on veterans could be interpreted to mean that the president was callous to the plight of disabled veterans.

Thus in 1934 when Cutting won reelection in New Mexico by a narrow margin, the administration, through James A.Farley, endorsed the effort mounted by Dennis Chavez to challenge his victory. Norris and other progressives protested to the president about the shabby treatment Cutting was receiving.

In May 1935, Cutting, en route to Washington from Santa Fe, was killed in a plane crash. Chavez, his Democratic opponent in the Senate race, was appointed his successor. As Chavez was being sworn in, Senators LaFollette, Norris, Johnson, Nye, and Henrick Shipstead strode silently out of the chamber as an expression of their frustration, anger, and disgust with the treatment Cutting had received from the Roosevelt administration. This startling and unprecedented action broke the "clubby" atmosphere of the Senate and engendered on the part of most progressives further suspicion of just how progressive the president really was.

While both Robert M. LaFollette Jr. and Hiram Johnson were becoming increasingly critical, they remained on cordial—even intimate—terms with the president. Roosevelt had asked both men to serve as delegates to the London Economic Conference. Both refused. Despite reservations, they, like Cutting, voted for New Deal measures. But LaFollette in many instances sought amendments that would either expand benefits or advance those most likely to be effective. The New Deal did not pursue its progressive impulse fast enough for him. In 1934 both Senators sought reelection. However, the president's response was markedly different from the treatment Cutting received. In Wisconsin, he spoke expressing his gratitude for LaFollette's support and made patronage appointments available to him; indeed, FDR probably rendered LaFollette more support than he did any Democrat in 1934. And he similarly supported the candidacy of Hiram Johnson in California. In neither case did he openly endorse their reelection.

LaFollette reciprocated in 1936. He organized and then chaired the Progressive National Committee, pledged to ensure Roosevelt's reelection. He also spoke on the president's behalf throughout mid-America. While Johnson voted by absentee ballot for Roosevelt, he literally sat out the election despite a request from the president for assistance. Previously both senators had played significant roles in endorsing the measures constituting the so-called second New Deal. LaFollette played a key role in supporting Social Security and tax reform. Johnson enthusiastically spoke in favor of these measures along with the labor-relations bill and holding-company legislation. Following the election, LaFollette championed Roosevelt's court-packing plan. He said the President was taking his election "mandate" seriously in seeking to curb the power of the Supreme Court, which had played havoc with the New Deal. Norris reluctantly agreed. He saw procedural problems in the proposal but certainly supported its intent. Johnson played a leading role in opposing the president.

Although LaFollette increasingly disagreed with Roosevelt on foreign policy and defense proposals, on domestic matters he and the president were still largely in accord. In 1939 the president let LaFollette know of his interest and belief in the senator's work as Chairman of the Senate Civil Liberties Committee investigation of unfair labor practices and violation of basic liberties by large corporations. By 1940 though LaFollette and the president openly disagreed on foreign-policy issues, both supported each other's election. LaFollette's reaction to Wendell Willkie was similar to Norris's. He symbolized big business, Wall Street, and everything progressives had fought against. His views on foreign policy did not differ widely from those of the President, but Roosevelt held progressive views on domestic issues and that was enough for LaFollette. While Roosevelt recognized LaFollette's isolationist views, he knew that LaFollette could be counted on more than his opponents in Wisconsin to back him on domestic issues. He encouraged prominent Democrats to campaign in Wisconsin on LaFollette's behalf and possibly provided assistance to his financially strapped campaign.

Despite their disagreements, both men remained on friendly and cordial terms. But with the introduction of the Lend Lease bill following Roosevelt's reelection in 1940, relations between the two literally came to an end. LaFollette considered Lend Lease "a green light for war" at a time when American security was not threatened. Hiram Johnson had arrived at this conclusion earlier, during Roosevelt's second term.

Johnson was first attracted to FDR as a fellow opponent of the "power trust." Though Johnson distrusted most Democrats and was suspicious of all "internationalists," he had high hopes for the Roosevelt presidency. Like the other progressive Republican senators, he voted for New Deal measures during the first hundred days, although he grumbled privately about some of them.

At the outset Roosevelt catered to Johnson's enormous ego and frequently invited him to the White House for private luncheons and formal dinners and to numerous meetings. Moreover, Roosevelt never raised issues that would have brought him into conflict with Johnson and the Senate progressives: tariff revision, membership in the World Court, and modification of war debts. And when Johnson seized the initiative in 1935 and secured passage of legislation forbidding loans to nations in default of war debts, Roosevelt signed the measure. When Johnson led the successful fight against American participation in the World Court, Roosevelt graciously accepted defeat without a break in their friendship. Johnson cast his first significant vote against the New Deal on the Reciprocal Trades Agreement bill. Nevertheless, he was still welcome at the White House and through James A. Farley continued to receive patronage plums in California. Like the other progressives, Johnson, as already noted, actively endorsed the measures called the "Second New Deal."

In 1937, after not participating in Roosevelt's campaign for reelection, Johnson informed the president that he would oppose him on the Supreme Court bill. Johnson led the Senate fight, which resulted in a stunning defeat for the administration. It was his last triumph in the Senate. Thereafter, it was all downhill for the relationship between Johnson and FDR. By 1939, with the outbreak of war in Europe, Johnson was already a bitter critic of the president. He played a leading role in opposing every defense and foreign-policy initiative the administration proposed. The extent of Johnson's anger, indicative of the enormous chasm between him and the president, is suggested in his response to offhand remarks by Roosevelt at an August 1940 press conference. Johnson said:

> My real acquaintance with Mr. Roosevelt began when I fought for him in 1932. Had I followed him in his attempted packing of the Supreme Court and his veiled and un-American deeds leading us down the road to war and dictatorship, I would have been a perfect liberal and progressive, and what glory would be mine![5]

Before the election he gave a radio address on behalf of Wendell Willkie, stressing the dangers of a third-term presidency. By 1940 Johnson's health was deteriorating and he was unable to play an active role in the Senate, but his barbed attacks on Roosevelt's interventionist policies continued to December 7, 1941.

From this account focusing on Norris, Cutting, LaFollette, and Johnson, several brief conclusions are evident. Progressive Republicans in Congress supported Roosevelt's New Deal as the federal government became a dispenser of relief, a creator of jobs, and a source of capital. They endorsed the New Deal's effort to stretch a safety net under the economy to rescue citizens from a free fall to economic disaster.

Roosevelt's relations with the Senate progressives was at best an uneasy one, Norris being the notable exception. As president, FDR had the continuous task of convincing them that, devoted to progressivism as he was, he could not go as far as they wished and had to compromise to secure as much as he did. To be sure, the Senate progressives had difficulty agreeing with one another and with other colleagues on issues and measures coming before them. Through three campaigns Norris and LaFollette were able to support Roosevelt for reelection. It was foreign policy, what Hiram Johnson called "interventionism," that stretched the relationship to its breaking point: Reluctantly Norris went along; reluctantly LaFollette went into opposition, and Johnson did so almost hysterically. The response of Norris, Cutting, LaFollette, and Johnson accurately reflects, I believe, the attitude and range of views of their progressive colleagues to Roosevelt and the New Deal.

NOTES

1. Senator Burton K. Wheeler, proceedings of a conference of Progressives (n.p., n.d.).

2. Richard Lowitt, *George W. Norris: The Persistence of a Progressive, 1913–1943* (Urbana: University of Illinois Press, 1971), p. 510.

3. FDR speaking in McCook, Nebraska, from *Lincoln Star*, September 29, 1932 as quoted in *George W. Norris: The Persistence of a Progressive, 1913–1932*, (Urbana: University of Illinois Press, 1971), p. 557.

4. Richard Lowitt, *George W. Norris: The Triumph of a Progressive, 1933–1944*, (Urbana: University of Illinois Press, 1978), p. 150.

5. See the *New York Times*, August 4, 1940.

CHAPTER TWO

The Congressional Mavericks: The "Radical" Populist-Progressive Heritage and the New Deal

Dennis N. Mihelich

Historians generally acknowledge that the roots of the New Deal lay in the earlier Populist and Progressive reform movements. The so-called Roosevelt Revolution culminated a half century of a reform impulse that sought an accord with the new urban-industrial order. Although many New Deal measures marked a significant departure from the status quo, they were moderate, compromising solutions compared to the demands of left-wing reformers bred on the "radical" Populist-Progressive heritage. The historiography of Populism and Progressivism presents a wide array of conflicting interpretations. Early attempts to construct a general profile of the average reformer or to build conceptualized models of the reform movements differed as to their status, class, outlook, intent, motivation, goals, and achievements. The models usually contained as many caveats as generalizations.[1] More recently scholars argue that Populism and Progressivism defy universal definition, but that a discernible element of radicalism existed within their broad ideological diversity. This indigenous "radicalism"[2] emanated from a view from the bottom of the social spectrum and a concern for the "plain people," as the Populists called themselves. In their battle against entrenched wealth and economic monopoly they turned to the national government as their ally. They accepted greater government action in the social and economic realms, provided the government remained democratic. Based on those principles, the Populists demanded that the government end "oppression," "injustice," and "poverty;" that it effect a redistribution of the wealth; and that it nationalize the monetary, railroad, and communications systems. The Progressives added proposals for curbing the power of the courts, for factory legislation, and for a comprehensive social security system. For the radicals within those movements, political democracy no longer sufficed; social and economic democracy became prerequisites of a well-ordered society.

In 1934 the electorate swept into office a sizeable number of congressmen nourished on that radical tradition. During the 74th Congress they organized as the Progressive Open Forum Discussion Group, commonly referred to by the press as the Mavericks (see appendix). Members accepted the New Deal as a minimal approach, while they constructed a comprehensive legislative program considerably to the left of President Franklin D. Roosevelt's. Their earnest desire for rapid, substantive change emphasized economic and social justice at the expense of property rights. Industrialism presented the potential for abundance, and the democratically exercised power of the national government, they believed, should guarantee the basic necessities of life to all. They refused to equate capitalism with democracy. The former merely represented a manner of economic organization; the latter symbolized the best of American traditions that deserved strengthening and expansion. The Mavericks decried the primacy of the profit motive, which overshadowed concern for the social good. They demanded a society based on equality of opportunity and an economy of planned abundance.

The Mavericks illuminated the essentially mild liberalism of the New Deal, but also revealed the continued minority status and relative ineffectiveness of the radical position in the United States. Special circumstances in particular constituencies produced a radical tradition that in hard times could dominate state politics,[3] but even with the massive swing to the left that occurred with the elections of 1934 and 1936, the radical bloc during those sessions of Congress constituted less than 10 percent (about forty members maximum) of the House of Representatives. Thus, while the Mavericks generated copious media attention, in terms of ideological impact, the bloc at best acted as a "ginger group,"[4] bubbling up lively debate. Their positions, however, did counter those of the laissez faire conservatives and helped to make FDR's liberalism more acceptable as the compromise position. Most important, they contributed to the success of the New Deal by consciously not being ideologues. The group practiced a "half-a-loaf" strategy[5]; that is, after failing to win their left-wing version of a piece of legislation, they did not join the conservatives to derail the New Deal bill. Thus, despite the rejection of indigenous radical solutions to end the Great Depression and to establish economic security, the Mavericks made a significant contribution to the New Deal.

In national politics the Mavericks represented the coalescence of a number of distinct grassroots movements. In Wisconsin, Thomas R. Amlie, former congressman and former Nonpartisan League official, unified local discontent then combined with the remnant of the organization originally built by Robert LaFollette Sr. to rejuvenate the Progressive Party in 1934.[6] Its platform asserted the failure of capitalism and proclaimed a fundamental harmony of interests between farmers and laborers in building a new order: Demands for public works, adequate relief, protection for unions, the regulations of hours, and social security legislation complemented agrarian planks calling for extended farm credit, the guaranteed cost of production, and the regulation of farm-implement monopolies and grain and livestock exchanges.[7]

Next door in Minnesota, the Farmer-Labor Association wrote "the most extreme document ever drawn up by an American party actually holding political power."[8] It avowed the bankruptcy of capitalism and endorsed the public ownership of mines, transportation, communications, utilities, banks, insurance companies, and "factories."[9] The party sent three incumbents to the 74th Congress and increased its strength to five for the next session. The delegation included John Kvale, an organizer of the Mavericks; Henry Teigan, former secretary of the North Dakota Socialist Party and editor of its newspaper, the *Iconoclast*; and John Toussaint Bernard, whom many considered the most radical member in Congress.[10]

On the West Coast, muckraker author Upton Sinclair sparked a movement to End Poverty In California (EPIC), which envisioned the abolition of capitalism and the emergence of an economy based on the principle of production-for-use. Despite his personal defeat in the gubernatorial election of 1934, the turmoil Sinclair helped to foster resulted in the election of several left-wing Democratic representatives, including Byron Scott and H. Jerry Voorhis, who joined EPIC because it meshed with his Christian socialism.[11] The California radicalism spread northward and influenced events in the state of Washington, where Howard Costigan organized the Commonwealth Builders, a conglomeration of groups that favored production-for-use. The organization played an instrumental role in electing representatives who rendered yeoman service with the Mavericks, including Democrat John Coffee, who, as a private citizen, had written FDR a letter urging him to adopt a more leftward position.[12]

Many other areas of the country that did not experience organized radical movements nonetheless elected left-wing representatives. New York City contributed Republican Vito Marcantonio, the "Pink Pachyderm of Congress"[13] and the former campaign manager for Fiorello La Guardia, Republican of New York. Although he later became associated with the Communist Party,[14] Marcantonio's early radicalism emanated from the visible contrast between the American dream and the realities of life in his district (East Harlem), an urban slum populated by Italians, Jews, Puerto Ricans, and blacks.[15]

Finally, it was an atypical Southern Democrat, Maury Maverick, a product of San Antonio politics, who emerged as the popular spokesman for the radical bloc and whose distinctive, symbolic surname provided the press with a catchy sobriquet for the group. Maverick claimed to have read every copy of the *Appeal to Reason*, and in order to experience the ravages of the economic crisis firsthand, he and two friends donned hobo garb, rode the rails, and lived in Hoovervilles. Subsequently, he reorganized a War Veteran Relief Camp, established by the state of Texas for a remnant of the Bonus Army that had marched on Washington, D.C. in 1932, into the Diga Colony, a cooperative, self-sufficient economic unit. The experiment in communal living, however, disintegrated rapidly and convinced him of "the utter futility of make-shift economies" and of the need for national action.[16]

Maverick and his radical cohorts entered the House of Representatives in 1935 and rapidly coalesced into the loose knit, multiparty Progressive Open Forum Discussion Group. As the new Congress assembled, left-wing members began discussion about organizing to facilitate "progressive" cooperation.[17] On March 9, 1935, John Kvale (Minnesota, Farmer-Labor Party) and Gerald Boileau (Progressive of Wisconsin), both of whom had been associated with the twenty-man La Guardia bloc during the Hoover administration, convened an initial meeting, which selected a policy committee consisting of Boileau, Maverick, Democrat of Texas, Kent Keller, Democrat of Illinois, George Schneider, Progressive of Wisconsin, William Lemke, Republican of North Dakota, Melvin Maas, Republican of Minnesota, and Fred

Gilchrist, Republican of Iowa. A week later it presented a sixteen-point program signed by thirty-four congressmen.

The Mavericks consisted primarily of young men new to national politics. The middle- and far-western states contributed most of the associates. In the East, only Pennsylvania provided a significant number of members. The group converted a storage area on the fifth floor of the Old House Office Building into a private work sanctuary[18] and held ad hoc meetings on the average of once per week, "usually in a rather dingy room over one of the second-rate restaurants that cluster about the Capitol."[19] Guest speakers included labor leaders or government officials who usually attended to discuss pending legislation.[20] Individual Senate progressives maintained working arrangements with the bloc on an informal basis, usually attending meetings when the discussion topic lay within their field(s) of interest.[21]

The Mavericks maintained a pro-New Deal posture, but relations with the White House fluctuated because the bloc failed to establish regular lines of communication and because Roosevelt rarely included members as part of his House floor leadership team on a particular piece of legislation. Occasionally, the group annoyed presidential advisers such as Thomas Corcoran when they refused to toe the line closely. On occasion, other New Deal administrators courted the Mavericks to demonstrate congressional backing on an issue. That information was then used to persuade FDR that there was congressional sympathy for the administrators' legislative proposal.[22] Bloc members, in turn, periodically aired their irritation concerning the president's unwillingness to hear their counsel. For example, John Hoeppel, Democrat of California, complained that FDR consulted only older representatives who did "not appreciate and understand, as we younger Members of Congress do, the desperate plight of our people."[23] Roosevelt obviously understood the nature of the political carping: It did not distort his political vision, and he subsequently supported the reelection bids of bloc leaders such as Maury Maverick.[24]

Because of its multiparty nature (3 Farmer-Labor, 7 Progressives, 7 Republicans, and 17 Democrats signed the first policy paper), the bloc refrained from establishing a formal institutional structure. Meetings were open to all interested lawmakers, presiding officers rotated, and individual members reserved the right to vote their conscience. This independence frustrated members who wished to transform the group into a new third party. Moreover, bloc cohesiveness suffered because of personality clashes, divergent policy self-interests, and sectionalism—the latter especially on agricultural issues.[25]

Nonetheless, discussions sometimes produced a consensus. On those occasions, the group chose designated speakers to present arguments and/or amendments during floor debate and certain members to act as liaisons with targeted colleagues.[26] Although the bloc dispensed with a permanent chairman, the media crowned Maury Maverick as "the moving spirit, guiding genius and general out-in-front man." His colorful personality and stamina suited him to the task, but his lack of diplomacy alienated people. His direct manner and emotional language produced headlines, but at times cost votes.[27] Alfred Bingham, a personal friend and editor of

Common Sense magazine, labeled Maverick "one of the best haters in America" and claimed that "an hour's talk with him is to give one a new concept of the English language as an instrument for expressing dislike."[28]

The Mavericks affiliated "for the purpose of advancing liberal and progressive legislation" designed to eliminate "special privilege" and to ensure "economic and social justice" for everyone. Specifically, they advocated federal regulation of the credit system and congressional control of the value and issue of money, government ownership of "all natural resources and monopolies vested with a public interest," federal aid to education, the creation of a social security system, and the funding of public works at the prevailing wage. For the farmer they demanded the guaranteed cost of production plus a reasonable profit and long-term debt refinancing at 1.5 percent interest. Operation of the remortgaging plan depended upon the creation of a revolving fund obtained through currency inflation. For its urban constituency, the platform also called for reduced interest rates on home loans. They wanted labor assured of its right to bargain collectively and protected by maximum-hours legislation. To effect income redistribution, they urged the abolition of tax exempt securities and steeply graduated rates for the income, inheritance, and gift taxes. Moreover, the platform insisted that the government protect civil liberties, avoid foreign entanglements, and remove the profits from war. Finally, the Mavericks demanded revision of the House rule regarding committee discharge petitions.[29] In order to control the huge majority in the new Congress, Democratic House leaders pushed through a rule requiring 218 signatures (previously 145) to discharge a bill stalled in committee. Obviously, the rule hindered the activities of an organized minority such as the Mavericks, but it remained in force throughout both sessions of its existence. (See footnote 6, p. 92.)

In general terms, the Mavericks program did not reveal its radical nature. The specific dimensions of individual proposals, however, illuminate the decidedly left-wing position. One example from each of the two congresses in which the bloc operated will suffice to demonstrate its homegrown, populist-progressive radicalism. First, "Maverick" Matthew Dunn, Democrat of Pennsylvania, chairman of the House Subcommittee on Labor, was strategically placed to pave the way for the full committee to report out a social security bill sponsored by Ernest Lundeen of Minnesota, Farmer-Labor Party. The draft directed the Secretary of Labor to establish a system of unemployment insurance that covered all farmers and workers over the age of eighteen who were involuntarily unemployed. It stipulated that compensation equal the average local wage, and it included a cost-of-living escalator. Those forced to work only part time would receive an earning supplement to adjust their pay to a full-time equivalency. Members of labor and farmer organizations would elect commissioners to administer the system within guidelines established by the Secretary of Labor. The bill also directed that the other forms of social insurance—sickness, old age, maternity, industrial injury and disability—follow the same patterns of compensation and governance. Estimating the cost of the program at 4 to 6 billion dollars annually, based on 10 to 14 million unemployed, the proposal envisioned all monies coming from new taxes on "inheritances, gifts, and individual incomes of $5,000 a year and over."[30]

Thus, the radicals combined social security with tax reform and wealth redistribution, whereas the New Deal bill sidestepped the use of taxation in favor of a reserve fund supported by participants in the system. The two approaches differed further in that the Lundeen bill provided for a democratic administration by worker and farmer representatives, and it covered all occupations for the entire period of unemployment, in contrast to the strictly limited coverage sponsored by Roosevelt. The president criticized the radicals' version as too expensive, although the committee report indicated that the necessary appropriations equalled only "the cost of truly adequate relief." In return, the Mavericks attacked the reserve-fund system as highly unpredictable and found the payroll tax most obnoxious, arguing that the employer's share would be passed on to the consumer in higher prices. Thus, they reasoned, the worker stood to absorb a double dose—lower wages because of the tax for his/her contribution and lower real earnings through an increase in the cost of living.[31]

The bloc followed a familiar strategy, trying to substitute by amendment the Lundeen bill for the administration bill. That maneuver met defeat 52 to 204 and received even less backing when supporters demanded tellers. The absence of recorded roll-call votes while the House proceeded as a committee of the whole protected anonymity, but the teller form forced representatives to file past counters in the well of the chamber. This visible, but still unrecorded, vote produced only forty proponents. Colleagues who wished to do so for any reason could identify individual voters, ensuring that only the most committed (most likely the signers of the Mavericks platform) continued to support the measure.

In a last-ditch effort to stall the passage of any social security legislation, conservative Republicans offered an amendment to recommit the administration bill to committee. At this juncture the Mavericks revealed the fissures in the multiparty coalition. The entire Progressive and Farmer-Labor delegations, plus ten Democrats, supported the recommit motion, while Maury Maverick and the other Democrats in the bloc defended the president's bill. For them at this point, contributing as loyal Democrats carried greater significance than registering a futile ideological contrary vote. The motion failed by more than 100 votes and minutes later the administration bill passed with overwhelming support, 372 to 33 with 2 answering present and 25 not voting. Only five members of the bloc—Usher Burdick, Republican of North Dakota, Hoeppel, Democrat of California, Kvale, Farmer-Labor of Minnesota, Lemke, Republican of North Dakota, Lundeen, Farmer-Labor of Minnesota, and Marcantonio, Republican of New York—refused to back the bill on the final tally, while Gardner Withrow, Progressive of Wisconsin, did not vote.[32]

The social security strategy was typical. The Mavericks legislative outline on any particular issue stood considerably to the left of FDR's. The bloc maneuvered to substitute its version or to amend the administration bill to align more closely with its goals. Sometimes it was able to nudge the New Deal leftward in terms of expanded coverage or higher appropriations. Most of the time, however, a majority of the bloc reluctantly supported the New Deal version of a bill rather than contribute to its defeat. The scenario produced frustration, but the group continued to meet, to plan, to agitate, and to make headlines. In 1938, as the second session of the 75th Congress began, journalist Harlan Miller reported that a band of thirty-four "Young Turks" (Miller identified Maury Maverick as the "sultan," although the Texan rejected the title) gathered nocturnally every Wednesday at Renkel's Cafeteria, a restaurant that provided "a square meal for 50 cents."[33]

A month of those meetings produced a new ten-point platform, which a contingent of thirty-three persons presented to Roosevelt as a blueprint to revive a fighting New Deal. The agenda included familiar but unfulfilled demands for labor and agricultural legislation, expansion of Social Security, nationalization of the Federal Reserve system, and the renewal—following the 1937 cutbacks—of large-scale government spending, especially in relief expenditures. Also numbered among their chief desires were tax reform ("low taxation on consuming power and active, competitive business; and high taxation on speculation, idle wealth, and monopoly"), a nationwide land use program that included resettlement and soil-conservation projects, a permanent public-works program, and a simplification of the system of government credit agencies "to provide credit for secured loans for low cost housing, agriculture, small business, home owners, and public works." Finally, the Mavericks petitioned the president to support a national planning proposal to increase and regulate industrial production.[34]

The Mavericks' planning scheme accepted the basic outline of Technocracy, a utopian program that envisioned a modern industrial society, led by engineers, which provided prosperity for all. It mixed in ideas advocated by bloc member Kent Keller, Democrat of Illinois, in *Prosperity Through Employment* (1936) and Mordecai Ezekiel in *$2500 a Year* (1936). Keller argued that the national government had the duty to guarantee "universal employment," and Ezekiel claimed that $2500 per annum would allow the average family to live in "modest abundance," which the government should ensure through programs to run industries to capacity, to manufacture every product in demand, to employ all workers, and to distribute income so the workers could consume all they produced.[35]

The resulting Industrial Expansion Act (IEA), introduced into the House by Maverick, Amlie, Voorhis, and Robert Allen, Democrat of Pennsylvania, resembled a "radically" remodeled National Industrial Recovery Act. It envisioned authorities that prepared annual production plans. The plans, however, had to provide for increased production, thus substituting the concept of abundance for the principle of scarcity. The authorities would include only the basic and heavy industries, approximately twenty, from the areas of mining, manufacturing, construction, and transportation, although the national government would own and control the key natural resources and public utilities, including the railroads. Moreover, the plans had to provide for the redistribution of wealth by limiting profit to 10 percent of the annual increase in earnings, while guaranteeing wage increases that did not come from price increases. The act also provided for an "ever-normal warehouse," whereby a government agency would purchase surplus goods at a discount then hold them off the market. Subsequent plans would eliminate the excess gradually in order to minimize economic disruption from overproduction. Finally, the IEA called for the creation of a new federal housing authority to coordinate regional and local plans that would direct the efforts of the thousands of small companies involved in this preeminently significant sector of the economy.[36]

Introduced as the conservative backlash against the New Deal began to mount, the bill never made it out of committee. The Mavericks made it one of six points of a platform they would use for the congressional elections of 1938.[37] Cognizant of a changing attitude, they participated in the president's plan to liberalize the Democratic party and they presented the electorate with a clear left-wing choice. The voters disdained the option; 20 of the 38 signers of the platform met defeat. The vanquished included 4 of the 5 Minnesota Farmer-Laborites and 5 of the 7 Wisconsin Progressives. Also, most of the recognized leaders of the bloc—Maverick, Amlie, Kvale, Boileau—were retired in the Republican congressional comeback.

That the Mavericks and the New Deal both ended in 1938 was more than a coincidence. Both benefitted from the mood that produced the second 100 days, and both suffered from the subsequent controversy—the abortive Supreme Court reform, the sit-down strikes, the recession of 1937, the attempted party "purge" of 1938. The conditions that had sparked the local radicalism in 1934 were largely extinguished four years later. During its brief foray on Capitol Hill, if opportunity existed because the country lay prostrate in the midst of an economic debacle, the Mavericks failed to radicalize the United States—not a single one of the radical features of any of the planks in the group's various platforms became the law of the land.

The two examples described here demonstrate some reasons for that failure. The Mavericks acted as the left-wing of the New Deal coalition, but the group was not in the pivotal position to provide votes for passage or defeat of a bill. The House discharge rule further curbed the influence of organized minorities. While occasionally internal problems weakened the bloc's effectiveness, external forces sealed its fate. Yet, group membership gave these neophyte representatives confidence. They rejected the traditional deferential posture of newcomers, and as vocal activists they became media stars, fawned over by newspaper and radio reporters. They got their message out; the entrenched American value of individualism, however, blunted the message's collectivist theme.

Maury Maverick's personal failure with his Diga Colony presaged the Mavericks' failure in Congress. As soon as the former Bonus Army marchers found work in a Reconstruction Finance Corporation funded military project, the experiment in communal living disintegrated because "not a man in the crowd understood cooperation for the common good."[38] The radical Populist-Progressive ideology could succeed at the local level, but American pluralism and regional diversity doomed national farmer-labor unity. Moreover, American individualism, even during the Great Depression, confined the indigenous radicalism to a minority status. It contributed to the debate and minimally it helped mold the solution, but it was not an acceptable alternative in American national politics.

21

NOTES

1. A representative sample of books interpreting Populism and Progressivism in their national scope includes Lawrence Goodwyn, *Democratic Promise: The Populist Movement in America* (New York: Oxford University Press, 1976); Samuel P. Hayes, *The Response to Industrialism, 1885–1914* (Chicago: University of Chicago Press, 1957); John D. Hicks, *The Populist Revolt* (Minneapolis: University of Minnesota Press, 1931); Richard Hofstadter, *The Age of Reform* (New York: Knopf, 1955); Gabriel Kolko, *The Triumph of Conservatism* (New York: The Free Press of Glencoe, 1963); Arthur Link, *Woodrow Wilson and the Progressive Era, 1910–1917* (New York: Harper, 1958); George Mowry, *The Era of Theodore Roosevelt, 1900–1912* (New York: Harper, 1958); Robert Wiebe, *The Search for Order, 1877–1920* (New York: Hill and Wang, 1967).

2. On first use I put the term "radical" in quotation marks to indicate the relative nature of the word. In this chapter, the term refers to a non-Marxian, indigenous ideology that rejected capitalism, accepted an intrusive national government, and demanded public ownership of some of the means of production. For the United States the position was radical in comparison to the laissez faire ideology of the late nineteenth and early twentieth centuries and to that of New Deal liberalism. The latter sought to tinker with capitalism in order to save it. The Mavericks did not call themselves radical for obvious reasons, using instead terms such as liberal, but especially progressive.

3. For a discussion of this phenomenon see Richard M. Valelly, *Radicalism in the States: The Minnesota Farmer-Labor Party and the American Political Economy*, (Chicago: University of Chicago Press, 1989), pp. 1–15, 165–73.

4. Jonathon Mitchell, "Front-Fighters in Congress," *New Republic*, vol. 83, June 19, 1935, p. 157.

5. Author's interview with H. Jerry Voorhis, May 21, 1970.

6. Harold M. Groves, "Radical Parties (V): The Wisconsin Progressive Party," *Common Sense*, vol. 4, May, 1935, p. 19; Donald R. McCoy, *Angry Voices*, (Lawrence: University of Kansas Press, 1958), pp. 46–52, p. 201, note 32.

7. *Progressive*, March 2, 1935, p. 2 and March 9, 1935, pp. 1–2.

8. George H. Mayer, *The Political Career of Floyd B. Olson*, (Minneapolis: University of Minnesota Press, 1951), p. 171.

9. Herbert Lefkovitz, "Olson: Radical and Proud of It," *Review of Reviews*, vol. 91, May 1935, p. 36.

10. Voorhis interview. He stated that Bernard was "probably a communist."

11. Jerry Voorhis, *Confessions of a Congressman* (Garden City: Doubleday and Company, 1948); Claudius O. Johnson, "Jerry Voorhis: 'What is Right Rather than What is Expedient'," in J. T. Salter, ed., *Public Men In and Out of Office*, (Chapel Hill: University of North Carolina Press, 1946), p. 326.

12. John M. Coffee to FDR, June 3, 1935, FDR Mss, FDR Library, Hyde Park, PFF 2581. See also *New York Times*, April 7, 1935, Section IV, p. 7 and June 7, 1936, Section IV, p. 10; Mary McCarthy, "Circus Politics in Washington State," *Nation*, vol. 143, Oct. 17, 1936, pp. 442–444; Cole Stevens, "Sunrise in the Northwest," *New Masses*, vol. 22, Dec. 29, 1936, pp. 13–14; "Progressives in Seattle," *New Republic*, vol. 92, Oct. 20, 1937, p. 285.

13. *New York Times*, March 22, 1935, section IV, p. 6.

14. Reinhard H. Luthin, *American Demagogues, Twentieth Century*, (Boston: Beacon Press, 1954), pp. 208–214.

15. Alan Schaffer, *Vito Marcantonio, Radical in Congress*, pp. 10ff (Syracuse: Syracuse University Press, 1966); Salvatore John La Gumina, *Vito Marcantonio, The People's Politician*, (Dubuque, IA: Kendall Hunt Publishing Co., 1969), p. iv.

16. Maury Maverick, *A Maverick American*, (New York: Covice, Friede Publishers, 1937), pp. 48–63, 152–3, 167–176.

17. Floyd B. Olson to Maury Maverick, January 21, 1935, Maverick Papers, "General Correspondence," University of Texas Archives, Austin; *Progressive*, January 5, 1935, p. 1 and January 12, 1935; *New York Times*, February 24, 1935, pp. 1–2.

18. *Washington Post*, July 14, 1937, Scrapbook, Maverick Papers.

19. Voorhis, *Confessions*, p. 30. Aubury W. Williams, executive director of the National Youth Administration, recalled that one of the establishments frequented was a seafood restaurant named Hall's. See Richard B. Henderson, *Maury Maverick, A Political Biography*, (Austin: University of Texas Press, 1970), p. 76.

20. Voorhis interview. Harold Ickes reported his presentation to the group on the topic of executive reorganization in *The Inside Struggle, 1936–1939*, vol. 2 of *The Secret Diary of Harold Ickes*, (New York: Simon and Shuster, 1954), p. 374.

21. Voorhis interview.

22. Ibid.

23. *Congressional Record, Proceedings and Debates of the First Session of the Seventy-fourth Congress of the United States of America,* vol. 79, part 6, May 2, 1935, (Washington: United States Government Printing Office, 1935), pp. 6813–6814.

24. Walter King to Maverick, July 2, 1936; Maverick to Robert S. Allen, July 6, 1936; Maverick to George Biddle, August 1, 1936, Maverick Papers.

25. Judith K. Doyle, "Out of Step: Maury Maverick and the Politics of the Depression and the New Deal" (unpublished Ph.D. dissertation, University of Texas at Austin, 1989), pp. 258–280; James J. Lorence, *Gerald J. Boileau and the Progressive-Farmer-Labor Alliance* (Columbia: University of Missouri Press, 1994), pp. 98–164; Donald L. Miller, *The New American Radicalism: Alfred M. Bingham and the Non-Marxian Insurgency in the New Deal Era* (Port Washington: Kennikat Press, 1979), pp. 112–136.

26. Voorhis interview: *The Progressive*, April 20, 1935, p. 1.

27. Voorhis interview.

28. Alfred M. Bingham, "Unbranded: Maury Maverick, Spokesman for New America," *Common Sense*, vol. 6, February, 1937, p. 23.

29. *Congressional Record*, vol. 79, part 4, March 20, 1935, p. 4128; *New York Times*, March 17, 1935, p. 33.

30. *Congressional Record*, vol. 79, part 5, April 3, 1935, pp. 4971–4972.

31. Ibid.

32. Ibid., April 18, 1935, p. 5969 and April 19, 1935, pp. 6068–6070.

33. *Washington Post*, January 28, 1938, Scrapbook, Maverick Papers.

34. *Philadelphia Record*, February 9, 1938, Scrapbook, Maverick Papers; *Progressive*, February 19, 1938, p. 1; original text of the ten-point program supplied to the author by Voorhis.

35. Kent Keller, *Prosperity Through Employment* (New York: Harper and Brothers Publishers, 1936), p. 214; Mordecai Ezekiel, *$2500 a Year* (Harcourt, Brace and Company, 1936), pp. v–vi.

36. Robert Gray Allen, "The Answer is Jobs," *Common Sense*, vol. 6, May, 1937, p. 13; "American Commonwealth Federation," *Common Sense*, vol. 6, May, 1937, p. 24; Mordecai Ezekiel, "AAA in Reverse," *Common Sense*, vol, 6, June, 1937, p. 12; Thomas R. Amlie, "The Answer to Fascism: Political Significance of the Industrial Expansion Act," *Common Sense*, vol. 6, August, 1937, pp. 8–10; Robert Gray Allen, "The Answer is Production," *Common Sense*, vol. 6, November, 1937, p. 17; Herbert Harris, "This Bill Bears Watching," *Survey Graphic*, vol. 27, April, 1938, pp. 227–232, 246–248; Donald L. Miller, *The New American Radicalism: Alfred M. Bingham and the Non-Marxian Insurgency in the New Deal Era* (Port Washington: Kennikat Press, 1979), pp. 139–141; Mordecai Ezekiel, *Jobs for All Through Industrial Expansion* (New York: Alfred A. Knopf, 1939).

37. *Congressional Record*, vol. 83, appendix, June 11, 1938, pp. 2584–2585.

38. Maury Maverick, *A Maverick American*, (New York: Covice, Friede Publishers, 1937), pp. 167–176.

CHAPTER THREE

FDR and the Nye Committee: A Reassessment

MATTHEW WARE COULTER

The Senate Special Committee on Investigation of the Munitions Industry, often called the Nye Committee after its chairperson, Senator Gerald P. Nye, was created in 1934 to examine the armament and munitions industries of the United States and propose regulatory legislation. Four Democrats—Bennett Clark of Missouri, Homer Bone of Washington, James Pope of Idaho, and Walter F. George of Georgia—and three Republicans—Nye of North Dakota, Arthur Vandenberg of Michigan, and W. Warren Barbour of New Jersey—served on the committee.

The reasons for Nye's selection to chair the investigation will probably never be known. The minutes of the meeting at which he was chosen by the committee have never been found. Senator Pope later said the committee hoped to demonstrate a spirit of bipartisanship. Nye had expected Senator Clark to chair the investigation.

The committee completed its hearings in early 1936 and released its final reports that summer. By 1936, committee members had taken opposing sides over the question of President Woodrow Wilson's role during the period of United States neutrality in World War I. In the Senate, conservative Southern Democrats attacked the committee on a variety of grounds, and the full Senate voted to curtail further funding for the investigation.

Gerald P. Nye, isolationism, appeasement, and the "merchants of death" are so closely intertwined in American history that untangling them presents an exceedingly difficult task. A recent textbook, for example, treats the matter in this fairly typical way: "Nye's committee concluded that profiteers, whom it called 'merchants of death,' had maneuvered the United States into the First World War for financial gain. Most of the Nye Committee's charges were dubious or simplistic, but they added momentum to the growing isolationist movement."[1] This chapter demonstrates that there are other contexts in which to consider the Nye Committee and that from these, new insights into the committee can be drawn.

For a topic so widely covered in United States history courses, the Nye Committee has received little detailed attention from historians. Only one book-length study of the munitions investigation has been published, John E. Wiltz's *In Search of Peace: The Senate Munitions Inquiry, 1934-1936.*[2] Focusing on the "merchants of death" theme, Wiltz used the phrase over thirty-five times in his book and found the Nye Committee's chief accomplishment to be the inadvertent debunking of the "merchants of death" thesis, which he defined as the assertion that "people who profited from war...bore responsibility for war."[3] One wonders how Wiltz might have approached the topic had the 1934 book *Merchants of Death* never been published. As Richard Dean Burns later noted, Wiltz's "belief that the Nye Committee's findings invalidated much of *Merchants of Death*'s central argument is most difficult to challenge." But Burns also found that Wiltz's "characterization of the mid-1930s...undoubtedly stems from the temperament of the 1950s." Starting from a more neutral position, allowing the "merchants of death" concept a place in the story, but not preassigning it the central role, opens up new avenues for a synthesis of the munitions investigation within the history of the 1930s.[4]

The relationship of the committee to American intellectual history, for example, has been largely unexplored. Stephen Raushenbush,[5] the committee's chief investigator, closely followed his respected father's teachings on the Social Gospel. Walter Rauschenbusch, writing in his 1907 *Christianity and the Social Crisis*, found that "the rapacity of commerce has been the secret spring of most recent wars." In 1912 the senior Rauschenbusch wrote that the "big interests that build dreadnoughts and manufacture ammunition are a very powerful factor in keeping the nations armed to the teeth in times of peace." Stephen Raushenbush carried such teachings into his work for the Nye Committee, but by the mid-1930s his father's Social Gospel views were under attack from Reinhold Niebuhr, an American theologian. In his 1932 book, *Moral Man and Immoral Society*, Niebuhr rejected the Social Gospel explanation of war. "Neither is it true that modern wars are caused solely by the modern capitalistic system with its disproportion of economic power and privilege," he wrote. Important intellectual underpinnings of the Nye Committee were under challenge even as it began to form, and by mid-1935 Niebuhr's views had ascended over the Social Gospel for most liberal Christian leaders. Wiltz has little to say on these developments, devoting one sentence to Walter Rauschenbusch and making no mention of Reinhold Niebuhr.[6]

The evolving cultural scene of the mid-1930s likewise receives little consideration from Wiltz. While he explains that Nye's views were often similar to those of the Jeffersonians and (William Jennings) Bryanites, and provides a good overview of the Progressive background of Stephen Raushenbush, Wiltz fails to account for how these worldviews, well represented in the thinking of the First New Deal, were superseded by the Second New Deal's emerging welfare state. The Second New Deal aimed to reduce slightly the power of big business while increasing the power of government and labor, thereby bringing into a better balance three major elements of modern industrial society. The yeoman farmer, the central figure of Jeffersonian and Bryant political philosophy did not play a critical role in the mix, making Nye's view increasingly obsolete as the munitions investigation proceeded.[7]

Transpiring events transformed the political climate. The Nye Committee took an eight-month break from hearings from April 1935 to January 1936. In this interval the Second New Deal began, and Reinhold Niebuhr launched his journal of ideas, *Radical Religion*. Other events marked a change of the guard, as some icons of the Progressive Era and the Roaring Twenties left the scene. Jane Addams, probably America's best known pacifist, died in June. In August, Will Rogers was killed in a plane crash. The next month Huey Long was assassinated. By the end of the year, Charlie Chaplin was editing his last silent feature film, titled, appropriately enough, *Modern Times*. When the Nye Committee reopened hearings in January 1936, it operated in a different intellectual, cultural, and political context from its earlier sessions.

The isolationism–appeasement approach has also complicated consideration of Franklin D. Roosevelt's relationship to the Nye Committee. Historians have offered widely varying assessments of his role, ranging from zealous support to wary distrust. James MacGregor Burns concluded that FDR had "strengthened the isolationist cause by virtually joining it" and cited the Nye Committee as an "egregious case in point...[in which] Roosevelt was no innocent bystander." Wayne S. Cole found the President giving reluctant support to the investigation, noting that the "attitudes, interests, and strength that the Senate Munitions Investigating Committee represented were more formidable than President Roosevelt was prepared to challenge head-on during his first term in the White House." Selig Adler agreed with Cole, finding that FDR yielded to public opinion and only "halfheartedly" supported the investigation. Robert Dallek argued that Roosevelt supported the Nye Committee but encouraged it to consider international solutions to the arms traffic. Kenneth S. Davis found that the investigation was "from the first...regarded with a suspicious eye, a wary dislike, by Franklin Roosevelt."[8]

As was often the case with President Roosevelt, the correct answer was all of the above. FDR approached the Nye Committee with purpose, but his purpose is obscured when the munitions investigation is considered within the confines of isolationism and internationalism. Roosevelt, the "politician's politician" who claimed no particular ideology, supported the Nye Committee when it suited his political goals and clashed with it when it did not. Thus, FDR warmed to the munitions investigation and the interests it represented in the election years of 1934 and 1936, while he challenged or ignored the actions and ideas of the committee in 1935 and 1937. Viewed from the perspective of national politics, instead of within the context of isolationism and internationalism, Roosevelt's approach to the investigation becomes more understandable.

Secretary of State Cordell Hull set out the isolationist framework in his *Memoirs*, published in 1948. "With the Democratic Senate majority going along with the Nye Committee, the President and I felt that our only feasible step was a sort of marking time," he wrote. "There was no hope of success and nothing to be gained in combating the isolationist wave at that moment." Hull's analysis overlooked the role that the administration played in making the munitions investigation possible in the first place, with the support of twenty-two senators contingent upon presidential influence. After the State Department announced support for a munitions inquiry, the measure still lacked majority support in the United States Senate and only some sharp parliamentary maneuvering by Nye and Arthur H. Vandenberg allowed the resolution to pass on April 12, 1934. No "isolationist wave" swept legislators in behind the Nye Committee. The administration could have easily prevented the investigation, probably by doing nothing but certainly by opposing it.[9]

Instead, Roosevelt authorized Hull to endorse the measure. The political aspects of a munitions investigation could hardly have escaped consideration by a master politician like FDR, with his decision coming as big business and big finance completed their break from the administration during the climax of the battle for the Securities and Exchange Commission Act. His sensitive political antennae had already sensed a growing split with business leaders and, as he endorsed the munitions investigation, the beginnings of future political opposition encouraged by officials of the DuPont Corporation. Lammot DuPont had already vented biting criticism of New Deal policies, published in the corporation's annual report. Considered within the framework of New Deal politics, a munitions investigation virtually guaranteed negative publicity for many of the industrial and financial leaders opposing administration policy, with the DuPonts in particular forming a leading target. The Delaware-based corporation received a full chapter of treatment in *Merchants of Death*.[10]

The selection of the Republican Nye to chair the committee surprised many observers. "Had I dreamed that an isolationist Republican would be appointed I promptly would have opposed it," Hull later wrote. Roosevelt, however, showed no such concerns. He enthusiastically endorsed the investigation in a May 18 statement, speaking of a "mad race in armaments which, if permitted to continue, may well result in war. This grave menace to the peace of the world is due in no small measure to the uncontrolled activities of the manufacturers and merchants of engines of destruction." Three weeks later FDR met with committee members, talking favorably about "clipping the wings of the arms manufacturers" and even of abolishing air forces. In August FDR travelled east by rail across the northern Great Plains, building support for Democrats in the upcoming election. He included a stop at Devil's Lake, North Dakota, to appear with the Republican Nye. Acting at the President's request, Nye introduced Roosevelt to an audience of 35,000 people. During the period leading up to the elections, FDR gave much more than grudging, halfhearted support to the Nye Committee.[11]

After returning to Washington, Roosevelt received a visit from Jouett Shouse, former Executive Chairman of the Democratic National Committee, and learned about a soon-to-be-announced political organization called the Liberty League. Shouse secured Roosevelt's agreement to endorse the organization, which received nearly one-third of its funding from the DuPont family. Pierre, Irénée, and Lammot DuPont, top officials in the DuPont corporation, served in leadership positions for the League. FDR realized that the League represented interests hostile to his policies, and when his promised endorsement came it proved to be rather qualified. "An organization that only advocates two or three out of the Ten Commandments may be a perfectly good organization," he told reporters, "but it would have certain shortcomings in having failed to advocate the other seven or eight."[12]

FDR's prescience in supporting the munitions investigation now paid a handsome political dividend. Two days after the Shouse meeting, Nye Committee investigators began searching through DuPont company records. Within one month the committee had the DuPonts on the witness stand and under scrutiny as potential "merchants of death." That a Republican headed up the inquiry suited Roosevelt's needs, perhaps even better than if a Democrat had held the post. Three days of DuPont testimony in September generated plenty of headlines, showing the DuPonts as profiteers to the extreme in the World War I. FDR tried to join the attack on the DuPonts. Soon after their testimony began, he received a letter from a former United States official who had investigated claims made by munitions companies to the government at the end of World War I. After reading that one of the claims "involved the DuPont Company, and some things I learned about this particular claim was such that it would not look well in print," FDR sent the letter to White House appointments secretary Marvin McIntyre with instructions to get the facts. The Justice Department followed up on the matter, but found nothing substantial.[13]

Following fourteen days of hearings in September, the committee adjourned until after the elections. Voters registered a stunning endorsement of Roosevelt's New Deal, with the Democrats gaining seats in both the House and Senate. Soon afterward the relationship between the Nye Committee and the Roosevelt administration started to sour. On November 18 the *New York Times* reported that Nye had accused the United States government of "acting in partnership with the 'merchants of death.'" He called for a tax on war profits to curb the munitions makers' lust for money. Less than a month later, Roosevelt took some wind out of the committee's sails by announcing formation of his own group to study the war profits issue. The administration committee, headed by Bernard Baruch, was viewed by many as a vehicle to undermine the munitions committee. Nye suspected as much, telling reporters that "if this is an attempt to halt the investigation, it is not the first one we have encountered during the late weeks."[14]

Tension between Roosevelt and the Nye Committee continued on through the rest of the hearings. The committee's investigation of the shipbuilding industry, with hearings conducted in the spring of 1935, threatened Roosevelt's plans for strengthening the United States Navy. The study of war profits led to a direct confrontation, with the committee endorsing a much more radical approach than that supported by Baruch. Roosevelt wrote Hull in late February to request a meeting to discuss war profits, attaching an unsigned memorandum that described how the Nye Committee might use the issue against the administration. The memorandum argued that weapons exports provided a means to "test killing implements and a nucleus for a war-time munitions industry by maintaining an export market for instruments of death. Of course, it is absolutely indefensible and we could not be put in a position of excusing it. If the Nye Committee should anticipate in reaching this conclusion it would put the administration in an embarrassing position." The memorandum concluded that this was "what the Nye Committee is now doing, and obviously intends to do, is to embarrass the administration." Embarrassing the DuPonts was one thing, embarrassing the administration another. Roosevelt's honeymoon with the Nye Committee was definitely over.[15]

Meeting with committee members on March 19, Roosevelt indicated agreement with their war-profits proposals and then steered them into the thicket of neutrality legislation. The president's performance in the meeting has prompted historians to speculate on his motivations. Wiltz saw Roosevelt's behavior as rather undisciplined, suggesting that FDR acted "on impulse" in directing the committee onto the neutrality question. Wayne Cole offered several possibilities, concluding that FDR was probably not focused on the issues discussed. Robert Dallek depicted a more purposeful Roosevelt, finding that the president put the Nye Committee onto neutrality as a means of "taking the issue away from the Senate Foreign Relations Committee." In Dallek's analysis, Roosevelt feared that the Foreign Relations Committee would demand an impartial neutrality bill and he hoped that, by working with the munitions committee, he might get a bill allowing presidential discretion to punish an aggressor. Robert A. Divine suggested that FDR may have lost patience with the State Department's slow progress on neutrality and was "using the Nye Committee as a way of forcing the State Department to act."[16]

It seems more likely, however, that Roosevelt wanted to sidetrack the troublesome investigation. A discretionary neutrality bill, allowing the President to suspend trade with one belligerent country while continuing it with another, could expect to find even less favor from the Nye Committee than from the Foreign Relations Committee. Roosevelt's earlier efforts to gain control over the war-profits question show that he had given serious consideration to that issue and undermine the suggestion that he acted impulsively and with little forethought. Roosevelt knew the Foreign Relations Committee had jurisdiction over neutrality legislation and could be expected to keep control over the issue. The diversion came at a critical time. While the munitions committee struggled with neutrality for nearly a month before giving up on it, mostly due to the jurisdictional question, the House of Representatives rejected the munitions committee's war-profits proposals and voted for the administration's plan.[17]

Roosevelt may have regretted the move later when Nye organized a majority of the committee's senators for a filibuster in August, as Congress prepared to finish work on several key Second New Deal bills, and he threatened to halt progress until a neutrality bill passed. The resulting Neutrality Act of 1935 included much of what the leaders of the munitions committee wanted and left very little discretion to the President. The administration managed to make the law temporary, with its provisions effective for only six months. FDR signed the bill and soon afterward revealed his thoughts in a letter to former Woodrow Wilson confidante Edward House. "You may be interested to know that some of the Congressmen and Senators who are suggesting wild-eyed measures to keep us out of war are now declaring that you and Lansing and Page forced Wilson into the war!" he wrote, surely having Nye and munitions committee in mind. "The trouble is that they belong to the very large and perhaps increasing school of thought which holds that we can and should withdraw wholly within ourselves and cut off all but the most perfunctory relationships with other nations. They imagine that if the civilization of Europe is about to destroy itself through internal strife, it might just as well go ahead and do it and that the United States can stand idly by."[18]

During the final months of 1935 the administration continued to have problems with the investigation as the resumption of hearings approached. The committee

31

planned to investigate the role played by bankers in drawing the United States toward the Allies in World War I, with the inquiry set to coincide with debate over extension of the temporary neutrality legislation. The examination of banking records from the war years generated diplomatic problems with the British and French governments; Hull and Roosevelt had tried to dissuade the committee from this inquiry. The hearings would delve into the workings of the Wilson administration, in which FDR had served as Assistant Secretary of the Navy, and probably criticize the only other Democratic president of the twentieth century. The hearings would spotlight Nye, who many observers, including Roosevelt, saw as a possible presidential candidate in 1936. Additionally, the President would have to fight Nye if he wanted a discretionary neutrality bill. FDR might well lose the battle again, starting off an election year with a legislative defeat. By this time, too, the President and many of those close to him were concerned that the munitions investigation was contributing to isolationist sentiments at a time of international tension. Roosevelt had little reason to support the munitions committee in late 1935 and early 1936.[19]

The banking inquiry provided the dramatic high point of the Nye Committee hearings, with J. P. Morgan testifying in person. An issue little involved with war finance or munitions makers, however, generated an uproar that brought down the Nye Committee. Reviewing the Allied "secret treaties" from World War I, Nye noted that Wilson had "falsified" (i.e., lied about) his knowledge of these agreements before the Paris Peace Conference. When newspaper headlines carried the story, southern Democrats in the Senate rose to defend the former President, a fellow southerner, and lash out at the munitions committee. Tom Connally of Texas and Carter Glass of Virginia led the attack, with support from Kenneth McKellar of Tennessee, Alben Barkley of Kentucky, James Byrnes of South Carolina, and Majority Leader Joseph Robinson of Arkansas. With the senators making clear their opposition to further funding, the Nye Committee's time was running out.[20]

The southern Democrats represented the more conservative elements of the party, with no northern or western Democrats or any Republicans speaking against the munitions committee. By 1936 many southern Democrats were uneasy with Roosevelt's New Deal, being more comfortable with the earlier Democratic tradition represented by John W. Davis or even Al Smith. In January 1936, Davis and Smith made common cause with the Liberty League and the DuPonts to oppose Roosevelt's reelection. Smith addressed the first annual Liberty League dinner on January 25, attacking Roosevelt and calling the New Deal a "socialist platform." At least twelve members of the DuPont family attended. Davis, who served as legal counsel for J. P. Morgan during the Nye Committee hearings, was also present, as were some congressional southern Democrats. From a political perspective, the munitions committee found itself out on the left with the administration in the center and some conservative Democrats, most Republicans, and the Liberty League on the right. The munitions investigation had driven a wedge between itself and the administration, and when the attack came from the right, the Nye Committee received no support from Roosevelt. If FDR wanted to campaign from the left, the pesky Nye Committee may have looked like an obstacle ripe for removal.[21]

Presidential politics increased in intensity as the committee completed its work, publishing a series of reports in June. Shortly after the last report appeared, Roosevelt received the Democratic nomination for President. FDR delivered a rousing convention speech attacking the "economic royalists" and launched into his triumphant reelection campaign. Facing Republican Alf Landon, who received generous support from the "economic royalists" of the Liberty League, and having little to fear from the defunct munitions committee, Roosevelt reached out to Senator Nye much as he had in 1934. Interior Secretary Harold Ickes suggested the move, seeing Nye as the key to attracting peace-minded voters to the Roosevelt campaign. Ickes wanted the President to make a strong peace speech, after which Nye would issue a statement endorsing Roosevelt. FDR liked the idea and responded quickly, delivering his noted Chautauqua speech four days later.[22]

"I hate war," the President concluded after vividly describing the horrors of modern combat. FDR did not blame bankers and munitions makers for the bloodshed, instead finding many causes of war. Of all the causes, however, governments could effectively legislate against only one: the "economic source" of war could be controlled by neutrality and war-profits laws. Warming to this theme, Roosevelt embraced the thinking of the munitions committee. "Industrial and agricultural production for a war market may give immense fortunes to a few men," FDR said, without having to name the DuPonts or other economic royalists, but "for the nation as a whole it produces disaster." Calling war profits "fool's gold," the President ridiculed the arguments offered for shipping supplies and extending credit to belligerent nations. "If we face the choice of profits or peace, the nation will answer—must answer—'we choose peace,'" he stated. But FDR parted with the majority of the munitions committee in assessing current legislation. He believed policies already in effect would reduce war profits, whereas most members of the committee found the current laws full of loopholes and virtually unenforceable.[23]

The speech set out much of what the peace movement wanted to hear, and also supported some of the findings of the munitions investigation. Harold Ickes pursued his plan to bring Nye onto the Roosevelt bandwagon, asking the White House to invite the North Dakota senator to visit Hyde Park. Ickes had a clear idea of what he wanted, hoping Nye's statement would "show very clearly that those elements in this country who would profit from a war, namely, the international bankers and the munitions makers, are all on the side of Landon." He phoned Roosevelt on August 22, and, after learning that Nye was waiting at the moment to see the President, told him to encourage Nye to tie the arms makers and bankers to Landon in any statement. Despite the efforts of Ickes and Roosevelt, the statement never came forth. Further efforts to get Nye's endorsement continued on into October, but he did not get off the fence. Nye left it for voters to connect Landon with the "merchants of death."[24]

Presidential speechwriter Samuel Rosenman saw the Chautauqua speech as Roosevelt's first effort to "warn the people of the United States and the world of the dangers which lurked in all dictatorships." Rosenman found Roosevelt returning to the same theme in the "Quarantine the Aggressor" speech of October 1937. Coming fourteen months after the Chautauqua speech and during a year without any national elections, "Quarantine the Aggressor" again emphasized the horrors of modern warfare and stressed Roosevelt's desire to follow a peaceful policy. In the earlier speech FDR said "I hate war." In the later address, he noted that "America hates war." There was an important difference between the two addresses, however, with the latter making no mention of war profiteers as impediments to peace. Unlike the fall of 1934 or 1936, views expressed by the munitions committee were of little political value to the President in the fall of 1937.[25]

Taken out of context, President Roosevelt appeared to waffle in his posture toward the Nye Committee. He initially endorsed it enthusiastically, then supported it halfheartedly, and finally viewed the hearings skeptically. His approach was often shaped by the political purposes he could make of the munitions investigation and its hearings. FDR first used the hearings to confuse his opponents in the 1934 elections, but then retreated when the investigation threatened to jeopardize his own rearmament plans and challenge administration positions on war profits and neutrality. When the hearings ended, FDR once again embraced the thinking of the committee in time for the 1936 election. By standing on the platform in North Dakota with Gerald P. Nye in August 1934 and meeting with him at Hyde Park in August 1936, Roosevelt sought the political backing of Nye and of the forces and interests that supported his investigatory committee.

Roosevelt's relation to the Nye Committee had little do with whether the investigation proved or disproved the "merchants of death" thesis. FDR's tacit endorsement of the Liberty League, his Chautauqua speech, and consideration of the political impact of the munitions investigation figured little in Wiltz's analysis. As Richard Dean Burns pointed out, Wiltz's study emerged from the temperament of the cold war 1950s. The Nye Committee folded comfortably into isolationism and appeasement, both anathema to the internationalist and containment doctrines of the 1950s and early 1960s. Nye Committee members led the fight for neutrality legislation in 1935; and five weeks after FDR signed the bill into law, Mussolini's Italian forces invaded Ethiopia. The munitions committee held its last hearing on February 20, 1936. Less than three weeks later, Hitler's army rolled into the Rhineland. For much of this aggression the Nye Committee pointed the finger of blame at munitions manufacturers, whereas later generations of historians held the committee responsible for fueling isolationist opinion that led to appeasement. Wiltz saw the committee promoting a "national distraction during a critical period"[26] of American history. Nye, Raushenbush, Roosevelt, and others connected with the investigation, however, viewed the munitions committee as something more than a distraction. Perhaps historians could benefit from doing likewise.

Acknowledgment
Portions of this chapter were previously published in Matthew Coulter, *Senate Munitions Inquiry of the 1930s: Beyond the Merchants of Death* (Westport, CT: Greenwood Press, 1997). The author and publisher have given permission to publish this material here.

NOTES

1. James A. Henretta, and others, *American's History*, 2nd ed. (New York: Worth Publishers, 1993), p. 818.

2. John E. Wiltz, *In Search of Peace: The Senate Munitions Inquiry, 1934–1936* (Baton Rouge: Louisiana State University Press, 1963).

3. Ibid., pp. 3, 231.

4. Richard Dean Burns, "Introduction" in Helmuth Carol Englebrecht and Frank Cleary Hanighen, *Merchants of Death: A Study of the International Armament Industry* (1934; reprint, New York: Garland Publishing, Inc., 1972), pp. 9–10.

5. After the First World War, Stephen Raushenbush "de-Germanized" his name by dropping the c's.

6. Walter Rauschenbusch, *Christianity and the Social Crisis* (1907; reprint, New York: Macmillan, 1912), p. 270; Rauschenbusch, *Christianizing the Social Order* (New York: Macmillan, 1912), p. 279; Reinhold Niebuhr, *Moral Man and Immoral Society* (1932; reprint, New York: Charles Scribner's Sons, 1949), p. 16; Richard Wightman Fox, *Reinhold Niebuhr: A Biography* (New York: Pantheon Books, 1985), pp. 158–168; Wiltz, *In Search of Peace*, p. 50.

7. Wiltz, *In Search of Peace*, pp. 26–27, 50–51.

8. James MacGregor Burns, *The Crosswinds of Freedom* (New York: Alfred A. Knopf, 1989), p. 155; Wayne S. Cole, *Roosevelt and the Isolationists, 1932–1945* (Lincoln: University of Nebraska Press, 1983), p. 62; Selig Adler, *The Uncertain Giant, 1921–1941* (New York: Macmillan, 1965), p. 65; Robert Dallek, *Franklin D. Roosevelt and American Foreign Policy, 1932–1945* (New York: Oxford University Press, 1979), p. 86; Kenneth S. Davis, *FDR: The New Deal Years, 1933–1947* (New York: Random House, 1986), pp. 553–554.

9. Cordell Hull, *Memoirs* (New York: The Macmillan Company, 1948), 1, p. 400; Dorothy Detzer, *Appointment on the Hill* (New York: Henry Holt and Company, 1948), pp. 160–163.

10. Special Committee on Investigation of the Munitions Industry, Hearings, Part 17, pp. 4244–4246; "DuPont's Income Increased in Year," *New York Times*, January 31, 1934, p. 25; Englebrecht and Hanighen, *Merchants of Death*, pp. 22–37.

11. Hull, *Memoirs*, 1:398; "Roosevelt to Link Arms and Chocolate," *New York Times*, May 18, 1939; J. Pierrepont Moffat diary, cited in Cole, *Roosevelt and the Isolationists*, p. 149; Wayne S. Cole, *Senator Gerald P. Nye and American Foreign Relations* (Minneapolis: The University of Minnesota Press, 1962), pp. 58–59; Nye papers, container 15, Herbert Hoover Presidential Library, West Branch, Iowa.

12. Arthur M. Schlesinger Jr., *The Coming of the New Deal* (Boston: Houghton Mifflin Company, 1958), p. 486; Roosevelt to William E. Dodd, August 25, 1934, Franklin D. Roosevelt Papers, President's Personal File, FDR Library, Hyde Park; Donald Day, ed., *Franklin D. Roosevelt's Own Story: Told in His Own Words from His Private and Public Papers* (Boston: Little, Brown and Company, 1951), pp. 221–222.

13. "Begins Munitions Inquiry," *New York Times*, August 18, 1934, p. 26, and "$1,245,000,000 Work to DuPonts During War," September 13, 1934, p. 5; Charles F. Brown to Roosevelt, September 15, 1934; Roosevelt to MacIntyre, September 24, 1934; and J. Edgar Hoover memorandum, October 10, 1034, all in R.G. 60, Department of Justice file 235644, National Archives.

14. "11 Alumni Honored by City College," *New York Times*, November 18, 1934, section II, p. 1 [Senator Nye spoke at the ceremonies honoring the alumni.] and "Roosevelt Will Ask Laws to Take Profit Out of War; Baruch to Offer Program," December 13, 1934, pp. 1–2; Dorothy Detzer telegram to state leaders of the Women's International League for Peace and Freedom (WILPF), December 13, 1934, WILPF-U.S. section records, Document Group 43, Swarthmore College Peace Collection, Swarthmore, PA.

15. Roosevelt to Hull, February 23, 1935, R.G. 59, 811.13/582, National Archives.

16. Wiltz, *In Search of Peace*, 175; Cole, *Roosevelt and the Isolationists*, p. 154; Dallek, *Franklin D. Roosevelt and American Foreign Policy*, 102; Robert A. Divine, *The Illusion of Neutrality* (Chicago: The University of Chicago Press, 1962), pp. 87–88.

17. *Foreign Relations of the United States, 1935*, 1:339–40; *Congressional Record*, 74th Congress, 1st Session, pp. 5325–5326.

18. "Filibuster Threat Made," *New York Times*, August 21, 1935, p. 1; *Congressional Record*, 74th Congress, 1st Session, 13775–13797; Elliot Roosevelt, ed., *FDR: His Personal Letters, 1928–1945* (New York: Duell, Sloan and Pearce, 1950), 1, pp. 506–507.

19. Hull, *Memoirs*, 1, pp. 401–403; Elliot Roosevelt, ed., *FDR: His Personal Letters, 1928–1945*, 1, pp. 452–453; Felix Frankfurter to Henry L. Stimson, October 1935, Stimson papers, microfilm.

20. Special Committee Investigating the Munitions Industry, Hearings, Part 28, p. 8509–8514; *Congressional Record*, 74th Congress, 2nd Session, pp. 504–512, 564–577.

21. "Smith Threatens Revolt on Roosevelt Leadership; Calls New Deal Socialism," *New York Times*, January 26, 1936, pp. 1, 36–37.

22. Frank Freidel, *Franklin D. Roosevelt: A Rendezvous with Destiny* (Boston: Little, Brown and Company, 1990), pp. 202–203; Harold L. Ickes, *The Secret Diary of Harold L. Ickes* (New York: Simon and Schuster, 1953), p. 661.

23. "President Roosevelt's Chautauqua Address on International Affairs," *New York Times*, August 15, 1936, 4.

24. Ickes, *The Secret Diary of Harold Ickes* (New York: Simon and Schuster, 1953), pp. 663–665, 698.

25. Samuel I. Rosenman, *Working with Roosevelt* (New York: Harper Brothers, 1952), p. 108; "President Urges 'Concerted Action' for Peace and Arraigns Warmakers; League Committee Condemns Japan," *New York Times*, October 6, 1937, p. 1. [The text of the speech is in this edition on pp. 1, 16.]

26. Wiltz, *In Search of Peace*, pp. 231–232.

CHAPTER FOUR

'Die Velt, Yene Velt, and Roosevelt':
The New Deal In The Jewish Community

MARC DOLLINGER

When Jews first immigrated to the New World in 1654, they met resistance from New Amsterdam's governor, Peter Stuyvesant, who feared that the new arrivals would become destitute and petition the colonial authority for relief. The Dutch West Indies Company, which employed Stuyvesant, cautioned him not to expel immigrants whom it believed could offer valuable commercial services to the local economy. After some negotiation, the three parties reached a compromise: Jews would be allowed to settle in New Amsterdam, provided they agreed to take care of their own poor and needy. This agreement, later known as the Stuyvesant Pledge, evolved into a sacred American Jewish promise to reject government support and establish their own philanthropic and social welfare agencies.

At the turn of the twentieth century, the Stuyvesant Pledge continued to hold great symbolic power, despite centuries of population growth and an industrialized economy which made social welfare self-sufficiency next to impossible. The Jewish community still prided itself on its impressive philanthropic and social welfare organizations. Over a 250-year period, American Jews from Spain and later Germany and eastern Europe, developed one of the most sophisticated private philanthropic systems in the United States. Organizations such as the American Jewish Committee, Hebrew Immigrant Aid Society, Joint Distribution Committee, and the later American Jewish Congress raised monies and distributed them to needy Jews in the United States and throughout the world.

Within a generation, however, Jewish leaders began a systematic assault on what had become an anachronistic promise. Burdened with the massive immigration of eastern European Jews, Jewish leaders began to reassess their responsibility to "care for their own." When the Great Depression pressed the nation's private social welfare programs beyond their limits, one prominent Jewish leader, Isaac Rubinow, a Cornell University economist and architect of the Social Security system, rose at a national convention for Jewish social workers and asked pointedly, "What do we owe to Peter Stuyvesant?"[1]

The answer was surprising. Not only did Jewish communal organizations abandon their age-old promise, but they led the charge for greater federal government involvement in relief and recovery. American Jews, steeped in an eastern European tradition that valued communitarian solutions to social welfare problems, challenged traditional conceptions of American poverty, which placed the primary responsibility for poverty on the individual and the main burden for recovery on private philanthropy or local government. American Jews stood in the forefront of the movement for the government dole, believing that the human will for self-improvement outweighed the inclination towards pauperism. When the U.S. Congress approved millions of dollars in welfare relief, the Jewish community spear-headed the drive for community control, guaranteeing its clients the best possible care and defining a central feature of New Deal liberalism—the enfranchisement of local political leaders as a means to guarantee the success of Roosevelt's national reform plan.[2]

Demographic changes within the Jewish community inspired corresponding national political change. As America's eastern European Jews challenged their assimilationist-minded German-American coreligionists for control of organized Jewish life, they developed a definition of Americanism founded on tolerance, pluralism, and an embrace of ethnic difference. At a time when New Deal programs placed all Americans under the same economic umbrella, eastern European American Jews demonstrated that government programs could be redirected to benefit Jewish educational, cultural, and character-building programs. Their desire to maintain a strong Jewish subculture within the larger framework of an activist federal government challenged conventional thinking on the question of ethnic persistence during the New Deal years.[3]

Jewish affinity for New Deal-style programs inspired nothing less than complete devotion to its chief architect, Franklin D. Roosevelt. On election day 1932, Jewish Americans posted a solid 82 percent vote in favor of the former New York governor. In later elections, Jewish support for the incumbent chief executive would rise to an astronomical 90 percent. The Jewish community embraced the Democratic standard bearer so completely that Judge Jonah J. Goldstein once remarked that American Jews had but three worlds (*velten*); *die velt* (this world), *yene velt* (the next world), and Roosevelt.

The marriage between American Jews and Roosevelt's New Deal proved beneficial for both. The administration inherited the legacy and expertise of an American Jewish community committed to New Deal-style politics while the Jewish community enjoyed unprecedented access to the corridors of power, official confirmation that they had "made it" as Americans after only a single generation on this country's shores. By the end of the New Deal, the American Jewish community had moved from archaic slogans of Jewish self-sufficiency to the realization that its economic future was tied to that of the nation. American Jews established themselves as solid Democratic voters committed to activist government and a progressive social welfare platform. The Jewish community formally rejected its colonial promise: It owed nothing to Peter Stuyvesant.[4]

When the stock market crashed on October 24, 1929, Jewish leaders, in a reaction typical of the period, expressed little fear of impending crisis. The American Jewish Committee, meeting just three weeks after the Wall Street plummet, failed to mention the economic downturn in any of its proceedings. Jewish Family Welfare Agencies experienced only slight increases in expenditures and in the number of cases served. Fundraising efforts by local Jewish Federation Councils continued unaffected throughout the 1930 campaign as relief costs among the largest Jewish agencies increased just 7 percent.[5]

By 1931, though, Jewish social welfare organizations felt an economic pinch. More Jews applied for aid than in any previous year. Jewish social workers witnessed increases in case loads, expenditures, and applications for service. The American Jewish Committee disclosed that for the fiscal year, "practically every local Federation in the country was compelled to reduce its budget." The Chicago Jewish charities announced that for the first time in their history, they ended the year with a deficit. In Cleveland, early plans were made both to expand contributor pools and to economize operations. In every relief category, Jewish agencies carried a greater burden.[6]

By the winter of 1931–1932, relief figures peaked at a new high. As the snow melted in the spring of 1932, Jewish social welfare organizations faced new, more difficult challenges. Demand for social service increased, but contributions to Jewish philanthropic appeals decreased. The Bureau of Jewish Social Research reported 50 percent increases in relief while contributions declined 30 percent. Jewish agencies sought out bank loans to cover their relief commitments. As the nation continued to sink into economic collapse in the first half of 1933, so, too, did Jewish agencies. A third more Jewish Americans sought relief in 1933 than in the previous year. In thirteen large cities, federations reported a decline in contributions from $8.8 million in 1930 to $5.9 million in 1933.[7]

American Jews responded to the economic crisis by stepping up their campaign for government relief. Overwhelmed by the sheer numbers of poor and unemployed, American Jews rejected the prevailing individualist social and economic ideology and embraced a collectivist stance that acknowledged systemic inequalities. They answered the conservative charge that government aid created a welfare-dependent nation by pointing to the novelties of a modern industrial economy and by arguing, as other American liberals had since the nineteenth century, that the "worthy poor" should not be penalized for poverty caused more by economic factors than moral transgression. By distinguishing between worthy and unworthy, American Jews justified government aid while they addressed the fear of overreliance on the state.[8]

The community's call for federal intervention challenged traditional American ideas about the nature of poverty, redefined the role of the national government in welfare relief, and forged a new relationship between the Jewish community and the state. During the New Deal years, Jewish organizations insisted on federal intervention to help ease the burdens weighing heavy on their social welfare agencies. Ironically, the organized Jewish community's increased reliance on the state nourished a Jewish cultural revival. Freed from responsibilities for relief, Jewish philanthropies concentrated on creating Jewish educational and religious programs.

This novel fashioning of New Deal programs offers a new interpretation of the state's relationship to ethnic Americans. The most recent studies of 1930s ethnic life conclude that the overwhelming economic demands of the era necessitated abandonment of ethnic identity to embrace a more universal political culture. Gary Gerstle, in his exhaustive labor history of Woonsocket, Rhode Island, *Working Class Americanism: The Politics of Labor in A Textile City: 1914-1960*, contended that "New Deal icons like the Blue Eagle...offered individual Americans security and a sense of belonging to a greater whole in a time of deep distress. These symbols and terms," he concluded, "thus encouraged adjustment rather than rebellion, conformity rather than dissent."[9]

Lizabeth Cohen, in her award-winning study of depression-era Chicago, *Making A New Deal*, asserted that local ethnic networks collapsed under the weight of federal intervention. It was a time, Cohen asserted, "when the nation moved...from diverse social worlds circumscribed by race, ethnicity, class, and geography to more homogeneous cultural experiences." This diminution of ethnic identity, according to Cohen, led Chicago laborers to petition for a larger governmental role. The New Deal, she contended, weakened communal ties. "People would depend on the government," explained Cohen, "the way they once had depended on [ethnic organizations]." Cohen's findings conflict with the experience of both national and local Jewish organizations. While Cohen posited that "ethnic workers would never again accept so easily the hierarchical authority of the ethnic community," this chapter demonstrates how one religious minority used New Deal programs as a vehicle to forge stronger institutional bonds.[10]

The shift from private to public aid in the United States developed slowly and revealed profound fears about involving government in the traditional sphere of private philanthropy. Historically, the federal government expected private philanthropies and local governments to assume primary responsibility for welfare relief. "Care of the poor," one New Dealer affirmed, "has been recognized from earliest colonial days as fundamentally a function of local government." This attitude, borrowed from the nineteenth-century English economist Thomas Malthus, "held that the poor were responsible for their own misery and destitution, that they had no 'right' to public relief." Laissez-faire reigned supreme.[11]

Opponents of activist government dominated American politics throughout the 1920s and into the 1930s. Senator Thomas Gore of Oklahoma wrote in 1931 that "you could no more relieve the depression by legislation than you can pass a resolution to prevent disease." Conservative Americans remained skeptical of government involvement. Artificial tinkering in the up and downs of the economy, they reasoned, could only unbalance the natural rhythm of supply and demand, job production and unemployment, growth and recession. Economic downturns, like physical ailments, could best be remedied by following nature's course, and government action was not natural.[12]

Critics of government relief spending insisted that success or failure in the economic world reflected an individual's moral fitness. Invoking the memory of the late nineteenth-century industrial giants who opposed government regulation, conservative opponents of the New Deal adhered to the principle that the economic cycle rewarded those most fit for advancement and punished those lacking the appropriate human qualities. Bright, keen, and intelligent Americans would find a way to prosper. Those who were lazy and uninterested would end up impoverished. The federal government could not be held responsible for problems created by individual vices.[13]

American Jews argued that the unique size and scale of the 1930s depression mandated a change in social policy. "Victims of the depression who are able and willing to work but can find none through no fault of their own," argued Maurice Karpf, dean of the Graduate School for Jewish Social Work, "should not be forced to apply to charity but should be aided by the government whose duty it is to care for its citizens." Marc Grossman, the president of Cleveland's Jewish social service bureau, concurred, observing that the depression brought new clients who were "physically and mentally fit." In previous years, Jewish social service agencies assisted only those unable to care for themselves. With the business downturn, Grossman discovered a new group of needy who "were merely victims of a change in the economic structure affecting the entire population." By distinguishing their needs as a Jewish minority from their rights as American citizens, communal leaders justified their support for federal aid and led liberal America down the path to activist affirmative government.[14]

Jewish social workers pointed out that most of the nation's poor did not lose their jobs due to mental or even physical defect. The moral fitness argument, Karpf explained, could not be waged in an economy where otherwise productive and competent people went jobless.[15]

American Jews, with virtual unanimity, called for more local, state, and, eventually, national government activity. In the midst of an economic crisis that knew neither ethnic nor religious bounds, Jewish liberals reasoned, basic relief and welfare needs were the domain of the government. As early as 1918, the reform movement called for a government-sponsored unemployment insurance program as well as a pension fund for elderly Americans. In 1923, Jewish social service agencies questioned "the need, desirability, and propriety of separate Jewish agencies." During the 1920s, Jewish organizations urged municipal governments to take a more active role in the social welfare needs of their community while Isaac Rubinow worked up plans for a national social security system. By 1931, representatives from Catholic and Protestant philanthropies as well as leaders from the Polish American, German American, and African American organizations joined the Jewish community in calling for greater governmental action.[16]

Jewish leaders justified their call for federal relief by pointing to the catastrophic Great Depression and reminding their constituents that only large-scale solutions could remedy widespread economic problems. "Economic adjustment is a national and social problem," Benjamin Glassberg, a Milwaukee social worker, contended in 1931, "It is not a specifically Jewish problem." The following year, Ben Rosen concluded that "It is becoming less and less apparent that there is a special Jewish responsibility" for relief. "If in any large degree," the executive director of New York's Federation for the Support of Jewish Philanthropic Societies petitioned, "either the governmental or the semi-public agencies would be able to take over or to relieve us of the necessity for raising the funds for our relief activities, either broadly or narrowly defined, that would be helpful."[17]

The following year, Benjamin Selekman of Boston's Federation of Jewish Philanthropies proposed an eight-point plan that called for "the development in the United States during the depression of an elaborate program of public social work, particularly in the field of relief." Harry Lurie, the director of New York's Bureau of Jewish Social Research, acknowledged that the Jewish community was "beginning to see more clearly that the Jewish family agency actually functions in a supplementary capacity and that its future is tied up with the destinies of the entire public welfare movement." Other leaders concurred. Henry Monsky, president of Omaha's community chest and welfare fund and later national president of B'nai B'rith, recognized "that the Jewish group is an integral and inseparable part of the larger community and must adjust itself to a program of active participation in and entire cooperation with the social agencies that minister to the social needs of the community as a whole." He explained, "It is totally illogical, to my mind to hold ourselves aloof as a special and segregated group and to refuse to accept or refrain from the enjoyment of the aid and assistance justly due to our group...from the public agencies."[18]

Jews considered themselves a distinct ethnic community, not a distinct economic community. They focused on that separation to justify support for government aid. Solutions to basic economic problems, Jewish leaders reasoned, extended beyond the means of the private relief agency. Isaac Rubinow held that "the economic position of the American Jew today and even more so his position tomorrow is irretrievably interwoven with the economic present and future of the American people." He believed that American Jews had "penetrated American economic life, so much so that to separate them would be as difficult a process, if not as unscrambling eggs, than at least as it would be to separate the light from the dark particles in the sands in the sea." "Jewish poverty is not a result of intra-group conditions," he explained, "It is part and parcel of the whole economic and social problem of wealth production and wealth accumulation of the country as a whole."[19]

Though often overburdened and understaffed, local, state, and finally federal government agencies responded as best they could to the new demands. The experiences of Milton Meltzer, a fourteen-year-old Jewish boy from Worcester, Massachusetts, personified the earnest but fruitless relief efforts by local authorities. With unemployment at 25 percent and a winter storm blowing, Meltzer recalled that in 1932, his city government hired citizens to clear the streets. While he was careful to credit his local government for all it did, Meltzer ultimately admonished that "the cities, counties, and states were not prepared to meet the crisis." Meltzer's experience was typical of most Americans who found traditional means of alleviating unemployment ineffective in the face of the Great Depression.[20]

Plans for state-sponsored relief began in 1929 when the New York legislature, at the request of Governor Franklin Roosevelt, authorized a commission to study the feasibility of a state social security plan. Not until 1931, though, did the New York legislature approve a $20 million grant for unemployment relief. Later that year, New

Jersey allocated almost $10 million for the same purpose while in Pennsylvania, Governor Gifford Pinchot called a special session of the state legislature to secure additional funds for the state's welfare, health, and labor departments. Similar scenarios played out in Wisconsin, Rhode Island, Kentucky, Oklahoma, New Hampshire, Maryland, and California. "Never before in the history of the United States," reflected Josephine Brown, later an assistant to Harry Hopkins, "had state governments invested so heavily in relief for any purpose. These unprecedented appropriations established once and for all the responsibility of state government for relief of persons in need, not only in this unemployment emergency but in any emergency."[21]

As local and state agencies increased their commitment to relief, Jewish welfare organizations grew more dependent upon public aid for their survival. "Between 1929 and 1932," *Jewish Social Work* reported, "new public agencies were set up in Chicago, Philadelphia, and New York, to name only three cities. In each case, primary responsibility for relief was assumed by the public agency, the Jewish agency readjusting its program to meet needs otherwise not met." Reports issued in 1931 from New York, Brooklyn, Philadelphia, Chicago, and Detroit indicated that the majority of Jewish social work cases were not handled by Jewish agencies. Another study of some fifty-two Jewish communities found "increased responsibility assumed by governmental agencies for programs of unemployment relief and emergency funds."[22]

At a meeting held five months before the 1932 presidential election, the National Conference of Jewish Social Service called on Congress and the president "not only to alleviate present and immediately impending suffering, but to lay the foundations for the effective prevention of similar social and economic catastrophes in the future." Conference delegate Linton B. Swift criticized President Hoover's continued insistence that "the American method of assisting the unemployed is through private charity." Dr. Ben Selekman, executive director of Boston's associated Jewish philanthropies, alerted the delegates to the probability that they, as Jewish social workers, would "have to redouble [their] efforts and take the lead, if necessary in getting the proper kind of governmental action in alleviating distress due to unemployment." Jewish America demanded that the federal government take decisive action to head off the worsening depression, but the Hoover administration failed to turn the economic tide, and they looked to the Democratic nominee, Franklin D. Roosevelt, and his proposed New Deal for American society.[23]

Soon after his election, Franklin Roosevelt and his advisers formulated federal plans for economic recovery. After his inauguration, the new president took to the radio to deliver the first of his famous "fireside chats." Gathered around their radios, listening to their national leader, Jews, like other Americans, took notice of the president's urging and worked hard to help bring the nation to recovery. American Jews would come to share a special relationship with Roosevelt and liberal politics: it was the New Deal that marked the emergence of Jewish Americans as prime performers in the unfolding drama of national political change. Between the beginning of the "Roosevelt Revolution" in 1933 and the outbreak of war in 1941, Jews entered the political mainstream en masse.[24]

During his first 100 days in office, the president kept his messengers busy en route from the White House to the Capitol Building, initiating an unprecedented campaign for legislative reform. The "alphabet soup" agencies, as they came to be known, addressed problems in areas as diverse as agriculture, business, finance, and labor. Organizations such as the Agricultural Adjustment Administration (AAA), National Recovery Administration (NRA), Civilian Conservation Corps (CCC), and Works Progress Administration (WPA), attempted to arrest the deteriorating economy and stimulate growth.

Almost immediately, New Deal programs slowed the downward spiral and helped put the nation on the long road to recovery. Isador Lubin, the commissioner of the United States Department of Labor's Bureau of Labor Statistics, reported in May 1934 that income for the average American had increased 27 percent over the previous year, and unemployment rates had decreased. Over half the Americans who lost their jobs between 1929 and 1933 found employment between April 1933 and April 1934. Jewish philanthropies noted an upward turn in contributions. Due in large part to aggressive public relief and works programs, Jewish social service agencies reduced their relief budgets for the first time since the onset of depression.[25]

Jews greeted FDR's early recovery efforts with the same enthusiasm as other Americans. After the failure of President Hoover's more conservative approach, change, any change, offered hope. In newspapers and magazines, in synagogues and throughout their neighborhoods, the Jewish community welcomed the new president's reform program. In its April 1933 edition, for example, the B'nai B'rith *Messenger* urged "the Jews of America" to "serve as a leaven of social reconstruction." Isaac Rubinow, speaking before a national gathering of Jewish social workers only months after Roosevelt's inauguration, typified the hope of America's Jews when he affirmed that "it was the duty of social workers to force upon the attention of a bewildered world the necessity of a broad legislative economic program." On record as Roosevelt's most loyal supporters, American Jews looked to their new duty with both optimism and concern.[26]

In the months and years before the New Deal, American Jews could call for increased government aid with virtual impunity. Speeches, platforms, and resolutions offered idyllic hopes of a more utopian world, but they failed to account for the important concessions Jewish organizations would be asked to make in exchange for federal aid. With the flurry of New Deal legislation, Jews, like so many other Americans of the time, learned the art of political compromise. They knew that President Roosevelt needed their support to make the New Deal a success, just as they were reminded that government aid always came with strings attached.

As the U.S. Congress debated various relief bills, American Jews worked to guarantee that New Deal programs would respect the needs of minorities in a pluralistic society. Their concerns over federal projects mirrored reservations expressed by most private philanthropic agencies. Communal leaders wanted to ensure that the government in Washington would serve the special needs of the local ethnic community and that the standards of social welfare administered by the newly formed federal programs would match those performed by the older, more established local organizations. American Jewish leaders eased their concerns by supporting a cooperative arrangement with government.

The Jewish community did not have to wait long to test the new waters of affirmative government. Within eight weeks of his inauguration, Roosevelt secured passage of the Federal Emergency Relief Act (FERA), allocating $500 million "to provide for cooperation by the federal government with the several states...in relieving the hardship and suffering caused by unemployment." The measure stipulated that virtually all relief work administered by private agencies be turned over to the federal government.[27]

The FERA's effect on the Jewish community was immediate and profound. As Jewish relief cases were sent to the public social service agency en masse, the economic strains on the Jewish agencies eased. By the end of 1933, the majority of dependent Jewish families received aid from public agencies. Relief expenditures for Jewish family welfare agencies dropped from $4.04 million in 1933 to $2.38 million in 1934. The number of cases administered by Jewish agencies declined to predepression levels for the first time since the market crash.[28]

According to the Bureau of Jewish Social Research, "the F.E.R.A. ruling constituted by far the most influential factor in determining the relief, intake, case-count and staff trend for the Jewish family agency in 1933." "By executive order," the Bureau explained, "the Federal Relief Administration had accelerated a process which was and is changing the entire development of a family service program under Jewish auspices." The Bureau found that in large cities, "the Jewish community, as represented in its organized philanthropies, is today no longer charged with the responsibility of meeting all the relief needs of its submarginal groups. That function, perhaps permanently, has been delegated to the state." By the end of 1933, none of the twenty largest cities with a Jewish population had allocated the care of the majority of dependent Jewish families to a Jewish agency, and a 1936 survey of Jews in Minneapolis found that once "the philanthropic burden ha[d] been transferred from Jewish to general community responsibility, the long tradition of Jewish self-sufficiency ha[d] been broken."[29]

The Jewish communal embrace of FERA marked a major turning point for American Jews. Leaders of Jewish organizations rejected social welfare self-sufficiency and embraced government intervention. For the first time in modern history, Jews allied with a civil government dedicated to improving their quality of life. Frustrated in the old country by the anti-Semitic policies of czarist officials and thwarted in the United States by a generation of politicians dedicated to laissez-faire economic policies, the organized Jewish community reveled in Roosevelt's willingness to listen to ordinary Americans and lend a helping hand. The Jewish community applauded FDR's contention that government could serve as a force for positive social change with fifty years of loyal Democratic support. New Deal programs such as the FERA reaffirmed an optimistic Jewish assessment of the American political system: Government and private citizens could work together.

While almost all Jewish organizations welcomed New Deal relief money, no two agencies adjusted to the new arrangement in exactly the same way. In Baltimore,

Cleveland, St. Louis, and San Francisco, government officials played a large part in the whole welfare process. By contrast, their role in Indianapolis, Scranton, and Providence was more limited. As a general rule, most Jewish agencies enjoyed federal government support without losing a great deal of operational autonomy. That national policy stemmed from Roosevelt's calculated attempts to gain grassroots support for the New Deal by empowering local officials with fiscal control. FDR's strategy successfully gained support for the New Deal and strengthened the Democratic party machines throughout the nation.[30]

Political benefits aside, professional social workers sought local control for humanitarian reasons. Josephine C. Brown explained that "extravagance and waste were bound to occur when spending was so far removed from local controls, and such a regime would necessarily be more subject to political interference. Local citizens knew local conditions best." She concluded, "The nearer the administration of relief was kept to the community affected the sooner its evils would be detected and checked." Private agencies received government assistance without compromising their operational autonomy while the government saved the time and expense of creating duplicative social service agencies.[31]

American Jews also supported local control because they feared that government social workers would be unable to serve the particular needs of the Jewish community. For the Jewish agencies, operational autonomy meant maintaining specialized care for the Jewish poor. Jewish social service, Ben Selekman said, was devoted to "those activities which are so specifically Jewish that none but Jews can be expected to support them." Religious Jews required kosher food, often spoke Yiddish, and observed Jewish traditions. In Atlanta, for example, the Jewish agency retained its case load because recipients required "a good deal of service and we have assumed that our knowledge of the psychological and cultural background of our group gives us a better understanding of the problems of these clients." Only a social worker specially trained in Jewish customs, they argued, could properly care for the Jewish client.[32]

Jews addressed the often-heard complaint that government organizations lagged behind private agencies in their quality of client care. During the depression years, the Jewish social service agencies' quality of care and service surpassed that provided by government welfare programs. In 1930, for example, Jewish agencies provided an average relief check of $43.09 compared to an industry average of only $22.80. One Jewish social worker called upon private philanthropy "to stimulate the public agencies to an increasingly high standard of personnel and of service" while delegates at a 1933 meeting of the Southern New England Conference of the National Council of Jewish Federations and Welfare Funds concluded that the inadequacies of government relief and training constituted "good reason for the continued existence and independence of Jewish family welfare work."[33]

The same year, Jewish Family Welfare Executives "reemphasized the responsibility of the Jewish agency to improve the standards of public relief, to preserve the essential case work services for Jews and to extend the specialized services of a constructive nature not available through the public agency." In 1934, Ben Selekman warned his colleagues that "[u]ntil the public childcare agency maintains social work standards as high as those of the private, the Jewish community will probably insist upon maintaining dependent and neglected children of the Jewish faith as its wards."[34]

Communal leaders sometimes charged the government agencies with insensitivity towards the poor. Jewish social workers stressed the importance of remembering their clients' dignity and honor as they dispensed relief. Even the FERA, they pointed out, reflected the principle that the poor were somehow responsible for their own misfortune. In order to qualify for assistance, potential recipients were required to show up at a relief station in person and pass a means test verifying their economic status. Many complained of the humiliation involved with such a process, arguing that the focus should not be placed upon them as individuals, but rather on society as a whole.[35]

With some trepidation, Jewish social workers moved their clients to the public rolls. Yet, in the final analysis, Jewish social workers accepted the limitations of federal relief and acknowledged that the future of their social work programs depended on continued government funding. Fears about government interference eased as Jewish agencies succeeded in securing government subsidies without relinquishing their responsibility as primary caseworkers. A 1933 Bureau of Jewish Social Research study confirmed a cooperative spirit between Jewish social service organizations and government. In the years after 1933, Jewish agencies continued to serve special-need cases and, whenever possible, encourage the federal government to hire Jewish social workers to serve the public agency's Jewish clientele.

Appropriations from the FERA expired in 1935. Most Americans on relief rolls shifted to the Works Progress Administration (WPA) to build public works projects. The rest transferred back to Jewish agencies for care. State relief funds were quickly exhausted as primary responsibility fell once again upon local communities. In St. Louis, for example, "where 25,000 employable men and women were transferred from the relief rolls to federal works projects," Jewish clients "shunted from the public agency to the private, and from the private to the public." Yet, while Jewish agencies bore increased financial burdens after 1935, they never again faced the desperate situations they had in 1932 and 1933.[36]

By May 1934, Isador Lubin reported that average per capita weekly income had grown 27 percent in a single year. At the nadir of the depression in 1933, thirty-nine of the largest Jewish family agencies cared for approximately 31,000 families. After implementation of the FERA, that number dropped to 23,000. In 1935, relief expenditures dropped below predepression figures and continued to decline throughout the remainder of the decade.[37]

The increased government aid provided by New Deal programs not only relieved a great financial burden for Jewish philanthropies, but also forced Jewish fundraising organizations to justify their existence. "The impact of vast social changes," Benjamin Selekman explained at a 1936 meeting of the Conference of Jewish Federations and Welfare Funds, "has given new challenge once again to the Jewish tradition of communal responsibility. For, like all people, American Jewry faces today the central problem of our times—adaptation to rapidly moving economic and social forces." Selekman called on his coreligionists to explain how they could justify and protect their community's specific interests at a time when all Americans were realizing the universality of economic depression. He understood the irony of supporting government aid when that meant challenging the Jewish organization's raison d'etre. An embrace of government action not only promised great social and political rewards, but also demanded accommodation and compromise as well.[38]

Jewish social workers, led by second-generation American Jews of eastern European descent, took advantage of their new-found resources to increase support for Jewish cultural, educational, and social activities. Eastern European American Jews advocated strengthening character-building programs as a way to preserve Jewish traditions at a time when most had left the Orthodox fold of their parents and grandparents. Enjoying the rights and privileges of citizenship, these second- and third-generation American Jews sought some way of guaranteeing the survival of their heritage.

In earlier years, Jewish communal life in the United States had been controlled by German American Jews. Forced out of Europe by the political upheaval of the 1840s, thousands of established, middle-class, professional German Jews immigrated to the United States where they enjoyed great success in business and commerce. When eastern European Jews immigrated en masse at the turn of the twentieth century, the German Jewish community funded numerous absorption, education, and "Americanization" programs for the new arrivals. The German Jews supported a platform of assimilation and accommodation in American life, opposing most attempts to preserve traditional customs and beliefs long abandoned by their Reform movement.[39]

While assimilationist-minded German American Jews dictated the terms of Jewish communal life until the 1920s, the ever-growing eastern European American Jewish community coalesced to challenge its German brethren for control of organized Jewish life in the 1930s. Young Jews coming of age during the New Deal advocated the support of Jewish cultural life within the sphere of the private organization. "As the later Jewish immigrants, especially those from eastern Europe attained a more secure place in the [American Jewish] community," Ben Selekman explained, "they urged another directing impulse for Federation programs." The eastern European immigrants brought "the strong feeling that every Jewish child should be given a Jewish education." They looked to the government to provide aid and to themselves as guardians of the Jewish legacy in America. At a time of growing economic interdependence, these Jewish liberals posited a pluralistic vision of American democracy that encouraged American minority groups to forge stronger ethnic bonds. If American Jews could participate equally with other Americans in the national political process, they reasoned, then they should have equal right to protect their distinctive ethnic culture within the limits of their own communal organizations.[40]

Eastern European American Jews pushed for "character building" programs long before the New Deal. At the turn of the century, they supported Talmud Torahs as well as Jewish supplemental schools to make sure their children received formal religious instruction. In 1928, when Jewish educational programs constituted a mere 6 percent of Federation budgets, Jewish social workers called for a greater philanthropic commitment to Jewish cultural life. "Jewish organization cannot rest on pure philanthropy," Dr. John Slawson, the head of the Jewish Welfare Federation in Cleveland and later the executive vice president of the American Jewish Committee, argued. "It must not be based on a foundation of misery and woe. We should not duplicate state and private social instruments; we should supplement to the extent that our Jewish cultural interests make it advisable for us to do so. But our reason for being must be ethnic culture, and not only the maimed, the sick and the blind. Pathology should not be relied on solely as a community integrator."[41]

Slawson tried to steer his colleagues away from relief activities and toward the development of culturally rich Jewish organizations. "The [Jewish] Federation [Council] is no longer a Federation for philanthropy," he insisted, "but becomes a Federation for Jewish ethnic group expression. The dependent is no longer exploited for purposes of emotional satisfaction, but the cultural tone, in all of its manifestations, of the Jewish group as a whole becomes the concern of Jewish organized welfare endeavor—a cooperative enterprise on the part of all American Jewry."[42]

When the depression struck, it slowed the growth of character-building programs. A study on the effects of the depression on Jewish philanthropy revealed that by the latter half of 1930, Federations showed a "precedence of relief over all other needs. While a 1931 report to the National Conference of Jewish Social Service noted "no great changes" in Jewish child care agencies, health agencies, community centers, or national agencies, it did note budget cuts in Jewish education.[43]

By 1932, Jewish communal workers began to dismantle their character-building programs. Harry J. Sapper, reporting on the effects of the depression on intermediate-sized communities, noted that "The swing in the direction of devoting huge sums for relief has...made it necessary to eliminate cultural activities, and to reduce personnel and salaries, at a time when the facilities of these character building and morale saving units of community life are needed most." Kurt Peiser, executive secretary of the United Jewish Social Agencies in Cincinnati, reported that the "Federation is under great pressure and temptation to curtail seriously its allotments to educational constituents." He concluded that "Our work in the educational and recreational fields is being deserted rapidly."[44]

Increasing relief demands on Jewish organizations provoked a bitter debate over the wisdom of continuing character-building programs. Early in 1933, Rabbi Edward L. Israel of Baltimore exhorted his coreligionists to remember the importance of Jewish cultural activities, even in the face of great economic burdens. "One after another," he lamented, "splendid character-building services which represent the true genius of modern social work have collapsed while the cry has gone up, 'Not a penny for anything except relief.' Even those constructive agencies which are weathering the storm are practically entirely incapacitated from lack of funds." Rabbi Israel represented those Jews who sought to develop an educational foundation for Jewish life within the sphere of the private agency.[45]

Jacob Golub, another Russian immigrant and president of the National Council of Jewish Education concurred. "Jewish education finds itself between two opposing antagonisms," he noted. "On the one hand there is the group that is basically assimilationist and regards Jewish education as an attempt to impose an outmoded religion and the belief in a set of myths upon the modern generation. On the other hand," Golub continued, "the traditional religionists, taking their religion very much in earnest, regard Jewish education as religious education...designed to make the young conform to the beliefs and rituals of traditional Judaism."[46]

Opponents of character building programs saw relief of the hungry as the Jewish community's first priority. According to one social worker, "Any appeal for Jewish culture or other communal needs becomes a very difficult matter from an ethical point of view. If it is to be made an appeal in competition with the needs of the hungry, and the starving, and the widows, and the orphans, if it be a question between feeding the needy and giving up communal and cultural values, we are all human enough to give precedence to the feeding of the hungry."[47]

While those supporting bread over education ostensibly did so out of compassion for needy Jews, proponents of character-building programs charged that the "false opposition of bread versus education" was merely a guise for assimilationist Jews to halt the growing influence of more isolationist and religiously traditional Jews. Albert P. Schoolman, director for the Central Jewish Institute, reminded his colleagues that "no poor parents have come clamoring to Jewish schools that these be closed and that the school funds be given them for relief, that the children's Jewish education be neglected and that bread and clothing be given them instead." As far as Schoolman was concerned, "the first and most compelling challenge that is brought forth out of the very lowest depths of economic misery produced by the depression is the now familiar cry 'in times of depression, what shall it be, bread or education?' " Schoolman thought it "significant that this apparent dilemma is being posited by those in our community who are physically satiated, but Jewishly, spiritually starved, and not by those whose body may be hungry but whose Jewish spirit has not been emaciated."[48]

Schoolman's veiled reference to assimilationist German American Jews points out the inherent contradiction in the bread-versus-education debate. Assimilationist-minded American Jews could not argue for increased government aid on the one hand and then criticize Jewish education for taking needed relief funds on the other. "Does the cry of bread versus education really present mutually exclusive alternatives?" Schoolman wondered. It did not. Assimilationist-minded Jews sought to capitalize on the depression to achieve an ulterior motive—the more rapid Americanization of the traditional community. Schoolman was accurate when he concluded that "the policy of bread at the expense of education will yield no bread but will consume education."[49]

With the bread-versus-education debate muted by the assumption of relief cases by the government and with the weakening of the assimilationist-minded German

American Jews, proponents of Jewish educational, social, and recreational programs expanded their character-building programs. By 1935, these programs were, according to the executive director of the New York City Federation, "large and growing fields" and commanded over 60 percent of local Federation expenditures. According to Harry Lurie, the shift from relief to character building constituted "a shift of emphasis from the submerged part of the community to the community as a whole and from merely physical and economic need to cultural and spiritual satisfaction."[50]

In 1937, Jewish educators reported "marked improvements" in school classrooms, buildings, and decorations. Harry Glucksman, in his presidential address to the National Conference of Jewish Social Welfare, stressed that "our profession is now in a strategic position to enlarge its field of influence by becoming directly involved in the total pattern of Jewish group life." A social worker reported, "Great changes have taken place in society and particularly in the Jewish situation...the emphasis in Jewish life has changed from preoccupation with the unfortunate minority of maladjusted, the poor and helpless to an almost general concern with problems affecting Jews in all walks of life that arise from the fact that they are Jews." *The American Jewish Year Book*'s "Year in Review for 1936–1937" noted that "a sharp decrease in the economic difficulties experienced by Jewish schools" led to a strengthening of Jewish education. In Los Angeles, over half of the 1938 United Jewish Welfare Fund (UJWF) budget for local activities went for Jewish education, cultural and social programs. In 1939, that figure rose to almost 75 percent.[51]

The New Deal taught American Jews the wisdom of accommodation and compromise. "The most important lesson coming out of this emergency," the president of Cleveland's Jewish social service bureau concluded in an understated 1931 prediction of the decade to come, "is the fact that an unwilling Jewish community has come to realize that relief work can, under proper safeguards, be financed by public funds without detriment to the Jewish families thus served." Not only did the Jewish community learn the plausibility of government aid, it fashioned the Roosevelt reform program into a powerful advocate of American ethnic life. Jews led the call for federal government action, reflecting a faith in civil administration almost unknown in modern Jewish history. Jewish leaders spearheaded the drive for local community control of New Deal monies. Jewish social service clients enjoyed a higher standard of care and assurances that their particular religious needs would be addressed. The Roosevelt administration enjoyed the support of ethnic Americans and of state and municipal political leaders who shared the Jews' drive for greater fiscal and operational autonomy. And, in a consensus era when most Americans lined up behind the Democratic party and its standard bearer, the organized Jewish community showed how a common economic problem could be fashioned into a vehicle for greater multicultural expression. Judge Goldstein's famous quip about the three worlds for Jews only slightly exaggerated the Jewish community's love affair with FDR and his New Deal.[52]

NOTES

1. *Proceedings: National Conference of Jewish Social Service, 1933*, p. 7. The National Conference of Jewish Social Service (NCJSS), later renamed the National Conference of Jewish Social Welfare (NCJSW), brought together leaders in every field of Jewish social service to discuss papers of topical interest. The Conference served as the major forum for presenting ideas and opinions on the state of Jewish social welfare in America.

2. For more on how Roosevelt co-opted local leaders in his New Deal strategy, see Bruce Stave, *The New Deal and the Last Hurrah: Pittsburgh Machine Politics* (Pittsburgh: University of Pittsburgh Press, 1970). FDR's relationship to the state is chronicled in Michael S. Holmes, *The New Deal in Georgia*, (Westport: Greenwood Press, 1974) while Lizabeth Cohen's, *Making a New Deal: Industrial Workers in Chicago, 1919–1939* (New York: Cambridge University Press, 1990), and Charles H. Trout's *Boston, The Great Depression, and the New Deal* (New York: Oxford University Press, 1977) add to Stave's city-centered investigation.

3. See especially, Cohen, *Making a New Deal*.

4. In the electorate as a whole, FDR won support from a broad coalition of Americans. Election returns gave Roosevelt a commanding 57.4 percent majority over rival Herbert Hoover's 39.6 percent. Roosevelt had successfully forged an alliance of farmers and businessmen, southerners and westerners, African Americans and working class ethnic whites. Jewish support for Roosevelt rose to 85 percent in the 1936 election and increased again to 90 percent in both the 1940 and 1944 campaigns (Lewis, *The Jewish Vote: Fact or Fiction*, p. 45). In 1936, even Jewish socialists joined the liberal mainstream and voted for Roosevelt. See Werner Cohn, "Sources of American Jewish Liberalism—A Study of the Political Alignment of American Jews," unpublished Ph. D. dissertation, New School for Social Research, 1956, p. 87. By comparison, a *Literary Digest* poll of 21,606 Christian clergymen in 1936 showed that 70.22 percent opposed New Deal policies, while the majority of Protestant church members opted for Landon over Roosevelt in the 1936 presidential contest (Sidney Ahlstrom, *A Religious History of the American People*, Yale Press, 1972). For more on the New Deal and American Jews, see Leonard Dinnerstein, "Jews and the New Deal," *American Jewish History*, vol. 72, (June, 1983) as well as his "Franklin D. Roosevelt, American Jewry, and the New Deal," in Wilbur J. Cohen, *The Roosevelt New Deal: A Program Assessment Fifty Years After* (Virginia Commonwealth University, 1986).

5. *American Jewish Year Book*, vol. 32, 1930–1931, pp. 299–306; *Jewish Social Work, 1931*, p. 31; *Jewish Social Work, 1930*, pp. 45, 46; Harry Lawrence Lurie, *A Heritage Affirmed: The Jewish Federation Movement in America*, (Philadelphia: Jewish Publication Society of America, 1961). The first Jewish Federation Council

was organized in 1896 in Cincinnati. At the time known as "Federations of Jewish Charities," they were organized by the German Jews and provided relief, vocational training, and "Americanization" programs for the masses of new immigrants from eastern Europe. The Federation acted as the umbrella organization for the myriad of Jewish philanthropies devoted to the social, economic, and cultural needs of the Jews. *American Jewish Year book*, vol. 36, p. 65 and *Proceedings, National Conference of Jewish Social Service, 1932*, p. 77. For more information on the evolution of the Jewish Federation, consult Lurie, *A Heritage Affirmed: The Jewish Federation Movement in America* (Philadelphia: Jewish Publication Society of America, 1961); *American Jewish Year Book*, vol. 39, 1937–1938, pp. 90–91.

6. *American Jewish Year Book*, vol. 33, 1931–32, p. 381, 39; *Jewish Social Work, 1931*, p. 5. Between 1931 and 1932, total volume increased 12.7 percent. The number of active care cases increased 17.6 percent and the total amount of money spent on relief increased 33.7 percent. See *Jewish Social Work, 1931*, p. 7.

7. Robert Morris and Michael Freund, *Trends and Issues in Jewish Social Welfare, 1899–1952* (Philadelphia: Jewish Publication Society of America, 1966) p. 280; *American Jewish Year Book*, vol. 36, 1934–1933, pp. 67–68. See also *American Jewish Year Book*, vol. 34, 1932–1933, speech by Benjamin Selekman on the fundraising abilities of the Jewish federations. From "Notes and News," number 25, December 20, 1934, p. 10, quoted in Harry L. Lurie, *A Heritage Affirmed*, p. 423. The U.S. government's February 1934 "Monthly Labor Review" reported a decline of 21.2 percent in the cost of living between December 1929 and December 1933, *Jewish Social Work*, 1933, p. 12. The drop in private contributions to Jewish agencies of 18.4 percent in 1933 was more than offset by a gain of 69 percent from public agencies, *Jewish Social Work*, 1933, p. 12. By 1933, about "ninety-four percent of relief money came from public funds as compared to eighty-two percent in 1931, and seventy-five percent in 1929 and 1930." *Jewish Social Work*, 1933, p. 3.

8. Josephine Chapin Brown, *Public Relief: 1929–1939*, (New York: H. Holt, 1940), p. 15; *American Jewish Year Book*, vol. 39, 1937–1938, p. 128.

9. Gary Gerstle, *Working-Class Americanism: The Politics of Labor in a Textile City, 1914–1960* (New York: Cambridge University Press, 1989), p. 7.

10. Cohen, *Making a New Deal*, pp. 8, 362.

11. Brown, *Public Relief*, pp. 3, 39.

12. Brown, *Public Relief*, chapter one; Frances Fox Piven and Richard A. Cloward, *Regulating the Poor: The Function of the Public Welfare* (New York: Random House, 1971, 1993), p. 54.

13. Brown, *Public Relief,* pp. 112, 110.

14. *Proceedings, National Conference of Jewish Social Service, 1931*, p. 25.

15. From a lecture at the International Conference on Jewish Social Work, London, July 8–10, 1936, reprinted in the *American Jewish Year Book*, vol. 39, 1937–1938, p. 128.

16. Max I. Dimont, *The Jews in America: The Roots, History, and Destiny of American Jews*, (New York: Simon and Schuster, 1978); Cohen, *Making a New Deal*, pp. 223–227.

17. *Proceedings, National Conference of Jewish Social Service, 1923*, p. 69; *Proceedings, National Conference of Jewish Social Service, 1931*, p. 32.

18. *American Jewish Year Book*, vol. 34, p. 68–69. In 1934, the Reform movement's Central Conference of American Rabbis (CCAR) called for a forty-hour work week, the elimination of child labor, old age pensions, unemployment insurance, public works projects, and collective bargaining. The same year, both the Reform and Conservative movements in Judaism called for a tax system that was based on income redistribution rather than just revenue collection. See *Proceedings, National Conference of Jewish Social Welfare, 1938*, p. 37. The following year, the CCAR supported Roosevelt's social security program. See *Proceedings, National Conference of Jewish Social Welfare, 1938*, p. 38. In June 1931, the National Conference of Jewish Social Service passed a resolution calling on "the President of the United States to take such steps in the form of federal emergency relief on a large enough scale to alleviate existing and future suffering; construction of public works to stimulate and revive industry; the formulation of a comprehensive program of social insurance; and the creation of such commissions as will assure wise social administration of these and other necessary measures." *Proceedings, National Conference of Jewish Social Service, 1931*, p. 8; *Proceedings, National Conference of Jewish Social Service, 1932*, p. 99; *Proceedings, National Conference of Jewish Social Work, 1931*, pp. 54–55.

19. *Proceedings, National Conference of Jewish Social Service, 1934*, p. 28; *Proceedings, National Conference of Jewish social service, 1932*, p. 29; *Proceedings, National Conference of Jewish Social service, 1930*, pp. 101–102. For a biography of Max Rubinow, see J. Lee Kreader's Ph.D. dissertation, *America's Prophet for Social Security: A Biography of Isaac Max Rubinow* (Chicago: University of Chicago Press, 1988).

20. Milton Meltzer, *The Jewish Americans: A History in Their Own Words, 1650–1950* (New York: Crowell, 1982), pp. 235–237.

21. Letter from Franklin Roosevelt to Bishop Francis J. McConnell, April 16, 1929, appearing in Wilbur J. Cohen, ed., *The Roosevelt New Deal: A Program Assessment Fifty Years After*, p. xiv; Brown, *Public Relief*, pp. 90, 94–97; and Bruce M. Stave, *The New Deal and the Last Hurrah: Pittsburgh Machine Politics*, p. 110.

22. *Jewish Social Work*, published by the Bureau of Jewish Social Research, served as the main statistics gathering publication of the Jewish community, *Jewish Social Work, 1933*, pp. 15–16. The Bureau of Jewish Social Research reported that "the volume of need among Jewish agencies would have been vastly increased were it not for the rapid development of new public resources for unemployment relief and the continuance of public welfare service." *Jewish Social Work, 1931*, pp. 5, 8; though it should be noted that *Jewish Social Work*, later reported that "as compared with the non-sectarian and Catholic family agencies, the Jewish agency has shown a consistent lag in the use of public funds for relief purposes." *Jewish Social Work, 1933*, p. 4.

23. *Proceedings, National Conference of Jewish Social Service, 1932*, p. 217; Herman D. Stein, "Jewish Social Work in the United States, 1920–1955," in Marshall Sklare, *The Jew in American Society* (New York: Behrman House, 1974), p. 176. When President Hoover's Organization on Unemployment Relief concluded in August 1931 that the economic ills of the depression could be best solved by local charity, delegates to the Conference on Jewish Social Service objected. They rejected the commission's assertion that poverty resulted more from administrative problems plaguing local charity than from an absence of federal participation. See Josephine Chapin Brown, *Public Relief: 1929–1939* (New York: Henry Holt, 1940), chapter one; Frances Fox Pivin and Richard A. Cloward, *Regulating the Poor: The Functions of Public Welfare* (New York: Random House, 1971, 1993), pp. 51–52; Herman D. Stein, "Jewish Social Work in the United States, 1920–1955," in Marshall Sklare, *The Jew in American Society*, p. 176.

24. James MacGregor Burns, *Roosevelt: The Lion and the Fox* (New York: Harcourt, Brace, 1956), p. 164.

25. Isador Lubin, Commissioner, Bureau of Labor Statistics, United State Department of Labor, "Recent Economic Trends in Relation to Jewish Life," in *Proceedings, National Conference of Jewish Social Service, 1934*, p. 8. In 1935, forty-four Jewish agencies took 7,035 cases, 11.9 percent fewer than in 1934. *1935 Yearbook of Jewish Social Work: Part One: Service Trends in Family Welfare, Child Care, Care of the Aged, Hospitals, Clinics*, p. 2; "Recent Economic Trends," *Proceedings, National Conference of Jewish Social Service, 1934*, pp. 7–8; *Proceedings, National Conference of Jewish Social Welfare, 1935*, p. 26.

26. *B'nai B'rith Messengers*, vol. 47, April 1933, No. 7. p. 201; *Proceedings, National Council of Jewish Social Service, 1933*, p. 8; presidential address by Isaac M. Rubinow, "The Credo of a Jewish Social Worker," in *Proceedings, National Conference of Jewish Social Service, 1933*, p. 7. Just days after Rubinow's speech, the social policy committee of the NCJSS presented a detailed report outlining its position on increased government aid. See *Proceedings, National Council of Jewish Social Service, 1933*, pp. 104–111.

27. Just as the president signed the FERA into law, he advised delegates to a Human Needs Conference in early September 1933 that government aid would be only an emergency measure and ultimately the responsibility for relief would return to "individual citizens, to individual responsibility, and to private organizations." See Stave, *The New Deal and the Last Hurrah*, p. 114. FDR's first 100 days have been accurately characterized as "conservative" in that he did not nationalize the banking system, embraced big business, and remained staunch in his support for individual initiative over collective action. For more on the struggle Roosevelt felt from both the left and the right, see William Leuchtenburg, *Franklin Roosevelt and The New Deal, 1932–1940* (New York: Harper & Row, 1963); Barton Bernstein, "The New Deal: The Conservative Achievements of Liberal Reform," in Barton J. Bernstein and Allen J. Matusow, eds., *Twentieth Century America: Recent Interpretations* (New York: Harcourt, Brace, Jovanovich, 2nd ed., 1972); Jerald S. Auerback "New Deal, Old Deal, or Raw Deal: Some Thoughts on New Left Historiography," *Journal of Southern History*, February 1969, pp. 18–30.

28. *1935 Yearbook of Jewish Social Work*, part I, pp. 20, 22. Harry L. Lurie, former president of both the Jewish Social Service Association and the National Social Service Association, estimated that by 1934, between 70 and 90 percent of Jewish dependent families were receiving public relief. Jewish social service agencies reduced their relief budgets for the first time since the onset of the depression. *Proceedings, National Conference of Jewish Social Service, 1934*, pp. 7–8; *Proceedings, National Conference of Jewish Social Welfare, 1935*, p. 26.

29. *Jewish Social Work, 1933*, pp. 4, 1, 15. The findings reflected only the conditions of Jews in urban areas. For the few Jews who lived in rural areas, the report stated, "the Jewish agency still retains its traditional responsibility for dependency in its own community," from "The Minneapolis Jewish Communal Survey," in *Proceedings, National Conference of Jewish Social Welfare, 1937*, p. 93.

30. *Jewish Social Work, 1933*, p. 17. There were some cases where the federal government permitted the local Jewish agencies to administer all relief funds. This was the case in St. Louis. In Philadelphia, "private agencies have co-operated with the county relief board fully and wholeheartedly." *Proceedings, National Conference of Jewish Social Service, 1933*, pp. 39–42, 43. "In nearly all cities of any size," *Jewish Social Work* reported, "the Jewish agency made known to the

public agency its willingness to be of service to Jewish families on public relief."
Jewish Social Work, 1933, p. 21. The Bureau of Jewish Social Research reported in
1933 that "it was possible to classify these communities into three large groups...one,
where no public agency was to be found or where it did not dispense relief, the relief
function being discharged by the private agency (Baltimore, Birmingham, Cleveland,
Pittsburgh, St. Louis), two, where both public and private agencies carried on
independent work in the community, three, where there had occurred an actual
merger, wholly or in party, of the work of the two agencies (St. Paul, Erie)" *Jewish
Social Work, 1933*, p. 17.

31. Brown, *Public Relief: 1929–1939*, p. 113.

32. *Jewish Social Work, 1933*, p. 17, 26; see Oscar Leonard's comment in
Proceedings, National Conference of Jewish Social Service, 1930, pp. 112–113;
see, for example, responses by southern planters to the AAA, big business to the
NRA, and state governments to federal control of relief administration; *American
Jewish Year Book*, vol. 34, 1932–1933, pp. 69–70; *Jewish Social Work, 1933*, pp.
19–20.

33. *Jewish Social Service Quarterly*, vol. 7, no. 2, December 1930, p. 13; *Proceedings,
National Conference of Jewish Social Service, 1930*, p. 105; *Jewish Social Work,
1933*, p. 20.

34. *Jewish Social Work, 1933*, p. 16; *American Jewish Year Book*, vol. 36, 1934–
1935, p. 72.

35. James T. Patterson, *America's Struggle Against Poverty, 1900–1980*
(Cambridge: Harvard University Press, 1981), p. 58.

36. *Proceedings, National Conference of Jewish Social Welfare, 1938*, p. 23. Dr.
Solomon Lowenstein of New York's Federation of Jewish Philanthropies wrote that
"it is easier to raise money today than it was two or three years ago," from
Proceedings, National Conference of Jewish Social Welfare, 1936, p. 19.

37. *Proceedings, National Conference of Jewish Social Welfare, 1934*, p. 7;
Proceedings, National Conference of Jewish Social Welfare, 1938, p. 234; *American
Jewish Year Book*, vol. 39, 1937–1938, p. 90; *1939 Year book of Jewish Social
Welfare*, section 1, n.p. In Allegheny County, Pennsylvania, for example, private
funds composed 54 percent of all direct relief aid in 1922, while it totaled less than 1
percent in 1935. From Bruce M. Stave, *The New Deal and the Last Hurrah*, p. 109.

38. Speech by Benjamin Selekman, meeting of the National Conference of Jewish
Federations and Welfare Funds, *American Jewish Year Book*, vol. 36, 1934–1935, p.
65; "Federal Emergency Relief Administration Monthly Report," May 22 to June 30,

1933, pp. 1–2, quoted in *Public Relief, 1929–1939*, p. 146. At that time, 4 million families, or 18 million people, claimed some form of support from the public dole. As a proportion of the total population, one in every six families was dependent. These estimates were made by the Reconstruction Finance Corporation and are quoted in the FERA Monthly Report, May 22 to June 30, 1933, p. 1, quoted in Brown, *Public Relief: 1929–1939*, pp. 145–146.

39. The Reform movement of Judaism originated in enlightenment Germany and sought to combine the benefits of legal equality with the morality of Jewish law. For a complete history of the movement, see Michael A. Meyer, *Response to Modernity, A History of the Reform Movement in Judaism* (New York: Oxford University Press, 1988).

40. *Proceedings, National Conference of Jewish Social Service, 1936*, pp. 11–12; *American Jewish Year Book*, vol. 34, 1932–1933, p. 76; See Charles I. Schottland, "Federation and Community Building," *Proceedings, National Conference of Jewish Social Welfare, 1938*, p. 142. For an excellent analysis of the relations between German and eastern European Jews in America, see Naomi Cohen, *Encounter with Emancipation: The German Jews in the United States, 1830–1914* (Philadelphia: Jews Publication Society of America, 1984); Arthur Goren, *New York Jews and the Quest for Community: The Kehillah Experiment 1908–1922* (New York: Columbia University, 1970); and Deborah Dash Moore, *At Home in America: Second Generation New York Jews* (New York: Columbia University, 1970). A small minority of Jewish communal leaders simply rejected the avalanche of reform in an attempt to preserve the Stuyvesant Pledge. "What kind of Jewish heart have we now, that we can't take care of our own? Haven't we always taken care of our own?" one social worker admonished in 1938. *Proceedings, National Conference of Jewish Social Welfare, 1938*, pp. 23–24. "The Jewish case-working organization cannot turn over its load, or even a part of it [to the government]," another argued, "A group which has held high the banner of justice in its dealings with the underprivileged cannot shrug its shoulders and say 'under present conditions we cannot help ourselves'." *Jewish Social Work, 1933*, p. 20.

41. *Jewish Social Service Quarterly*, vol. 7, no. 1, September 1930, p. 1; *Proceedings, National Conference of Jewish Social Service, 1928*, p. 87.

42. *Proceedings, National Conference of Jewish Social Service, 1928*, pp. 88–89.

43. *Proceedings, National Conference of Jewish Social Service, 1932*, p. 90; *Proceedings, National Conference of Jewish Social Service, 1931*, pp. 41–46, 50.

44. *Proceedings, National Conference of Jewish Social Service, 1932*, pp. 86, 92–93.

45. *Proceedings, National Conference of Jewish Social Service, 1933*, p. 111.

46. *Proceedings, National Conference of Jewish Social Service, 1936*, p. 12.

47. *Proceedings, National Conference of Jewish Social Service, 1931*, p. 37.

48. Alexander M. Dushkin, executive director, Board of Jewish Education, Chicago, *Proceedings, National Conference of Jewish Social Service, 1931*, p. 49; *Proceedings, National Conference of Jewish Social Service, 1932*, p. 40.

49. *Proceedings, National Conference of Jewish Social Service, 1932*, pp. 40–41.

50. *Proceedings, National Conference of Jewish Social Welfare, 1935*, p. 1; *Jewish Social Work, 1935*, p. 20; *Proceedings, National Conference of Jewish Social Service, 1935*, p. 104.

51. *Proceedings, National Conference of Jewish Social Welfare, 1937*, pp. 53, 12, 60; *American Jewish Year Book*, vol. 38, 1936–1937, p. 235; *United Jewish Welfare Fund Yearbook, 1938*, p. 32–33; *United Jewish Welfare Fund Yearbook, 1939*, pp. 48–49.

52. *Proceedings, National Council of Jewish Social Service, 1931*, p. 27.

II

FDR and
Individual Congressmen

CHAPTER FIVE

Sam Rayburn and FDR

ANTHONY CHAMPAGNE

Sam Rayburn was Franklin Delano Roosevelt's key spokesman in the United States House of Representatives. So important was he to the New Deal's success in the House that Roosevelt said of Rayburn, he was "the most valuable man in Congress".[1] The relationship was two sided: Rayburn received valuable rewards for his loyal service to the New Deal. Like many lengthy political relationships, it was not without tension. Problems were resolved between the two because their alliance was in their mutual interest. It is the complexity of this alliance between a president of the United States and a congressman from a small northeast Texas farming district that this chapter explores.

Sam Rayburn was elected to the House of Representatives in 1912 where he remained until his death in 1961. In that time he served on only one standing committee of Congress, the Interstate and Foreign Commerce Committee. In 1931 Rayburn became chair of that committee when the Democrats organized the House, in 1937 he became majority leader, and in 1940 he became Speaker of the House. With the exception of four years when the Republicans controlled the House, he held the position of Speaker until his death. From 1953 through 1956, Rayburn was Minority Leader.

During the Franklin Roosevelt presidency Rayburn developed his reputation as a master legislator. Initially, Rayburn was John Nance Garner's protégé, not Roosevelt's. Before 1932, Rayburn had spoken to Roosevelt only once, in a telephone conversation when Roosevelt was Assistant Secretary of the Navy.[2] He first shook hands with the New York Governor at the 1932 Democratic National Convention.[3] At that time, Rayburn was an unquestioned "Garner man."

His allegiance to Garner rested on political indebtedness to the older Texan that extended over several years. In 1913 John Nance Garner moved from the House Foreign Affairs Committee to the Ways and Means Committee. It was a major change for Garner since not only was Ways and Means the tax-writing committee of the House, it was also the Democratic Committee on Committees. As the Texas member of Ways and Means, Garner could exercise substantial impact upon the careers of new congressmen such as Sam Rayburn. Perhaps because both Garner and Rayburn shared political ties with Texas Senator Joseph Weldon Bailey, Garner made sure that Rayburn got a prize committee assignment, Interstate and Foreign Commerce. That committee was one of the most important in the House since its chairman, James Mann, was a chief ally of Republican Speaker Joe Cannon. These two made sure that the jurisdiction of the committee was broad, including rail and water transportation, the Panama Canal, the Federal Trade Commission, the Federal Power Commission, and public health.[4]

It was a committee on which a hard working Congressman like Rayburn could make a substantial career, if he could continue to be reelected and if the Democrats retained control of the House. Before Rayburn attained much seniority, Democrats lost their House majority. After the 1918 elections, Republicans organized the House and remained in control until the Democrats regained power twelve years later as a result of a series of deaths of congressmen after the 1930 elections.

During those years, Garner climbed the hierarchy of the House, becoming minority leader in 1929. In 1931, Garner was elected Speaker, making him the nation's top elected Democratic official. With a mighty push from newspaper magnate William Randolph Hearst, Garner became a contender for the Democratic presidential nomination in 1932. Rayburn, Garner's protégé, was prominent in the Garner campaign. Rayburn knew the leading party contender was FDR. Yet, there was a possibility that Roosevelt's campaign would founder. If it did, Garner might get the nomination.[5] When the formal nominating process began at the Chicago convention, FDR led the balloting, but lacked the two-thirds of the delegate votes then required for the Democratic nomination.

Rayburn went to the convention as Garner's chief spokesman, and it was only Rayburn through whom Garner would communicate his convention strategy. Both were strong party men, Democrats who did not want a deadlocked Democratic convention as occurred in 1924. Both sensed the Democrats would win the presidency if the party could avoid destructive factionalism. When it was evident that Roosevelt was the apparent choice of the delegates, Rayburn obtained Garner's release of the delegates and handled the negotiations with the Roosevelt forces. Those actions led to Garner's nomination for the vice presidency.[6]

Garner's election as vice president and concomitant departure from the House moved Rayburn further up the leadership ladder in Congress. He was no longer just a longtime Texas congressman but a national power broker and chairman of a major congressional committee. In these roles, Rayburn supported Roosevelt's program and fathered key New Deal legislation such as the Emergency Railroad Transportation Act, the Truth in Securities Act, the Securities Exchange Act, the Interstate Motor Carriers Act, the Federal Communications Act, and the Utility Holding Company Act.[7]

In 1934 Rayburn described himself, with considerable justification, as being "a helluva New Dealer."[8] His leadership with New Deal legislation gave him an impressive record that enhanced his reputation both in the House and with the White House. That reputation was critical in achieving his goal of becoming Speaker of the House of Representatives.

Yet, these legislative efforts were not without costs. The Securities Exchange Act was opposed by the securities industry, which was instrumental in a major lobbying campaign against the bill. Rayburn claimed this campaign was "the most powerful lobby ever organized against any bill which ever came up in Congress."[9] The lobbying activities initially appeared to have stirred up his constituents. Rayburn, who rarely had constituent mail, received sacks of mail from his district expressing opposition to the bill. However, when Rayburn ordered his staff to reply to every letter with an explanation of his position, most of those letters were returned with postal notations of "Deceased" or "Moved Away." Rayburn inferred that the securities lobby had used addresses from outdated phone books to conduct a phony grass-roots campaign.[10] Understandably, this tactic did not deter him.

The battle over the Utility Holding Company Act exposed Rayburn to the more serious threat of the utility lobby, which flooded his office with letters, telegrams, and phone calls. In addition, the utility lobby, offered funds to unseat Rayburn. On the floor of the House, Rayburn attacked the lobby, "So much has been said, such a whispering campaign has been carried on, unequaled in my opinion by anything in the last half century. The fat cats from Texas would cuss me out like I was a horse thief." He was accused of being a socialist, and he claimed that John W. Carpenter, the president of Texas Power and Light, went to a banker in his district and asked him for an estimate of the amount of money it would take to defeat Rayburn. When the banker said Rayburn could not be defeated, Carpenter said the utility industry had the money to do anything.[11]

Promoting New Deal legislation, even when doing so placed Rayburn at some risk, put him in FDR's good graces and facilitated his becoming majority leader. On June 4, 1936, Speaker Joseph Byrns died, and majority leader William Bankhead became Speaker. John J. O'Connor of New York, chairman of the Rules Committee, became floor leader for the remaining two weeks of the session. O'Connor was considered to be a major contender for majority leader in the next session of Congress. He was a Tammany Hall, Irish Catholic politician who claimed that the South held a disproportionate number of leadership posts in Congress—as indeed it did—and that a northerner deserved to be leader. As chairman of Rules, he was in a powerful position to block New Deal legislation if he were angered. O'Connor had a tie to FDR since his brother, Basil O'Connor was FDR's former law partner and ran the Warm Springs Foundation [later the March of Dimes Foundation]. However, O'Connor was not a New Dealer. For example, he had sought to block the Holding Company Act.[12] Years later, James Roosevelt, the President's eldest son, observed that both Basil O'Connor and FDR "looked upon John O'Connor as someone they wished they didn't have to deal with." James added that he "would be amazed if there was any real evidence that father ever preferred to have John O'Connor as Leader."[13]

Signals from the White House indicated that Rayburn was the president's choice: Roosevelt asked Rayburn to head the Democratic Party's National Speakers' Bureau for the 1936 campaign.[14] Garner openly endorsed Rayburn and, following Huey Long's assassination in Louisiana, negotiated a deal where the Louisiana delegation could get back in the good graces of the administration by supporting Rayburn for the leadership. Senator Joe Guffy, a strong New Dealer and political leader in Pennsylvania, endorsed Rayburn and got the Pennsylvania delegation to do so. Northern political bosses—some of the Irish Catholic northern political bosses—such as Brooklyn Tammany leader Tom Cullen, Chicago's "Big Ed" Kelly, and Jersey City's Frank Hague endorsed Rayburn.[15] The hidden hand of Franklin Roosevelt seemed to be at work. That hand was apparent when Thomas Corcoran, known as "Tommy the Cork," met a ship carrying Postmaster General Jim Farley home from Europe. Farley intended to endorse O'Connor, but Corcoran instructed Farley to remain silent.[16]

Although Roosevelt never publicly endorsed Rayburn, it was evident that the Texan was the President's choice. At the Democratic caucus January 4, 1937, Rayburn was elected majority leader by a vote of 184–127.[17] That put him a step away from the speakership since he now held the second highest office in the House majority. Speaker Bankhead even then was suffering from poor health.

At first, Vice President John Nance Garner proved to be an important operative in the Congress, especially the Senate, presiding on behalf of the Roosevelt program.[18] However, with the sit-down strikes, the 1937 court-packing plan, the 1938 Wage and Hour Bill, and the 1938 effort by Roosevelt to purge the Democratic Party of his opponents, Garner became openly hostile to the administration.[19] Suspecting Roosevelt would seek a third term, which Garner adamantly opposed, the vice president sought to block that with his own candidacy. In 1938, he told his close friend, the journalist Cecil Dickson, that FDR would seek a third term and be a war president.[20] Early in 1939, at a gathering in the Washington Hotel where Garner lived, he told Rayburn and a few other friends that he would oppose FDR's quest for a third term any way he could.[21] The *Fort Worth Star-Telegram*, a paper published by Amon Carter, a wealthy, influential Texan and strong supporter of Garner, polled the Texas delegation regarding their choices for the presidency in 1940. Rayburn responded on July 31, 1939:

> I have your telegram. I am for that outstanding Texan and liberal Democrat John N. Garner, for the Presidential nomination in 1940, believing that if elected he will make the country a great President.[22]

The press interpreted Rayburn's statement as "a jolt to advocates of a third term for the President."[23] Added to that "jolt" was Rayburn's effort two weeks earlier to obtain a Texas delegation defense of Garner when John L. Lewis, a prominent labor leader, attacked Garner as "a poker-playing, whiskey-drinking, evil old man."[24] Only the opposition of Congressman Lyndon Johnson, a Roosevelt ally, prevented Rayburn from obtaining a delegation endorsement in defense of Garner.[25] Johnson apparently made it well known within the administration that he had kept Rayburn from defending Garner's name, an action which probably made Johnson look like a Roosevelt defender and Rayburn a Garner ally to the administration.[26] Adding to the tension between Rayburn and Roosevelt, was Rayburn's calling Garner a "liberal Democrat," seemingly a direct response to a recent Roosevelt speech critical of the "old Democratic Party" comprising the conservatives represented by Garner.[27]

Within two days, Stephen Early wrote Roosevelt that he had just received telegrams from Senator Morris Sheppard and Cecil Dickson, each requesting a presidential congratulatory message to Rayburn on Sam Rayburn Day. This celebration was held on August 22 in Denison, Texas, a key town in Rayburn's district and the recipient of the Denison Dam, the principal public works project in the district. For previous celebrations, congratulatory messages were sent to Denison. The year before, Roosevelt's telegram noted that it was Rayburn Day in Denison and that he joined "with the Booster Club in extending deserved appreciation to him for the work he did to make the Red River Dam Project possible."[28] In 1939 things were different. Early noted, "Ordinarily I would take care of this without troubling you but in light of Rayburn's recent declarations, I think it best to leave the decision to you."[29] FDR responded to Early, "Sorry—my absence makes it impossible etc."[30] Three days after Sam Rayburn Day, Early wrote Senator Sheppard and Cecil Dickson identical messages.

> I am sorry to advise you that your telegram of August thirteenth was among other letters and wires which were flown to the President and which were delayed several days en route because the Navy pilots were unable to deliver to the Tuscaloosa due to the heavy fogs which prevailed along the coast at that time.
>
> Your request for a message on the occasion of Sam Rayburn Day, therefore did not reach the President until after the celebration at Denison was concluded.[31]

This was, of course, a signal to Rayburn—one he would certainly get from his friend Dickson if not from Sheppard—that it would be difficult to walk a tightrope of loyalty to both FDR and to Garner. Later, when Alla Clary, Rayburn's secretary, sent a photograph to the White House for a routine presidential autograph, Missy LeHand returned it unsigned.[32]

Rayburn presented his dilemma to Roosevelt, perhaps with less success than he had anticipated. Before endorsing Garner, Rayburn met privately with FDR.

> One night at a banquet, I said to the President, "I want to come up and talk some politics with you." Roosevelt would always perk up when you mentioned politics. He said come down to the White House the next morning and come to his bedroom. When I got down there, he was still in bed. He started talking about war in Europe. I said, "Mr. President, I didn't come here to talk of war in Europe but of war brewing in Texas." I told him, "If you are a candidate, you can get the nomination," and he agreed. Then I told him Texas was going for Garner, and I was going to go along with John.
>
> He looked out the window at the Washington Monument for the longest time. Finally, he said, "That's what you ought to do. I understand your situation perfectly." Then he said, "But Sam, John can't be nominated, and he couldn't be elected if he was nominated." Right then, I knew he was going to run for another term.[33]

Rayburn may have suffered more than slights for his loyalty to Garner. In 1940 several individuals thought they had Roosevelt's nod for the vice presidency, Rayburn was one of them.[34] It may be—for FDR was not above such scheming— that Roosevelt was dangling the vice presidency in front of Rayburn as a way of urging him to be loyal to Roosevelt during the tensions that resulted over Garner's candidacy. There was a fairly compelling argument in favor of Rayburn: He was a remarkably able legislator who had backed the New Deal and he was a Garner friend who would appeal to the Garner supporters upset with Garner's departure from the ticket. He was also a populist enemy of Wall Street and proponent of the Holding Company Act, a campaign asset since Wendell Wilkie, the Republican nominee, was a utility company executive.

As the convention opened, Roosevelt provided newsmen with a list of persons he considered acceptable vice-presidential nominees. Topping the list was Rayburn, followed by Senator James Byrnes, Democrat of South Carolina, then Missouri Governor Lloyd Stark and Supreme Court Justice William O. Douglas. Others who thought they had FDR's approval were Postmaster General James Farley, Louis Johnson, Senator Burton K. Wheeler of Montana, Jesse Jones, Indiana Governor Paul McNutt, and Secretary of Agriculture Henry A. Wallace. Farley considered Rayburn a "red-hot candidate for Vice President."[35] However, the Texas delegation was split between Rayburn and Jesse Jones, although the vote when it was finally taken within the Texas delegation was 88 to 7 in Rayburn's favor. Rayburn thought there was a chance, especially when he received a phone call from Roosevelt, who said, "Sam, I want you to do me a great favor." The Texan was certain Roosevelt was going to ask him to serve on the ticket, but FDR stunned him by asking Rayburn to make a seconding speech for Henry A. Wallace. With considerable reluctance, Rayburn agreed.[36]

Whatever tensions existed between FDR and Rayburn seemed to die quickly. Rayburn was a key figure in developing the "harmony" agreement in Texas where the delegation to the 1940 convention would support Garner on the first ballot, would endorse the Roosevelt record, and would shun a "Stop Roosevelt" move-ment. That agreement lessened, but did not eliminate differences in Texas between Garner forces and New Dealers.[37] Rayburn, working with Lyndon Johnson, also raised large sums of money for Democratic House candidates, helping keep the House Democratic. Rayburn, it became clear, was crucial to tapping the funds of Texas oilmen made rich by the discovery of the East Texas oil field.[38]

Four years later, the choice of a vice presidential candidate arose again. Then when Rayburn's name came up, FDR told Congressman Lyndon Johnson that Rayburn lacked a world viewpoint, that he had never travelled outside of North America, that labor would oppose him, and that he was needed in the House.[39] Without presidential backing, the Speaker could not hope to be on the party ticket. The less well-known junior senator from Missouri, Harry Truman, got FDR's nod and the nomination.

Ordinarily the relationship between Rayburn and Roosevelt was pleasant enough, although several members of the Administration disliked Rayburn. Secretary of the

Interior Harold Ickes, for one, did not look with favor on Rayburn. His diary contains evident enjoyment of several embarrassments and slights to Rayburn. Whether these embarrassments and slights were real or were creations of Ickes' imagination is uncertain.[40] Even Marvin McIntyre seemed to poke fun at what he called Rayburn's "literary effort" over NBC radio on October 28, 1942.[41] The usual pettiness among individuals within the administration did not bother Rayburn. What was a continual source of concern to him was FDR's lack of consultation with members of Congress and congressional leaders. Rayburn persistently urged Roosevelt to improve his communications with the legislative branch.

From Rayburn's perspective those communications were often inadequate, but Roosevelt made an effort to ensure greater consultation with the leadership. For example, in 1943, Marvin McIntyre wrote the Director of the Bureau of the Budget,

> I have just been informed that at the Cabinet meeting the other day, the President said he wanted all hands to refrain from sending up legislative drafts; he wanted the leadership consulted in advance.[42]

Six months later, Grace Tully wrote Roosevelt that Lyndon Johnson urged that Sam Rayburn and Representative John McCormack of Massachusetts,

> get together with [Senators] Jimmy Byrnes and Fred Vinson at least once every other ten days for discussion and for guidance that the two heads of agencies can give to them about the Administration's thoughts on legislation, as well as various policies.[43]

That prompted Roosevelt to speak with James Byrnes about the request.[44]

Sam Rayburn was a cautious man. When he pushed legislation, he wanted to win; he was reluctant to fight losing battles. His caution had long disturbed John Garner who wanted Rayburn to be more aggressive, urging him to "bloody his knuckles."[45] Roosevelt also may have thought that Rayburn erred in favor of caution. Perhaps the best example is a peculiar letter from Roosevelt to Rayburn, a copy of which was sent to McCormack.

> Because of our long-standing friendship and intimate association I know you will not mind if I write you in great confidence some thoughts which come to me since the failure of the Republicans, and certain Democrats, to override the veto of the Walter–Logan Bill. Courage—just sheer courage—brought that about.
>
> I know that there was much inclination on the part of Democrats—the friendly kind—the "cooperation" kind, to feel, ten days ago, that the veto would be over-ridden. When all is said and done that inclination amounted to a yielding to a probable defeat.

More courageous beliefs prevailed.

I myself must, as you know, be guided by the recommendations of the Democratic Leaders in the House, and while in no sense of the word do I want the advice of "yes men," I do want the advice of fighting leadership with the adjective "fighting" underscored.

When I got back on Monday last, I did not quite know what to make out of this particular problem—for some of my friends were pulling long faces and gave me the feeling that the veto would be over-ridden. Others among my friends were telling me that in thirty-six hours victory could be attained, by enthusiasm and team-work, to sustain the President.

You and I and John McCormack are facing a very difficult session. On the success of that session will depend the future reputation of the President and the Speaker and the Majority Leader. It will not help any of the three to meet with a series of defeats in the next Congress.

That is especially true if the three of us, or any one of the three accepts prospective defeat tamely. Therefore, I renew my ancient feeling that it is better to be defeated while going down fighting than it is to accept defeat without fighting.

The vote last Wednesday is proof of this theory. A very large number of prospective defeats—not all—can be turned into victory by carrying on a real honest-to-goodness fight, thereby cutting down the percentage of defeats. I know you will agree and I know that John McCormack agrees.

What I want to get across to you both before the new session begins is that good fellowship for the sake of good fellowship alone, an easy life to avoid criticism, an acceptance of defeat before an issue has been joined, make all of them, less for Party success and for national safety than a few drag-down and knock-out fights and an unwillingness to accept defeat without a fight.

You and John have an opportunity to salvage much that would otherwise be lost in the coming session, and you and I know that this means day and night work, taking it on the chin, getting knocked down occasionally, but making a come-back before you are counted out.

I am saying this for the sake of the Party. I am saying this more greatly for the sake of the Nation.

And I know you will understand—and do your bit.[46]

The letter prompted an enthusiastic response from McCormack who stated that he "thoroughly agree[d]."[47] There is no record of a response from Rayburn. Rayburn considered the letter to be patronizing, and he told McCormack that Roosevelt had to show more respect for the legislative branch if he wanted cooperation. When he and McCormack visited Roosevelt to propose closer cooperation, Roosevelt agreed.[48]

For Roosevelt, communication with the legislative leadership did not always mean that he would listen, a trait that on at least one occasion caused Rayburn to flare at the President. The court-packing plan introduced by Maury Maverick, a rather unpopular congressman, had gone nowhere. FDR, however, had been assured by staff that he could bring the bill to the floor despite a hostile Judiciary Committee if a somewhat revised version was introduced by the highly regarded congressman Fred Vinson. That scheme was abandoned over the opposition of Rayburn and Bankhead, but not before Roosevelt had belittled Rayburn's comment that the bill was not even popular in his district. Rayburn burst out, "Looky here, Mr. President! By God, I'm talking to you. You'd better listen."[49]

An issue of patronage also caused Rayburn to flare at FDR. Rayburn was close to Dr. W. M. Splawn, a scholar who had once been President of the University of Texas and a man Rayburn had relied upon during his chairmanship of Interstate and Foreign Commerce. FDR promised Rayburn that Splawn would be appointed to the Interstate Commerce Commission. When a vacancy occurred Splawn was not appointed. According to Cecil Dickson, at Roosevelt's meeting with the Democratic leadership, Rayburn sat away from FDR and refused to speak. FDR noticed. At the end of the meeting he asked Rayburn what the problem was. Rayburn replied, "You promised you would give the next appointment that came up on the Interstate Commerce Commission to Dr. W. M. Splawn and you didn't do it. You lied to me." Then, claimed Dickson, Rayburn turned his back on the president and walked off. FDR called Rayburn back and promised to fix the problem. Not long thereafter, Splawn was appointed to a vacancy on the ICC.[50]

Roosevelt was not the only partner in the alliance who sometimes refused to listen. Rayburn had an independent streak and simply blocked administration efforts to legislate federal controls over oil production. In 1930, the East Texas oil field with reserves of five billion barrels was discovered. Before long, the field had 25,000 producing wells. That oversupply of oil, coupled with the Depression, dropped the price of oil to ten cents a barrel. While the Texas Railroad Commission tried to regulate oil production, much oil was produced in violation of its production quotas. As a result, many oilmen desired federal oil regulation to limit well production and shipment of oil. Roosevelt supported this increase in federal authority. Against the administration's strong wishes, Rayburn bottled up the legislation in his committee.[51] The following year, Rayburn supported the Connally Hot-Oil bill, which provided for a federal penalty for interstate shipments of oil in violation of state law, and oil prices increased.[52]

Rayburn's leadership of the New Deal in the House was an important facet of his maintaining support in his Congressional district. In the New Deal years, he arranged to have a massive public works project built in his district, the Denison Dam and Lake Texoma. Known as the Red River project, it was especially important since it provided a source of jobs for Rayburn's constituents in the middle of the Depression. It was estimated that the project provided 17,000 new jobs in its first year. Lake Texoma is the tenth largest man-made lake in the United States, holding 2,722,000 acre feet of water. Located in both Texas and Oklahoma, it is formed by the Red and Ouachita rivers. Because the Red River is salty, there is little water use of the lake, but it protects thousands of acres from floods, provides recreation, and the dam supplies hydroelectric power.[53]

Rayburn knew the lake was an invaluable project for his district, and he fought for it with great tenacity. When Oklahoma's congressional delegation opposed the project, Rayburn, who was then majority leader, suggested that Oklahoma would therefore not get federal funds for any water project. As a result, opposition from the Oklahoma delegation was withdrawn.[54]

This was not the only obstacle to the dam project. Opponents in his district claimed that Rayburn was ineffective because he could not get authorization for the dam. In 1935, FDR promised Rayburn that funds for the dam's survey would be in the Works Progress Administration (WPA) budget. That was welcome news to Rayburn, who had been pushing for the dam for a decade without success. The thrilled Rayburn announced FDR's promise to the press. However, when the list of WPA projects was published, Rayburn's dam was not on the list. He was in a bind. Harold Ickes wrote FDR that he had received two long telegrams from Sam Rayburn regarding the Red River Project:

> He says that he is in an embarrassing position because of the publicity that he gave it after his talk with you about this project. He thought that money would be forthcoming for at least a preliminary survey, to be followed by more money for actual work on the project. He so announced through the press, as I understand it. Now his political enemies are twitting about his failure to deliver.

Ickes noted that the National Resources Committee had not favored the project.[55] Twelve days later the President received further unfavorable news about the project, causing him to write Marvin McIntyre, "Will you tell Sam Rayburn about it next time he asks but do not stir up the animals until then!"[56]

FDR understood that he had placed Rayburn in political jeopardy, especially because in the 1936 Democratic primary, Rayburn would face a Greenville printer, Jess Morris, who was a major political threat. The utility companies attempted to get even with Rayburn for his role in the Holding Company battle. They generously funded Jess Morris's campaign and Rayburn responded to the threat by intensively campaigning across his district.[57] To be secure in his reelection, he needed an announcement before the primary that funds had been approved to prepare the land survey for the dam.

In 1936, Rayburn campaigned as a New Dealer. Roosevelt was very popular in Texas and in Rayburn's district. With the announcement of a whistle-stop tour of the Southwest by Roosevelt that would include a stop in Denison, the Jess Morris faction became suspicious. The chair and secretary of the Jess Morris for Congress Club wired the president that "the Fourth Congressional District is so evenly divided in the present Congressional Campaign" that they would greatly appreciate "statements in papers and over radios" that the trip to Texas was "nonpolitical" and that Roosevelt was "taking no hand in local political races."[58]

The president would disappoint the Morris forces. In Denison, Roosevelt embraced Rayburn and then announced the approval of funds to begin the Denison

Dam survey.[59] John McDuffie, a former Alabama Congressman and close friend of Rayburn, wrote him, "Some people stay in Congress on cotton, others on dams. I thought you had built the dam at Denison, but if you did that how could you hold Denison with no dam to work for?"[60] Rayburn's victory was assured and in June 1938, Rayburn's position in his district was strengthened when Congress approved funding for the $54 million project.

The rewards for his labors on behalf of the administration were paying off on the home front. The dam was political gold to Rayburn. On Sam Rayburn Day the *Denison Herald* published a special edition in honor of their congressman. Not only did the paper praise him as an "indefatigable worker for the Red River dam," it described him as "one of the principal figures in Washington and right-hand man of President Roosevelt's New Deal administration."[61]

Rayburn further strengthened his position through appointments to executive posts. He arranged for his close friend and political ally in the district, Fenner Leslie, to be appointed special assistant to the United States Attorney in the Land Division of the Attorney General's office. Leslie worked closely with Lucius Clay to acquire land for the project. Another trusted political ally, Lee Simmons, was appointed to assess the property of landowners.[62]

Some of Rayburn's legislative battles damaged him in his district. It is clear, for example, that his sponsorship of the Public Utility Holding Company Act led to substantial utility-company funding of his opposition.[63] His work in support of pure food and drug legislation, according to D. B. Hardeman, led to drug-company funding of his opposition. His general support of the New Deal led to financial support of his opponents by wealthy anti-New Deal individuals such as oil tycoon Harry Sinclair.[64]

However, one Roosevelt bill that Rayburn sponsored probably brought him even greater political benefits in his district than did the Denison Dam. In January 1936 Sam Rayburn introduced in the House, and Senator George Norris of Nebraska introduced in the Senate, bills that would make the Rural Electrification Administration (REA) an independent, permanent agency. Rayburn believed his role in creating REA was one of his greatest legislative accomplishments. As part of the Emergency Relief Act of 1935, the first Rural Electrification Administration was created. The initial plan was that rural electrification would be a jobs program. Late in 1935, however, the program was revised so that farmers would join cooperatives, borrow money, and build and own electrical lines. The loans would then be repaid from the sales of electricity to farmers. That system became the basis for the legislation proposed by Rayburn and Norris. The legislation sailed through Congress and proved to be enormously popular with the small-farmer constituency that was Rayburn's district.[65] For the remainder of his career, when he spoke in his district, Rayburn routinely listed rural electrification as one of his primary accomplishments. In a letter to a critic of the Democrats, Rayburn listed the party's accomplishments and the first item was rural electrification.

> I might call your attention to just a few things that these Administrations, with my help, have done that no other Administration had ever thought of.
>
> There was no rural electrification, or practically none, in the United States when we came to power in 1933. Less than 3% of the farm houses in Texas were electrified then, and now with loans by the Government to the cooperatives, between ninety and ninety-five percent of our farm homes in Texas have electrification.[66]

The political bond between Sam Rayburn and Franklin Roosevelt was an enormously complex one. Ultimately, it was an alliance that worked throughout the Roosevelt era. In Sam Rayburn, Franklin Roosevelt found a markedly effective congressional leader, far more so than the previous Speakers with whom he worked, such as Rainey, Byrns, and Bankhead. Most importantly, given Roosevelt's experience with Garner, Rayburn's efforts as a Southerner and congressional leader were critical to the success of the New Deal.

When Rayburn did disagree, he was more reserved personally and more willing to cooperate and to lose arguments than Garner. He did insist that he be given the opportunity to present his views. His posture reflected the epithet that came to be associated with his career, "To get along, you must go along." In other words, cooperation is essential to success in Rayburn's Washington.

Though their alliance was strongly tested when Rayburn endorsed Garner for the Presidency in 1940, even that challenge resolved itself. Rayburn knew that if FDR ran in 1940, Garner had no chance, and his actions in supporting both Garner and the endorsement of the Roosevelt administration ensured there would be no enduring break in the alliance after Garner retired from the political scene. Their other difficulties were generally dealt with privately and often revolved around Rayburn's insistence that FDR give congressional leaders a greater consultative role.

Rayburn was never anointed with the vice presidency by Roosevelt, though it was dangled before him in 1940. His loyalty to the New Deal gained him many rewards. His name became synonymous with rural electrification, a program of enormous value to his constituents. Additionally, only a congressman whom FDR considered loyal, effective, and deserving could expect a public works project in his district as massive as the Denison Dam.

FDR was enormously popular in Rayburn's district, as he was in Texas generally. Rayburn's close ties to Roosevelt were favored by Rayburn's constituents. One must also understand that Rayburn was ambitious, a man whose dream since childhood was to be Speaker of the United State House of Representatives. Once elected to Congress, the lifelong bachelor's constituents and colleagues became his family. He had no significant outside interests. When Franklin Roosevelt entered the White House, Rayburn had already been in Congress for twenty years, and, although he was finally Chairman of the Interstate and Foreign Commerce Committee, he was still far from achieving his life's goal. His tries for the speakership upon the advancement of Garner to the vice presidency in 1933 and upon the death of Speaker

Rainey in 1934 failed. Franklin Roosevelt put him on the road to the speakership: first, by working with Rayburn when he was committee chair. This enabled the Texan to acquire an impressive legislative record. Second, FDR backed him for majority leader in 1936, which put him in line for the speakership when Bankhead died in 1940.

It was an ideal political alliance, and although there was always a distance in their relationship, a sense of respect or friendship developed. James Roosevelt said "[F]ather regarded Rayburn as a statesman."[67] When FDR died, Sam Rayburn sat alone in a small room and wept.[68]

NOTES

1. Lionel V. Patenaude, *Texans, Politics and the New Deal,* (New York: Garland Publishing, 1983), p. 57.

2. Booth Mooney, *Roosevelt and Rayburn: A Political Partnership,* (Philadelphia: J.B. Lippencott Company, 1971), p. 16.

3. Ibid., p. 30.

4. Ibid., p. 45.

5. Ibid., pp. 21–24.

6. D. B. Hardeman and Donald C. Bacon, *Rayburn: A Biography* (Austin: Texas Monthly Press, 1987), pp. 127–143.

7. Ibid., pp. 145–199; Mooney, pp. 42–63.

8. Alfred Steinberg, *Sam Rayburn: A Biography,* (New York: Hawthorn Books, 1975), p. 115.

9. Ibid., p. 117.

10. Ibid., p. 117.

11. Ibid., p. 127.

12. Anthony Champagne, "Sam Rayburn: Achieving Party Leadership," *Southwestern Historical Quarterly,* 90 (April 1987), p. 384.

13. James Roosevelt interview with Anthony Champagne, May 17, 1984, Sam Rayburn Library. John O'Connor was denied renomination and reelection in the 1938 purge. Details are in chapter eight of this volume.

14. Mooney, *Roosevelt and Rayburn,* p. 70.

15. Champagne, "Sam Rayburn: Achieving," pp. 380–392.

16. Mooney, *Roosevelt and Rayburn,* p. 80.

17. Champagne, "Sam Rayburn: Achieving," p. 390.

18. Patenaude, *Texans, Politics, and the New Deal,* pp. 39–42.

19. Ibid., pp. 43–51.

20. Ibid., pp. 43–51.

21. Cecil Dickson interview with Anthony Champagne, June 29, 1980, Sam Rayburn Library.

22. Gerald Griffin, "Rayburn Joins Garner Block for 1940 Race," *Baltimore Sun,* August 13, 1939, unpaginated, FDR Library.

23. Felix Cotten, "Young Democrats Back New Deal as Rayburn Bolts to Garner for '40," *Washington Post,* August 13, 1939, unpaginated, FDR Library.

24. Robert A. Caro, *The Years of Lyndon Johnson: The Path to Power*, (New York: Alfred A. Knopf, 1982), p. 572.

25. Ibid., p. 573.

26. Ibid., p. 573–574.

27. Griffin, "Rayburn Joins Garner."

28. Franklin D. Roosevelt telegram to Sam Rayburn, July 10, 1938, FDR Library.

29. Stephen T. Early to Franklin D. Roosevelt, August 15, 1939, FDR Library.

30. Franklin D. Roosevelt to Stephen T. Early, undated note on Early to FDR memo, August 15, 1939, FDR Library.

31. Stephen T. Early to Cecil Dickson, August 25, 1939 and Stephen T. Early to Morris Sheppard, August 25, 1939, FDR Library.

32. Caro, *The Years of Lyndon Johnson,* pp. 570–571.

33. Hardeman and Bacon, *Rayburn: A Biography*, p. 233. James Roosevelt thought FDR understood Rayburn's dilemma. He said, "My father was also enough of a realist to know that if you lived in Texas, you'd darn well better be for its 'favorite son.'" James Roosevelt, May 17, 1984 interview with Anthony Champagne.

34. Mooney, *Roosevelt and Rayburn*, pp. 134–135.

35. Hardeman and Bacon, *Rayburn: A Biography*, p. 240; Steinberg, *Sam Rayburn: A Biography*, p. 162.

36. Mooney, *Roosevelt and Rayburn*, p. 126.

37. Hardeman and Bacon, *Rayburn: A Biography*, pp. 238–239.

38. Caro, *The Years of Lyndon Johnson*, pp. 615–617. On February 13, 1942, Ed Flynn wrote FDR a memorandum stressing Rayburn's importance to Democratic fund-raising efforts, "In Texas particularly, the success of the fund raising campaign, which is probably the most important state in the union for fund raising, will be absolutely ruined if Rayburn does not go to Ft. Worth to make, not a political, but a patriotic speech. His merely being there will mean a great deal to the success of the fund raising campaigns." Ed Flynn to Franklin D. Roosevelt, February 13, 1942, FDR Library.

39. Hardeman and Bacon, *Rayburn: A Biography*, p. 301.

40. Ibid, p. 235.

41. Marvin McIntyre to Franklin D. Roosevelt, October 29, 1942, FDR Library.

42. Marvin McIntyre to Director, Bureau of the Budget, January 11, 1943, FDR Library.

43. Grace Tully to Franklin D. Roosevelt, June 8, 1943, FDR Library.

44. Franklin D. Roosevelt to James Byrnes, June 11, 1943, FDR Library.

45. Hardeman and Bacon, *Rayburn: A Biography*, p. 70.

46. Franklin D. Roosevelt to Sam Rayburn, December 23, 1940, FDR Library.

47. John McCormack to Franklin D. Roosevelt, December 28, 1940, FDR Library.

48. Hardeman and Bacon, *Rayburn: A Biography*, pp. 254–255.

49. Mooney, *Roosevelt and Rayburn*, pp. 93–94.

50. Dickson interview, June 29, 1980. Hardeman and Bacon tell a similar story about the Splawn appointment, although they do not mention Rayburn's calling FDR a liar or turning his back on the president. See Hardeman and Bacon, *Rayburn: A Biography,* pp. 493–494, fn. 12.

51. Hardeman and Bacon, ibid. pp. 162–163. Rayburn would not even respond to FDR's appeal that he thought something had to be done. Franklin D. Roosevelt to Sam Rayburn, May 23, 1935, FDR Library.

52. Steinberg, *Sam Rayburn: A Biography,* p. 122.

53. Hardeman and Bacon, *Rayburn: A Biography,* pp. 204–205; Anthony Champagne, *Congressman Sam Rayburn,* (New Brunswick: Rutgers University press, 1984), p. 52.

54. Ibid. pp. 52–53.

55. Harold Ickes to Franklin D. Roosevelt, November 30, 1935, FDR Library.

56. Franklin D. Roosevelt to Marvin McIntyre, December 16, 1935, FDR Library.

57. Hardeman and Bacon, *Rayburn: A Biography,* p. 204.

58. R.L. Warren and E.D. Barlow telegram to Franklin D. Roosevelt, June 10, 1936, FDR Library.

59. Hardeman and Bacon, *Rayburn: A Biography,* p. 206.

60. John McDuffie to Sam Rayburn, undated, Sam Rayburn Library.

61. Twelve-page special issue of *The Denison Herald*, July 11, 1938, Sam Rayburn Library.

62. Champagne, *Congressman Sam Rayburn*, pp. 53–54.

63. Hardeman and Bacon, *Rayburn: A Biography,* p. 187.

64. Larry Huffard, editor, *D.B.: Reminiscences of D. B. Hardeman,* (Austin: AAR/Tantalus, 1984), pp. 36, 73.

65. Champagne, *Congressman Sam Rayburn*, p. 48.

66. H.G. Dulaney, Edward Hake Phillips, and MacPhelan Reese, *Speak Mr. Speaker,* (Bonham: The Sam Rayburn Foundation, 1978), p. 210.

67. Roosevelt, May 17, 1984. James Roosevelt was clear, however, that it was not a social friendship between the two men. Part of the reason was, said Roosevelt, "Father did not make that many friends." Rayburn, on the other hand, "was a bachelor, therefore he did not socialize." Rayburn was able to maintain his influence at the White House in part because he never used friendship "to get father to do what he wanted."

68. Hardeman and Bacon, *Rayburn: A Biography,* p. 309.

CHAPTER SIX

Wright Patman's Entrepreneurial Leadership in Congress, 1929-1941

NANCY BECK YOUNG

Democrat Wright Patman represented Texas's First Congressional District from 1929 until his death in 1976. He garnered a national following early in his career. Unlike most freshmen legislators in the late 1920s and the New Deal, he took an immediate interest in the active advocacy of issues from the House floor. During the Herbert Hoover and the Franklin D. Roosevelt presidential administrations, Patman developed an entrepreneurial style of leadership that existed outside the formal House leadership structure. Patman's actions occurred at a time when new congressmen were expected to be seen and not heard. Indeed, Patman ignored the traditional seniority system as a method of advancement in favor of an individualistic style. Using steering committees with other members, public debates, speeches on national radio, and aggressive constituent solicitation, Patman continued his entrepreneurial leadership on issues ranging from early payment of a veterans bonus to reform of the Federal Reserve System (Fed). Scholarly analysis of the tactics he used in these legislative campaigns sheds new light on Patman's national significance.

Indeed, the Texas congressman's advocacy of the bonus and reform of the Federal Reserve placed him squarely in the national spotlight. The entrepreneurial leadership style Patman developed proved innovative because it gave the new congressman a national voice not readily available to more traditional congressman, and thereby aided his rapid rise to power. Furthermore, his independence merits scholarly analysis because of the significant challenges it presented to Franklin D. Roosevelt's presidency. Finally, academicians interested in the breakdown of the disciplined Congress and the evolution of the independent-agent style that peaked in the 1970s could profit from consideration of the Patman precedents.

What role did Patman's heritage play in the development of his leadership style? Like his more famous Texas colleagues, Sam Rayburn and Lyndon B. Johnson, Patman cannot be understood apart from his background. His rural East Texas roots shaped his political philosophy, and, from his upbringing, Patman gained a deep commitment to the farmers and small businessmen of his native region. Indeed, this rural ethos, more than anything else, defined his actions in Washington. Unlike some congressmen, he never forgot the problems of his district while serving in Congress. People from his district remember his friendly, down-home style, but back in Washington, D.C., he knew how to play power politics with the inside practitioners. His constant focus on the economic problems of rural America caused him to bring to the capital city a different voice that often sounded out of sync with the establishment concerns.

What kind of leader would Patman become? As a new Congressman during the Hoover years, Patman was unwilling to bide his time on the seniority ladder. Instead, he arrived in Washington in 1929 with plans for immediate activity. He often drew on his personal resources to further his legislative agenda. In 1932 when approached about the possibility of running for Governor of Texas, Patman declared "I am not in a position financially to make the race. I owe the same debts I owed when I came in, even including the mortgage on my home. A member of Congress, who conscientiously performs his duties and spends the money that is necessary for him to spend, cannot save anything." Patman carved his niche as a vocal critic of the system, and he often received more press than either of his state's two senators.[1]

During the Hoover years, Patman seemed more interested in protest than in pragmatic politics. His tendency to the dramatic colored the way in which other politicians responded to his leadership. He quickly assumed a leadership role in the fight for the immediate cash payment of the World War I veterans bonus. With this lofty agenda weighing on his mind, Patman desired an immediate impact. One observer noted "it has long been axiomatic that leaders rarely develop in the House of Representatives except by seniority. This axiom has been smashed in the last two years, however, by a young first termer from Texas. By using the demands of World War veterans on the Federal Treasury, Representative Wright Patman, Democrat, has attained such power that, as his second term begins he can throw shivers of apprehension into the ranks of both parties at will."[2]

The nuances of leadership styles cannot be appreciated apart from consideration of the issues to which they are applied. For Patman the issue that attracted most of his attention in the New Deal years was the pension program for World War I veterans more commonly known as the bonus. World War I veterans returned home with a severance bonus of less than $100. Noting the pay of domestic workers during the war, congressional advocates throughout the 1920s pushed for more equitable terms. Legislation passed in 1924 authorized adjusted compensation payment but only in 1945. As soon as he entered Congress, Patman sought immediate cash payment of the adjusted service certificates. He linked early payment of the adjusted service certificates with the larger cause of currency reform and a more equitable distribution of society's resources. Officials with the United States Veterans Bureau, though, doubted the wisdom of Patman's proposal. The arguments that he made in May 1929 launched what became a seven-year crusade. Patman's activities during this campaign for early payment are important not only for the political maneuverings he undertook but also for the revelations they contain about the maturation of his leadership style.[3]

Patman's actions in Washington were, in fact, a testing ground for a whole new style of congressional operations. Not only did he buck tradition by assuming a leadership role early in his first term, he also instituted various grassroots strategies unwelcome to the House leadership. In working for his legislation Patman did not rely solely on generating goodwill in Washington, but also recruited the support of those intended to benefit from early payment of the bonus. To that end, he sent numerous mailings of speeches and other documents to veterans. He urged former servicemen to organize within their local American Legion posts and to lobby their National Convention. The congressman believed that many of his colleagues would not support the bill until the American Legion had announced its preference. The Texan also formed coalitions within Congress among like-minded members and met often with his House colleagues to devise strategy. Understanding the value of numbers, Patman sought assistance from all Democratic nominees on the November 1930 ballot. Patman also contributed articles for the wire services to generate support for his cause nationwide.[4]

From the earliest days of this fight, the Texas congressman realized the importance of recruiting support not only from individual Legionnaires but also from the national American Legion, for that organization spoke with authority on Capitol Hill. But Patman also knew that the Legion in the late 1920s operated under a conservative structure. Unable to rely on the American Legion at the national level, Patman solicited the support of other veterans' organizations, including the Veterans of Foreign Wars (VFW) and the Disabled American Veterans (DAV).[5] This move had the dual effect of demonstrating to the public the support of the latter two organizations and sowing the seeds for a bitter rivalry between the Legion and the VFW. The feud that developed represented one failure of Patman's entrepreneurial leadership because the bickering between veterans' groups gave congressional opponents to the bonus another weapon for their fight.

In pushing his agenda, Patman did not overlook the main arena for action. To get around administration opposition to early payment, Patman perfected a rarely used parliamentary measure, the discharge petition, a document circulated among colleagues to force the committee in question, in this instance the Ways and Means Committee, to send the bill to the House floor. Needing 218 signatures, or a majority of the House, Patman encouraged veterans to lobby their representatives on behalf of the measure. Patman called on the first 100 signers to get one more member to join the fight. He also kept a careful list of members interested in meetings about the bonus. Patman circulated lists of the bill's supporters among members of Congress and the press.

Patman's leadership did not rely solely on making friends. When necessary, he feuded with other members of Congress. He publicized a disagreement with Congressman Hamilton Fish Jr., Republican of New York, to attract attention to his cause. Patman challenged tradition early in his first term when he published the names of his colleagues who had failed to sign the discharge petition while his bonus bill was still in committee.[6]

Realizing the importance of media backing, Patman also sought support from William Randolph Hearst's newspapers for his plan to pay the adjusted service certificates immediately. Patman pointed out that "your newspapers in the United

States can put this proposition over in sixty days." Patman's appeals to Hearst paid off, and the newspaper publisher pushed for early payment of the adjusted service certificates. Yet support from the Hearst chain did not ensure speedy passage. In his search for grassroots support, Patman did not overlook the advantages of modern technology, namely radio, for getting his message to the people. Father Charles E. Coughlin, the noted Detroit radio priest, asked Patman: "Have you ever been intrigued by a microphone: Is it not possible...to have either the National Broadcasting Company or the Columbia [Broadcasting System] donate an hour or so in the name of the ex-soldier so that you could appeal to the nation? Although I have never met you, I feel that you are made of the right stuff and that you are able to accomplish much by radio."[7] Nationwide radio appeals assumed a prominent place in Patman's arsenal. An effective speaker, he used these talks to generate publicity and advance his cause.

Public addresses provided another component of Patman's entrepreneurial leadership. When Congress recessed and Patman went home, he gave numerous speeches about the bonus. During June 1931, Patman made a speaking tour through the Midwest on behalf of the adjusted service certificates. While on the trip Patman held a strategy meeting with other leading advocates of the adjusted service certificates. On this tour Patman delivered a major speech in Chicago at a mass meeting that the Progressive Republicans of Illinois had arranged to plot strategy for defeating Hoover. The speech contained little in the way of substantive policy proposals; instead, the congressman chose themes with appeal for impoverished Americans. He complained that soldiers' actual wages amounted to little or nothing at all after mandatory deductions, while "alien slackers and alien enemies in America, who were exempt from military service, received from $15 to $70 a day working in Government shipyards and munitions plants. More than 33,000 millionaires were made during the World War and by reason of the country's misery and misfortune."[8]

Despite the various techniques Patman brought to his fight for the bonus, his style of entrepreneurial leadership proved insufficient to beat back administration and Republican congressional arguments against the bill. A compromise version of the Patman bill passed the House in 1932 but died in the Senate, leaving the issue for future battles in a new administration. In the aftermath of the 1932 bonus battle, thousands of Bonus Marchers, veterans from around the country who had moved into Washington throughout the year, heightened their protests against the government's lack of action. Hoover's use of the army to disperse the marchers hurt his candidacy for reelection, and that fall the governor of New York, Franklin D. Roosevelt, handily defeated Hoover.[9]

Patman failed to pass the bonus in 1932, but his crusade was not a complete loss. He used the problem of veterans' compensation to draw attention to himself and what he believed were neglected issues of resource distribution in the country at large. Heightened national publicity and a grassroots following allowed Patman to expand his entrepreneurial approach to congressional leadership in new directions. In the period 1929–1933 he created the coalition that passed the measure to pay the bonus in 1936. More important, he broadened the public's understanding of the problem from a simple matter of equitable compensation for soldiers to a larger discussion of currency expansion and reform. However, he limited his effectiveness by subscribing totally to his own rhetoric of protest. With a Democratic administration on the horizon, a question loomed: Would Patman moderate his demeanor and work with his party's established leadership, or would he fail to realize the importance of pragmatic politics and precipitate his own political demise?

Wright Patman hoped Roosevelt would support his plan for payment of the bonus linked to the currency reform measures that he had endorsed during his first four years in Congress. Patman was an enthusiastic supporter of Roosevelt well before the 1932 Democratic convention in Chicago. Yet, despite their shared liberalism, Roosevelt brought a world view of Eastern gentility and noblesse oblige to the White House, a view entirely different from the one that animated much of Patman's congressional activity. While the two men opposed most of the Republican policies of the 1920s, the new president employed a much more experimental approach to the problems of the depression than the rural-oriented Patman.

The relationship Patman forged with the new president demonstrates much about the nature of Congress's dealings with the White House during the New Deal and reflects the influence and independence of largely partisan Democrats on Capitol Hill. Despite his constant politicking on behalf of the president and the Democratic party, Patman had in mind an agenda of currency reform, and he used his entrepreneurial leadership skills to ensure its passage. Six months after the new president took office, Patman told constituents that "revolution is here now.... We're changing laws and business. The changes are so radical it's almost impossible to describe them. A hundred years from now historians will describe them as a revolution." Patman's public rhetoric and behavior never wavered in support of the president. For example, he marched in a parade from the Capitol to Union Station to greet the president upon his return to Washington in April 1934 and later told audiences in his district that "no president has ever hit Wall Street between the eyes as hard as Roosevelt."[10] Nevertheless, Patman was a leader of insurgent Democrats in the House on issues ranging from early payment of the veterans bonus to government ownership of the Federal Reserve.

The evolution of Patman's leadership skills became apparent as the New Deal progressed. To gain favor with the White House, Patman developed a pragmatic side for the entrepreneurial style of leadership he had forged during the Hoover years. While he still used unofficial steering committees, radio speeches, and other means of direct communication with his ideological constituency to gain support for paying the adjusted service certificates, expanding the currency, and later reforming the Federal Reserve, Patman had learned the art of compromise and negotiation with fellow congressmen for the sake of getting a bill out as he did in 1936 with the bonus legislation.

By the middle of February 1933, Patman launched his attack with a mass mailing to political and veterans groups that solicited their support. Despite media criticism for proposing a plan that would have unbalanced the budget, removed the United

States from the gold standard, and paid the soldiers with fiat money, Patman stressed the safeguards against inflation written into his legislation. The Texarkana congressman introduced his bill linking currency expansion with payment of the bonus on March 9, 1933, and lobbied Roosevelt for his support. However, Roosevelt ignored Patman's request. Patman temporarily bowed to the administration's opposition to the bonus. Yet Patman confidently added that "I believe after he tries all other plans that he will have to come to this plan as the best way to get money in circulation. However, I am not willing to throw any wrench in the machinery." Nevertheless, Patman generated a statement explaining his measure and his attempts to gain the administration's approval and sent it to supporters around the country. Despite public claims that he had backed off the bonus issue in deference to the president, Patman used a petition with the requisite signatures to compel the Democratic caucus to address his bonus bill in Congress. In turn, Democratic leaders promised Patman they would help him lobby the president if he would not force his measure on Congress.[11]

In January 1934, Patman was not ready to push the bonus over Roosevelt's opposition. He probably did not have the votes as like-minded Democrats in the first session of the 73rd Congress had not been able to defeat the president's economy program, a spending-reduction package that Roosevelt introduced as part of his 1932 campaign pledge to balance the budget. The discharge petition for his bill had been filed by Representative Ernest Lundeen (Farmer–Labor Party of Minnesota) in April 1933 and barely had one-third of the necessary signatures by January. Patman did not sign until the petition was nearly completed on February 20 when the last seventeen names were added. Then Patman forced the House to consider his bonus bill. Members supported Patman because they wanted the soldiers' vote in the coming elections. Patman denied his move was a challenge to the president. He reminded the press that the president had told the American Legion convention that the bonus would be paid when conditions warranted. The Texan then noted that payment of the bonus would be a good way to put the $3,140,000,000 in the Treasury to work.[12]

Roosevelt based his opposition to the bonus on the way pensions for Civil War veterans had been administered. The president told House members he would endorse the bonus only with "definite assurance" that there would be no demands for further payments to World War I veterans. "You know and I know what happened after the War between the States. Each year they got a little chiseling here and a little chiseling there until they got the Service Pension. The Act was passed in 1890."[13]

When he was unsuccessful in 1934, Patman lobbied key members of the House for their support for the new Congress taking office in 1935. Patman complained to his Democratic colleague from Texas, James P. Buchanan, chairman of the House Appropriations Committee, that "I received your very, very formal letter, with the same old story about leaving quickly and not having time to read, etc. Buck, I really want you to look this thing over and let me hear from you." Patman stressed, "I want to work with the administration, but at the same time I have certain views in regard to this matter that I would like to urge if it can be done without detriment to the administration. Look that statement over and let me have your opinion." Buchanan replied that "it will be better [for me] to discuss it at length with [Roosevelt], with the view of procuring his approval which, if we do, will insure the passage of the Act, and if we do not, in my judgment, it cannot become law."[14]

In December 1934, Patman expanded the reaches of his entrepreneurial leadership into the publishing world when he released two books that presented his argument for payment of the bonus. *Bankerteering, Bonuseering, Melloneering* had sections addressing the Federal Reserve, the adjusted service certificates, and the attempted impeachment of former Treasury Secretary Andrew Mellon in 1932. Patman distributed the section dealing with the bonus separately under the title *Patman's Appeal to Pay Veterans.* Designed for mass distribution, the books sold for 75 cents a copy or 100 copies for $25.00. The books had been planned for over a year and their release followed an extensive advertising campaign focused on veterans' publications and organizations. Patman asked the American Legion to purchase enough of the bonus books—10,000—to provide one for each post in the United States. He told one Legion official that, "I would like to contribute these booklets to the American Legion, but I am a poor man myself and have gone deeply into debt getting it ready for the press." However, by May 1935, prospects for financial success diminished when sales to Legion posts did not materialize, and Patman distributed the remaining copies to friends at no cost.[15]

The year 1935 proved crucial to Patman. He sensed that he was close to victory in the bonus fight. Therefore, Patman's leadership skills proved even more important. He arranged for a discharge petition for his H.R. 1 from the Ways and Means Committee, which had approved another bonus plan. In asking members to sign the discharge petition for H.R. 1, Patman declared "we do not consider this a reflection upon the Committee in any way, but we are merely protecting our rights and making sure that everything is being done that can be done to obtain consideration." Despite the petition drive, Patman asked the Ways and Means Committee for a hearing on the bonus. The parliamentary rule that brought the Patman bill to the House floor represented skillful maneuvering on both sides of the question. Opposition congressmen believed the Patman bill would not survive a veto override vote, but an alternative bill would. So they voted for the measure most likely to fail. Yet, when the House finally voted up or down on the Patman bill, it passed by a vote of 319–90, a veto-proof margin.[16]

Patman thanked the steering committee and praised their efforts. "The oldest members of the House of Representatives have informed me that our Steering Committee functioned efficiently in every way and never before in their experience have they witnessed such loyalty and one hundred percent cooperation nor such big victories against tremendous odds." Yet colleagues recognized Patman as "more responsible than any other man in the country, or any thousand men, for building up sentiment favorable to the adoption of bonus legislation.... The vast majority of the veterans voted with Patman. I think he is infinitely stronger with the veterans of the House and veterans of the country than is [Frank N.] Belgrano, [Jr., the National

Commander of the American Legion]. He is a clean, wholesome, upstanding man. He has fine ability, is industrious and well liked by his colleagues. The vote taken was distinctly a Patman vote."[17]

With victory achieved in the House, attention quickly shifted to the other side of Capitol Hill for the Senate battle. Administration officials realized there was still a good chance to defeat the bill in the Senate. Nonetheless, Vice President John Nance Garner, a Texas Democrat, observed "that damn thing's got a lot of strength down in the Senate." Patman expanded his advocacy role to the Senate when he lobbied members of the upper chamber. One contemporary observer noted that "when the battle shifted from the South to the North wing of the Capitol, the bonus generalissimo from the Lone Star State marched over and commandeered a rear desk in the Senate as his 'field headquarters.' No lobbyist was ever more vigilant than he." The Texas congressman "didn't take time out even for luncheon but stuck continually to his strategic observation post. He button-holed and wheedled Senators. He watched and checked every roll-call." The bill passed the Senate, but rumors indicated a probable presidential veto.[18]

When the fate of the bonus became questionable for 1935, Patman resorted to his steering committee for help. Patman called a steering committee strategy meeting on May 25, 1935, three days after the president announced his veto plans. Worried about the future of his bonus bill, Patman criticized Legion officials for not making an aggressive fight for the bonus between its passage in the Senate and the override vote. Patman arranged a meeting for his steering committee with Senator Elmer Thomas, an Oklahoma Democrat, and other Senate supporters to devise a compromise bonus plan. The House and Senate bonus advocates planned to reintroduce a bonus bill in the new session in January. In late July, Patman asked for steering-committee advice on a plan to revive the discharge petition for H.R. 1 from the Ways and Means Committee. That petition had been sidetracked when the Patman bill received a committee hearing in March. Patman believed that finishing the petition that summer would clear the way for consideration of the bill in January since the petition would remain valid into the next session. It required only sixty additional signatures. In early August, he circulated a list of House members who had not signed the petition. Patman suggested that if the White House would agree to go along in January, he could get Elmer Thomas to drop his push for adding the bonus to the tax bill. Patman then addressed an appeal to each House member who had voted to override the president but had not yet signed the petition.[19]

Yet Patman's bonus still faced competition from more conservative proposals in the 1936 session of Congress. Patman planned a conference with veterans' leaders in and out of Congress to unify the various forces before the January session of Congress. The steering committee met on January 2, 1936, and reaffirmed support for H.R. 1. Patman told steadfast backers of his support for the compromise. "This I cannot oppose as it will be construed as a fight over authorship," but he promised to "leave no stone unturned to get a rule that will make our bill in order." Members of the steering committee met with the American Legion, the Veterans of Foreign Wars, and Disabled American Veterans as well as bonus proponents in Congress to ascertain sentiment about a compromise. Patman and his steering committee decided to "divide the fight" and seek approval for immediate payment first and then address currency expansion. Patman saw that cooperation and compromise as the only way he would enjoy any credit for the passage of the new bill (H.R. 9870), which was almost certain in an election year. Patman's willingness to accept this compromise represented his growing maturity as a leader. He told his colleagues that "no major bill becomes a law without the sacrifice of a view or the compromise of opinion on the part of practically every Member of this Body." The unified bill became law after it passed the House and Senate in the middle of January. The president vetoed the bill on January 24, but both houses of Congress overrode within three days, the House on the 24th and the Senate on the 27th.[20]

By the time legislation to pay the bonus was passed in 1936, Patman's relationship to the rest of Congress was firmly established. His colleagues recognized him as a knowledgeable expert on financial and economic questions but rarely accepted all that he argued. In the span of only seven years, Patman had established his congressional niche through a combination of an entrepreneurial style of leadership with hardball politics. He adroitly merged the demands of issue advocacy with the pragmatic skills of a back-room negotiator and arm twister. His colleague, Congressman Maury Maverick, Democrat of Texas, noted that "no congressman has any influence with another. That's the reason that Wright Patman is the smartest member of Congress—he says very little to his colleagues but goes around the country making speeches. That is how he passed the bonus whether anyone likes it or not."[21] But Maverick was only half right, for Patman's victory rested on his hours of negotiation as well as his travels around the land. Despite the fact that the final adjusted service certificates bill as passed more closely resembled the proposal that Congressman Fred M. Vinson, Democrat of Kentucky, drafted for the American Legion, Patman was the man who made it all possible with his Herculean efforts dating back to his first days as a congressman. More importantly, Patman's constant push for the bonus attracted the attention of the White House since it offered a competing measure for providing relief and reform to the people suffering from the Great Depression and complicated Roosevelt's efforts at change.

Patman's entrepreneurial leadership was not limited to passing the bonus. Like his larger political philosophy, it transcended issues. Indeed, he used this style of advocacy to push his agenda for banking reform. Even before Roosevelt's inauguration, Patman noted in his diary that "the Solomons of finance have destroyed the temple." Patman served as secretary of the House Currency Reform Group during the early years of the New Deal and arranged for members to tour the U.S. Mint in Philadelphia on April 1, 1933. Deemed to have "the Texas intestinal stamina" and described as "one of the big men of the country" for his efforts to expand the currency, Patman pushed various legislative panaceas that he believed would increase the money in circulation.[22]

The Texan's leadership on the issue of monetary reform led to his cooperation with individuals holding questionable political agendas. Most notable was Patman's relationship with Father Coughlin. Patman worked with him from his earliest days as a bonus advocate, and he continued the relationship even when Coughlin's larger political and ideological agenda became questionable. In Patman's zealous efforts to forge an army for monetary reform, he made alliances with people like Coughlin who also desired currency expansion. Patman overlooked the extent of Coughlin's anti-Semitic, antidemocratic views and cooperated willingly with the priest throughout the 1930s. Part of the reason for Patman's association with Coughlin was due to one of the congressman's earliest mentors, Texan James H. "Cyclone" Davis, a protest politician and former member of Congress associated with the Farmers Alliance, the Populist Party, and the Prohibition movement. Davis remained fond of the priest and told Patman that "the political pimps of Wall Street would like to hush the voice of freedom as offered by Father Coughlin, Senator [Huey] Long [Democrat of Louisiana] and all who plead for the plundered masses against the predatory plundering classes."[23]

Robert M. Harriss, a New York cotton broker and Patman supporter, helped Patman raise funds for the distribution of Patman's speeches advocating currency expansion. Harriss sent one of Patman's addresses on the money question to Father Coughlin and suggested that the congressman meet with the priest while on a midwestern speaking tour in the fall of 1935. After their meeting, Patman sought an outlet for Coughlin's radio program in Texas and the Southeast. He gained access to the Louisiana radio market, but negotiations fell through with Dallas and San Antonio stations. Then Patman asked Dr. John R. Brinkley, the notorious goat-gland doctor and radio broadcaster, for time on his high-powered Reynosa, Mexico, station with a broadcast radius of 1500 miles. Harriss told Patman that "if [Coughlin's] radio talks could be heard in Texas it would be a great thing for you and especially for the people of Texas."[24]

In August 1936, Coughlin invited Patman to speak at the National Convention of the National Union for Social Justice. Patman did not want to accept the invitation because Coughlin had called Roosevelt a "liar" and a "betrayer," nor did he want to offend the priest with whom he had worked to secure passage of the bonus. He asked Sam Rayburn what he thought about using Coughlin's praise "before certain audiences [letting]...it be known that Coughlin is in accord with my views on everything else practically except supporting Roosevelt." Rayburn, however, believed Coughlin should be ignored entirely. While Patman followed Rayburn's advice on this occasion, he did not sever his connections with Coughlin, helping him the following year.[25]

At the same time Patman searched for broad solutions to monetary reform, he also focused his attention more narrowly on one agency of the government—the Federal Reserve System—which he believed had to be changed if any lasting improvements were to be made in the economy. Because of his battle with the Federal Reserve, one congressman remembered "Patman was always the recognized leader of the group of monetary reformers....He was always a very careful worker so that he didn't get too far out."[26]

Patman's 1937 legislative drive for government ownership of the Federal Reserve incorporated many practices used in his previous campaign for the bonus. A thorough researcher, he sought information about the earnings of banks belonging to the Fed and the earnings of national banks since 1929. In March 1937, Patman and Congressman Charles G. Binderup (Democrat of Nebraska) lobbied Democratic congressmen to join their steering committee for government ownership of the Federal Reserve. They sent a circular letter to 331 House Democrats announcing their plans for a steering committee. Sixty-five congressmen attended the first committee meeting and determined that their efforts would take a partisan tone. Patman told interested members that over the past two years he had distributed more than 500,000 copies of his speech, "Currency Instead of Bonds," nationwide and that as soon as a bill for government ownership was drafted and inserted in the *Congressional Record,* that document would also be mailed throughout the country. Patman and Binderup promised that all members who joined the steering committee would be listed as "co-framers, co-sponsors and co-authors of the bill upon request." They believed their organization would include approximately one-third of the House Democrats.[27]

Patman also drew support from allies outside of Congress. In 1937, Coughlin encouraged Patman's efforts to conduct a "national drive on rectifying the money" because "Mr. Roosevelt's financing system is breaking down irreparably." The priest asked Patman to send articles to *Social Justice.* Despite Coughlin's public use of anti-Semitic rhetoric, the congressman gave Coughlin permission to use his name and publish any of his public statements and promised that articles would be forthcoming. Patman recalled their previous battles together and declared "it pleases me very much to know that we will again be associated in this, the greatest of all fights, against the money changers. We are going to win; there is no question about it. We have the right side and our arguments cannot be answered." Patman's dalliance with Coughlin stemmed more from the political clout that the latter wielded than from any deeply ingrained anti-Semitism on the part of the congressman. Although Patman never hesitated to challenge the credibility of the financial community, his ideological ties to the priest revolved around their mutual critique of the monetary system and represented his willingness to use any medium available to bring his views forth to the American people.[28]

In early April, Patman and Binderup told their supporters they had over 100 Democratic members and expected half of the House Democrats to join the fight. In a steering committee meeting on April 13, 1937, 126 House members endorsed government purchase of $132,000,000 in stock from the 7,000 member banks of the Federal Reserve System; government ownership and operation of the twelve Reserve Banks, allowing all 14,000 FDIC member banks access to rediscount privileges with the Fed if their reserves were held in the Fed; receipt of profits by the Treasury; and placing all Federal Reserve Bank employees under the U.S. Civil Service. Patman told the press that there was little opposition to this proposal. Yet, the business and financial community worried that Roosevelt would approve the measure's passage as a trade-off for administration legislation.[29]

Both Patman and Binderup prepared separate bills that were submitted to the steering committee for a decision on which one to endorse. The committee backed the Patman measure. At the end of May, Patman introduced the steering committee bill and publicized a list of 150 House Democrats including four Banking and Currency Committee members who supported the measure. One published report described the text of the bill as "campaign fodder" as opposed to the typical "legalistic documents" usually introduced in Congress. Despite these criticisms, Patman and other leaders of the steering committee pushed their cause with, among other things, a "goodwill trip" on the Potomac River. Aboard a steamer about 100 members of Congress heard Elmer Thomas, Senator Lynn Frazier (Democrat of North Dakota), Patman, former Senator Robert L. Owen (Democrat of Oklahoma), and Professor Irving Fisher of Yale University, among others, make arguments for the government-ownership proposal.[30]

When nothing came of the government-ownership bill in 1937, House liberals proclaimed a brighter future in 1938. That fall and winter, Patman spoke before numerous groups to express his views on banking legislation. Patman planned another campaign to push government ownership of the Fed in 1938. He told local reporters that the twelve Federal Reserve Banks "are really not banking institutions; they are arms of the government, using the government's credit and should not be owned as now by private banks." Patman also worked with the Independent Bankers Association, an industry lobbying group, on legislation prohibiting the ownership of banks by holding companies.[31]

In early January 1938, Patman told the press he would seek a discharge petition if necessary to force consideration of his government-ownership bill by the full House. "I know it will be a hard fight but I don't believe the opposition is as strong as that we had in getting the bonus through." However, the House Banking and Currency committee undertook review of other legislation before Patman's government-ownership proposal. Patman told the steering committee members they should approach each Banking and Currency Committee member, the Speaker, the majority leader, and the Rules Committee chairman and ask for a hearing on H.R. 7230. Patman used the House floor to lobby the leadership for hearings on the government-ownership proposal. Patman's government-ownership bill went before the House Banking and Currency Committee in March and April 1938. Yet the measure failed to become law and demonstrated that entrepreneurial leadership was not always sufficient to see legislation through to enactment. One of the major factors in Patman's inability to swing enough support behind this radical reform bill was the abundant supply of money in the Federal Reserve.[32] Furthermore, his campaign for early payment of the bonus had a natural constituency, those who would benefit directly from the bill, but his call for government ownership of the Fed lacked this type of constituency. The loss of his latter piece of legislation did not cause Patman to drop entrepreneurial strategies, which he employed throughout his career. Instead, he hoped that greater attention to citizen education about economic inequities would produce the constituency he needed for legislative victories.

Comparison of the two issues—one successful and the other not—where Wright Patman applied his entrepreneurial leadership provides historians with a measure for evaluating the emergence of independent leadership strategies in Congress.

This study offers a critical understanding of his career. Indeed, contemporary opinion makers realized Patman's significance extended beyond being one among 435, because the congressman's entrepreneurial style of leadership combined with his abilities as a public speaker and his manipulation of the media enabled him to construct powerful coalitions pushing for alternative solutions to public problems.

NOTES

1. Wright Patman (WP) to Hugh Carney, May 12, 1932, in "Federal Reserve," Box 138B, Wright Patman Papers, Lyndon B. Johnson Library, Austin, Texas. Hereafter, unless otherwise indicated, all primary source material is from the Patman Papers, LBJL; Clippings, n.p. n.d., circa 1935 in WP Scrapbook no. 62.

2. *Baltimore Evening Sun*, December 11, 1931.

3. William Pencak, *For God and Country: The American Legion, 1919–1941* (Boston: Northeastern University Press, 1989), pp. 173, 185; *Congressional Record*, 71st Congress, 1st session, p. 2146; Harold W. Breining to Frank T. Hines, October 23, 1929; letter to James C. Roop, November 16, 1929; both in "World War Veterans—Bonus Correspondence, 1929–1930 April," Box 372, Herbert Hoover Presidential Papers—Subject File, Herbert Hoover Presidential Library, West Branch, Iowa (hereinafter cited as HPP—Subject File, HHPL); WP to Hines, November 26, 1929, in "Adjusted Service Certificates Correspondence General 1930 (31)," Box 62B; Roop to Herbert C. Hoover, December 3, 1929; letter to Hines, December 4, 1929; Lawrence Richey to Hines, December 5, 1929, all in "World War Veterans—Bonus Correspondence, 1929–1930 April," Box 372, HPP—Subject file, HHPL; Hines to WP, January 17, 1930, in "Adjusted Service Certificates Correspondence with Veterans Bureau and Treasury, 1930–1935," Box 1510C. For more information on the bonus episode see Roger Daniels, *The Bonus March: An Episode of the Great Depression*, (Westport: Greenwood Press, 1971); Donald J. Lisio, *The President and Protest: Hoover, Conspiracy, and the Bonus Riot*, (Columbia: University of Missouri Press, 1974).

4. WP to Platz, April 21, 1930, "Adjusted Service Certificates Correspondence General, 1930–1932 (24)," Box 62C. Patman distributed over 50,000 copies of his April 3, 1930 speech on the House floor to people around the United States. See WP Scrapbook no. 54. For an account of the American Legion's role in the bonus fight see Pencak, *For God and Country*, pp. 171–207. *Texarkana Gazette*, April 10, 1930; WP to Colleague, March 24, 1930, in WP Scrapbook no. 54; WP to Friend, October 14, 1930, in WP Scrapbook no. 54. See WP Scrapbook for a wide assortment of clippings.

5. Clippings in WP Scrapbook no. 54; WP to Edwin S. Bettelheim Jr., December 12, 1930, in WP Scrapbook no. 54; *Congressional Record,* 71st Congress, 3rd session, pp. 2185–6. For a popular history of the VFW see Bill Bottoms, *The V.F.W.: An Illustrated History of the Veterans of Foreign Wars of the United States* (Rockville: Woodbine House, 1991). *Washington Post,* December 28, 1930.

6. WP Scrapbook no. 54; *Dallas Morning News,* December 17, 1930; *Congressional Record,* 71st Congress 3rd session. pp. 620, 783, 897–902, 1214, 1502, 1773–9, 1669, 2465–70; WP to Walter Lambeth, December 16, 1930, in "Adjusted Service Certificates Correspondence General, 1930–32 (24)," Box 62C; Letter from WP, December 27, 1930; "The Following Members Asked to be Notified of Meeting for ASC Payment," both in WP Scrapbook no. 54; WP to Hamilton Fish, Jr., December 18, 1930, in "Fish, Hamilton—General," Box 124B; *New York Times,* January 1, 1931; Hamilton Fish *Memoir of an American Patriot* (Washington, DC: Regnery Gateway, 1991), pp. 37–39; *Brooklyn Eagle,* December 13, 1931; "Bonus-Burst," *Time* 17 (February 9, 1931): 11–12; *The Nation* 132 (February 4, 1931): 113; "The Week," *The New Republic* 65 (February 11, 1931): 337; for a picture see "The Veterans' Bonus—Calamity or Blessing?" *Literary Digest* 108 (February 14, 1931): 5. WP Scrapbook no. 54; "Bonus-Burst," *Time* 17 (February 9, 1931): 11–12. For a brief history of the discharge petition, which was still operative in the 1990s, see William J. Keefe and Morris S. Ogul, *The American Legislative System* (Upper Saddle River, NJ: Prentice-Hall, 1997, 9th edition), pp. 234–235.

7. WP to Frank Knox, November 18, 1930, "Adjusted Service Certificates Correspondence General, 1930–33 (25)," Box 62C; WP to William Randolph Hearst, [January 28, 1931]; Hearst to WP, January 29, 1931; both in "Adjusted Service Certificates Steering Committee Correspondence on H.R. 1, 1935," Box 1510A; Charles E. Coughlin to WP, December 30, 1930; WP to Coughlin, January 1, 1931, both in "Adjusted Service Certificates General Information, 1931–35," Box 1510A; Coughlin to WP, January 21, 1931, in "Coughlin, Rev. Charles E. General," Box 122C; Sheldon Marcus, *Father Coughlin: The Tumultuous Life of the Priest of the Little Flower* (Boston and Toronto: Little, Brown and Company, 1973), pp. 40–41, 186, 289.

8. *Texarkana Gazette,* March 7, 1931; *Jefferson Journal,* March 19, 1931, March 18, 1931; WP to Fay Ickes, May 29, 1931; L.N. Sicha, June 6, 1931; all in "American Legion Chicago Convention, 1931 (3)," Box 63A; WP speech, June 12, 1931, in "Adjusted Service Certificates Speeches 1931," Box 1510B; WP Scrapbook no. 55; *Washington Herald,* June 10, 1931; *Chicago Daily Tribune,* June 13, 1931.

9. "Expansion of the Currency and Payment of Adjusted Service Certificates," May 6, 1931, in "Adjusted Service Certificates 72nd Congress Legislation 1932," Box 1510B; *Congressional Record* 72nd Congress, 1st session, pp. 10720, 11077–8, 12844, 12852–5, 13020–33; 13083–6, 13751–3; Daniels, *The Bonus March,* pp.

116–121; "The Week," *The New Republic* 70 (June 22, 1932): 137; John Dos Passos, "Washington and Chicago," *The New Republic* 70 (June 29, 1932): 177–8; *The Nation* 134 (June 29, 1932): 709.

10. WP quoted in *Texarkana Press*, September 25, 1933; *New York Herald Tribune*, April 14, 1934; *Texarkana Press*, June 26, 1934.

11. *Congressional Record*, 73rd Congress, 1st session, p. 85; WP to "My Dear Sir," February 15, 1933, in "Adjusted Service Certificates General Information 1932," Box 1520C; WP to Franklin D. Roosevelt, February 16, 1933; Louis McH. Howe to WP, February 28, 1933, both in "White House Correspondence File no. 1," Box 82B; WP to George W. Armstrong, April 5, 1933, in "PQ March to April Special Invitation," Box 90, Armstrong Papers, UTA; "So-Called Bonus; Future Veteran Legislation; March on Washington and the National Economy League," April 25, 1933, in "Adjusted Service Certificates Speeches 1933," Box 1410B; Ray Murphy to Roosevelt, May 12, 1933, in Official File 95c (Soldiers Bonus 1933), Franklin D. Roosevelt Papers, Franklin D. Roosevelt Library, Hyde Park, New York (FDRP, FDRL); WP to T.B. Savage Jr., May 15, 1933, in "Adjusted Service Certificates Correspondence General 1933 (31)," Box 62B.

12. *Congressional Record*, 73rd Congress, 2nd session, pp. 363–364, 2938–2939; Daniels, *The Bonus March*, pp. 228–229; *New York Times*, January 12, 1934, January 14, 1934; *Congressional Record*, 73rd Congress, 2nd session, pp. 2883–2890; *New York Times*, February 21, 1934.

13. Roosevelt quoted in "The President's Conference with Members of the House of Representatives at 8:30 p.m., Sunday evening, April 15, 1934," in OF 419 (Congress of the United States April–December 1934), in FDRP, FDRL.

14. WP to James P. Buchanan, August 23, 1934, in "Adjusted Service Certificates Correspondence on New Plan for Adjusted Service Certificates Payment 1934 (18)," Box 62B; Buchanan to WP, August 25, 1934, in "House Speakership—74th Congress," Box 100C.

15. WP, *Banketeering, Bonuseering, Melloneering* (Paris: Peerless Printing Company, 1934); WP, *Patman's Appeal to Pay Veterans* (Paris: Peerless Printing Company, 1934), p. 76 (A copy is in ["Loose Material"] Box 878B); WP to O.B. Briggs Sr., January 4, 1934; WP to Yanofsky, November 26, 1934; WP to Frank N. Belgrano Jr., November 30, 1934; WP to George K. Broebeck, December 4, 1934; Belgrano to WP, December 5, 1934; WP to Yanofsky, December 6, 1934; WP to Belgrano, December 7, 1934, all in "Patman's Book General no. 1"; Yanofsky to WP, December 1, 1934; Briggs to WP, December 12, 1934; WP to Briggs, May 5, 1934, all in "Patman's Book General no. 2," all in Box 127C.

16. WP to South Trimble, February 8, 1935; Trimble to WP, February 9, 1935, both in "Adjusted Service Certificates General Information 1935 (46)," Box 1510C; *New York Sun*, February 20, 1935, February 21, 1935; *New York Times*, February 21, 1935, February 23, 1935, February 24, 1935; Attention of the member, n.d., in "Adjusted Service Certificates General Information 1935 (46)," Box 1520C; Broebeck to My Dear Congressman, February 21, 1935; WP to Robert L. Doughton, March 1, 1935, both in "Adjusted Service Certificates General Information 1935 (46)," Box 1510C; *Congressional Record*, 74th Congress, 1st session, pp. 4309–4314; Daniels, *The Bonus March*, pp. 233–235.

17. WP to "Dear Friend and Colleague," March 23, 1935, in "Adjusted Service Certificates Steering Committee Correspondence on H.R. 1 1935," Box 1510A; Cox to DeLacey Allen, March 23, 1935, in "Adjusted Service Certificates Correspondence General (36)," Box 61A.

18. Transcript, telephone conversation between John Nance Garner and Morgenthau, April, 9, 1935, in Morgenthau Diary, Book 4, p. 1691, Morgenthau Papers, FDRL; *New York Times*, March 24, 1935; Elmer Thomas to WP, April 12, 1935, in "Adjusted Service Certificates General Information 1935 (46)," Box 1510C; Martha H. Swain, *Pat Harrison: The New Deal Years*, (Jackson: University Press of Mississippi, 1978), pp. 99–103; Morgenthau Diary, April 18, 1935, Book 4, p. 247, Morgenthau Papers, FDRL; WP to "Dear Senator," May 2, 1935, in "Adjusted Service Certificates Steering Committee Correspondence on H.R. 1 1935," Box 1510A; *The United States News*, May 13, 1935, in "Mr. Patman's Political Files Campaign Material 1938," Box 77B; *Texarkana Gazette*, May 24, 1935.

19. WP to Steering Committee, n.d., in "Adjusted Service Certificates Steering Committee Correspondence on H.R. 1 1935," Box 1510A; WP to Murphy, May 31, 1935, in "Adjusted Service Certificates Correspondence General 1935 (36)," Box 61A; WP to Murdock to "All the Members of the Steering Committee of H.R. 1," June 6, 1935, in "Adjusted Service Certificates Steering Committee Correspondence 1935 (17)," Box 63B; *National Tribune*, June 13, 1935, in WP Scrapbook no. 62; WP to Dallas News, June 11, 1935, in "Adjusted Service Certificates Correspondence on Hobart Patman Debate 1935 (21)," Box 62B; WP to "Members of the Steering Committee," June 24, 1935; Letter from WP, July 22, 1935, both in "Adjusted Service Certificates Steering Correspondence on H.R. 1 1935," Box 1510A; Get H.R. 1 Ready for Quick Action in January," [August 2, 1935], in "Mr. Patman's Statements 1935," Box 20C; Memorandum for the President, August 6, 1935, in OF 95c (Soldiers Bonus 1935 March–December), FDRP, FDRL; WP to "Dear Colleague," August 15, 1935, in "Adjusted Service Certificates Correspondence General 1935 (42)," Box 61B.

20. WP to Sabath, November 4, 1935; Colmer to WP, November 11, 1935, both in "Adjusted Service Certificates Steering Committee Correspondence on H.R. 1 1935," Box 1510A; Colmer to WP, December 9, 1935; WP to Colmer, December 9, 1935; Colmer to WP, December 11, 1935; WP to James G. Scrugham, December 13, 1935, (sent to each member of the steering committee); Colmer to WP, December 16, 1935; all in "Adjusted Service Certificates Steering Committee Meeting of January 1, 1936," Box 1510C; WP to "Dear Colleague," January 2, 1936, in "Adjusted Service Certificates Steering Committee correspondence on H.R. 1 1935," Box 1510A; WP diary, January 2, 1936, in Box 1705; Thomas A. Rumer, *The American Legion: An Official History, 1919–69* (New York: M. Evans, 1990), p. 222; WP to Coughlin, January 3, 1936, in "Coughlin, Rev. Charles E. General," Box 122C; *New York Times*, January 3, 1936; *Washington Star*, January 3, 1936, January 5, 1936; WP to "Dear Colleague," January 4, 1936, in "Adjusted Service Certificates Steering Committee Meeting of January 1, 1936," Box 1510C; *New York Times*, January 7, 1936; *Congressional Record*, 74th Congress, 2nd session, pp. 220–250, 975–977, 1007–1015, Rumer, *The American Legion*, pp. 222–223; Roosevelt quoted in Morgenthau Diary, January 27, 1936, Book 16, pp. 49–52, Morgenthau Papers, FDRL; WP to Pat Harrison, January 28, 1936, in "Adjusted Service Certificates Correspondence General 1935–36 (44); Box 61B; Daniels, *The Bonus March*, pp. 240–1, 342; Roosevelt, *The Public Papers and Addresses of Franklin D. Roosevelt, With a Special Introduction and Explanatory Notes by President Roosevelt, Volume V, The People Approve, 1936*, (New York: Random House, 1938), p. 67.

21. Maury Maverick to Henry L. Mencken, April 23, 1937, in Box 83, Henry L. Mencken Collection, New York Public Library.

22. WP Diary, February 8, 1933, Box 1705; "All Members of the House of Representatives Invited. Inspection of the Mint at Philadelphia," n.d., in "Philadelphia Mint Trip, April 1, 1933," Box 1385C; For information on the meetings of the currency reform group see WP Diary, 1933, Box 1705; A.W. Lafferty to Roosevelt, March 26, 1933; Lafferty to WP, March 26, 1933; Lafferty to WP, March 23, 1933; WP to Lafferty, March 24, 1933; WP to Lafferty, March 28, 1933; Lafferty, "To Roosevelt and Congress The People Won—Execute Their Mandate Patman Silver Bill Hailed," [March 28, 1933]; Lafferty, "Roosevelt the Airpocket in his Program," [April 5, 1933], all in "Silver Ounce Bill H.R. 4102, File no. 1," Box 1315A; Harold G. Moulton to WP, April 30/34, in "Banking and Currency," Box 1315A.

23. Davis to Coughlin, March 10, 1935 in James Harvey Davis, *Memoir*, (Sherman: The Courier Press, 1935), p. 222.

24. Robert M. Harriss to WP, August 30, 1935; WP to Harriss, September 5, 1935; WP to Harriss, September 6, 1935; WP to Harriss, October 8, 1935; Harriss to WP, October 11, 1935, all in "Harriss, Robert M.," Box 124C; Marcus, *Father Coughlin*,

pp. 69, 71–179, 289; Jack O. Gross to WP, October 29. 1935; Brinkley to WP, November 2, 1935; WP to Fred Collins, November 4, 1935; Harriss to WP, November 7, 1935, both in "Harriss, Robert M.," Box 124C. For more information on Brinkley and his career see Gene Fowler and Bill Crawford, *Border Radio*, (Austin, TX: Texas Monthly Press, 1987).

25. Coughlin to WP, August 5, 1936; WP to Rayburn, August 8, 1936; Rayburn to WP, August 14, 1936; WP to Rayburn, August 28, 1936, all in "Coughlin, Rev. Charles E. General," Box 122C.

26. Transcript, Jerry Voorhis Oral History Interview, 1971, Claremont Graduate School, p. 27.

27. Leo T. Crowley to WP, March 2, 1937; Gibbs Lyons to WP, March 3, 1937, both in "Historical Material 1937–1954 Federal Reserve," Box 1617; Charles G. Binderup to Charles H. Leavy, March 18, 1937; WP and Binderup to "Dear Colleague," March 19, 1937, both in "Federal Reserve Banks—1937 H.R. 7230 (Steering Committee) (Government Ownership of) no. 1," Box 431A; *New York Times*, March 24, 1937; Various clippings in WP Scrapbook no. 1; "First Meeting of Steering Committee," March 24, 1937, in "Federal Reserve Banks—1937 H.R. 7230 (Steering Committee) (Government Ownership of) no. 1," Box 431A; *New York Times*, March 24, 1937; WP and Binderup to "The Following Members of the Steering Committee for Government Ownership of the Twelve Federal Reserve Banks," March 27, 1937; Memorandum from WP and Binderup, April 1, 1937, both in "mimeographed Statements and Letters—1937," Box 20C; WP Diary, March 31, 1937, in Box 1705; Memorandum from WP and Binderup, April 2, 1937, in "Mimeographed Statements and Letters—1937," Box 20C.

28. Coughlin to WP, April 15, 1937; WP to Coughlin, April 24, 1937, both in "Coughlin, Rev. Charles E. General," Box 122C; *Social Justice*, April 26, 1937, in WP Scrapbook no. 1.

29. "Committee Sponsoring Bill for Government Ownership of the Twelve Federal Reserve Banks," April 5, 1937; "Statement by the Steering Committee for Government Ownership of the Twelve Federal Reserve Banks," April 13, 1937, both in "Federal Reserve Banks 1937 H.R. 7230 (Special) (Government Ownership of)," Box 436A; *Wall Street Journal*, April 14, 1937; *New York Times*, April 14, 1937, April 17, 1937; New York *Journal of Commerce*, April 14, 1937, April 16, 1937; WP Diary, April 13, 1937, in Box 1705; WP to Harriss, April 13, 1937, in "Federal Reserve Banks 1937 H.R. 7230 (Steering Committee Boat Trip June 6, 1937)," Box 1617; "Announcement to the Members of the Steering Committee for Government Ownership of the Twelve Federal Reserve Banks," April 20, 1937, in "Federal Reserve Banks 1937 H.R. 7230 (Steering Committee) (Government Ownership of)," Box 436A.

30. WP and Binderup to "The Members of the Steering Committee for Government Ownership of the Twelve Federal Reserve Banks," May 19, 1937, in "Mimeographed Statements and Letters—1937," Box 20C; Brougham to Binderup, May 22, 1937; WP to Brougham, May 25, 1937, both in "Federal Reserve Banks 1937 H.R. 7230 (Steering Committee) (Government Ownership of)," Box 436A; *Washington Post*, May 27, 1937; *American Banker*, June 7, 1937; *Congressional Record*, 75th Congress, 1st session, pp. 5043, 1251A–1253A; *American Banker*, June 10, 1937; WP Diary, June 6, 1937, in Box 1705.

31. *New York Post*, August 30, 1937; "51st Annual Convention Iowa Bankers Association Golden Jubilee May 31st June 2, 1937," Program in WP Scrapbook no. 1; *American Banker*, 9/35, 1937; *Texarkana Gazette*, December 21, 1937; WP to R.F. Hollister, December 17, 1937, in "Bank Holding Company Bill (1938) H.R. 8991— 75th Congress, 3rd session," Box 64A.

32. *New York World Telegram*, January 7, 1938; *American Banker*, January 28, 1938; *Wall Street Journal*, February 1, 1938; WP to "Dear Colleagues," January 19, 1938, in "Federal Reserve Banks 1937 H.R. 7230 (Special) (Government Ownership of)," Box 436A; *Congressional Record*, 75th Congress, 3rd session, pp. 1010– 1011; *New York Herald Tribune*, March 3, 1938, March 4, 1938, March 6, 1938; *Congressional Record*, 75th Congress, 3rd session, pp. 802–804, 1547A–1555A; WP to Henry B. Steagall, April 19, 1938, April 23, 1938; Steagall to WP April 23, 1938, all in "Banking and Currency Committee—File no. 2 (1938–1939–1940)," Box 64C; *Government Ownership of the Twelve Federal Reserve Banks*, p. 507; Elgin Groseclose, *America's Money Machine: The Story of the Federal Reserve*, (Westport, CT: Arlington House, 1980), pp. 210–211; Owen to WP, May 24, 1938, in "Federal Reserve Banks, 1937 H.R. 7230 (Special) (Government Ownership of)," Box 436A.

CHAPTER SEVEN

A Southern Congressman Clashes with His Commander-in-Chief: James P. Richards, FDR, and the 1941 Neutrality Act

JOSEPH EDWARD LEE

United States Representative James P. Richards (Democrat of South Carolina), member of a politically prominent South Carolina clan, won election to Congress in 1932 by clinging tightly to Franklin D. Roosevelt's coattails. An aggressive candidate, Richards toppled an aged incumbent who had served in Congress since 1917. During the campaign, Richards stressed his World War I military service in France and his commitment vigorously to meet the challenge posed by the Great Depression. As a New Deal Democrat representing the rural north central section of the state, Richards supported Roosevelt's legislative initiatives 71 percent of the time. Endorsing the flood of change that flowed through the Hundred Days, Richards said of the president in the summer of 1933, "I admire him very much as he has shown his ability to take a position and stick to it. That is the real test of a president after all." He remained loyal to Roosevelt throughout the New Deal years and rarely strayed from the party line; a notable exception was the debate over the National Labor Relations Act of 1935. Richards' support of FDR's politics, domestic and foreign, continued unwavering for most of the decade. In March 1937, Richards, for example, now a member of the House Foreign Affairs Committee, applauded Roosevelt as "one of the greatest presidents in the history of our country."[1]

By autumn 1941, however, Richards' admiration for the commander-in-chief began to diminish. When Roosevelt suggested in November 1941 amendment of the Neutrality Act, and allowing American merchant ships to arm themselves and sail into war zones, Richards faced the most difficult decision of his early career. Would he support the president who he had followed throughout most of the New Deal years? Would he back the man who he had earlier reminded the American people possessed, by virtue of the Constitution, certain "discretionary powers" in foreign affairs? Or would James P. Richards find himself more comfortable with longtime administration foes like Hamilton Fish Jr., the Republican Congressman from New York? The answer resounded in Richards' eloquent "through-the-back-door" speech of November 12, 1941.

On the floor of the House, using time granted to him by Representative Fish, the South Carolinian reminded his colleagues of his earlier support of the administration's domestic and foreign policies. Conscription and Lend Lease had received Richards' assent. He recounted his position on "the non-involvement acts" of the mid and late 1930s. He explained, "I voted for these acts because I felt that such steps were for the best interest of the United States and would tend to keep the United States at peace rather than lead us toward war." The president's autumn 1941 request to permit armed American merchant vessels to enter war zones, however, posed a dilemma for the representative.[2]

Richards told the House, "I want to help England and her allies because, if the light of democracy goes out in Europe, the darkness there may easily spread to this continent." He quickly added, "At the same time, my first duty is to my own country, and the fact that I want to help some other nation against an aggressor is of secondary consideration when the welfare of my own country is involved." The president's proposal to dilute American neutrality "means that we will be totally engulfed in the boiling cauldron of war." He lamented that international law could not long protect United States merchant ships if they sailed into combat areas. International law had become impotent and, Richards said, "has already been raped and stabbed and is gasping for breath." It would only be a matter of time, Richards reasoned, before an American merchant ship became the prey of a Nazi submarine.[3]

The congressman admitted he was far from "neutral" in his own sympathies. He favored the allies, and he estimated 99 percent of his fifth congressional district's citizens did too. He alluded to Great Britain as "a good neighbor" and remarked, "I may support with my money, my property, and my substance a good neighbor who believes in my ideals against the bad neighbor who will possibly and probably give me trouble later on." There were limits, nonetheless, to how far James P. Richards would go in aiding "good neighbor" England. Richards predicted war if FDR had his way, and the congressman attempted to convince his colleagues not to risk "the blood of my children."[4]

He reminded the House that army maneuvers were currently taking place in his fifth district. Four hundred thousand soldiers were preparing for war. The maneuvers, in Richards' assessment, revealed a sobering fact. The soldiers "are not prepared, they are not fully trained, they are not fully equipped with tanks and guns, they have not yet been hardened to the life of camp and field." To send these men to war, and war was exactly what Richards anticipated if the Neutrality Act was revised, "would be suicide." He argued that before this step was taken, Great Britain must completely exhaust its own resources and manpower. Aid and material had already been given to England, and that nation "must show a will to use them to the limit before we should send our sons to bleed and die."[5]

Richards characterized Roosevelt's plan as a "through the back door" means of entering the conflict. If American soldiers were needed to defend democracy, they should be committed only after "an open, frank, straight-out declaration of all-out war." Since such a declaration and the accompanying national debate were not in the offing, Richards could not endorse what he considered a scheme to sneak "through the back door." Congress's decision on FDR's proposal was of monumental importance. The president had a responsibility in the matter, Richards emphasized, but Congress must also be held accountable for whatever decision it made. As Richards stated, "this vote, this act, this step, is a responsibility that Congress cannot shirk, that its Members must carry on their own shoulders not only now but as long as we live." Thus, what we find in this clash is a classic example of the executive and legislative branches battling over preeminence in the area of foreign policy, not unlike the debate concerning the proper response to Sadaam Hussein's 1990 invasion of Kuwait.[6]

Richards' experiences in the trenches of France during World War I returned to the legislator's mind. He spoke of the Old Hickory Division receiving more Congressional Medals than any other regiment. His pay for combat service, he recollected, ranged from $33 to $44 a month. Emotionally he remarked, "Many of our men, hundreds and hundreds of them, paid the supreme sacrifice." The soldiers all had made sacrifices of one kind or another in defense of democracy but, Richards argued, "There must be sacrifice, somewhere else besides the battle line, and we will never get that necessary spirit of sacrifice on the front or elsewhere by plunging this Nation into war by a cowardly policy here in Congress." Americans were not ready again to make the sacrifices they had made a generation earlier, Richards thought. The ravages of the Great Depression had weakened the United States and diluted its military's strength. Another war could not be undertaken "until we clear our decks at home."[7]

Nearing the conclusion of his comments, the South Carolinian pleaded, "I am thinking of the thousands and thousands of mothers' sons who may be sent to foreign soil and foreign seas and never come back." He added, "I am thinking of how Congress, in a moment of grand sentimentality, without realizing the mockery of it all, will direct the gathering up of a handful of dust and bones from Dakar, or Alexandria, or Leningrad, or Singapore, and have them brought here to be encased in another monument to the unknown soldier with the inscription 'here lies in honored glory an American soldier known only to God.'" If the nation must spill its youths' blood and erect another monument to their sacrifice, Richards pled, let that monument's inscription not read "sent to his death in a foreign land, through the back door, by Congress before he was properly armed or properly trained and without the undivided support of the people back home."[8]

His two sons, the older of whom was thirteen, were too young for military service, Richards told his colleagues. If America ever needed them, however, the congressman pledged that he would advise his offspring to rally to the cause "with prayer on their lips and a smile in their soul, and with an unconquerable belief in the justice of their cause." Then he said of his sons and indeed of America's collective sons, "May they never be called to battle untrained, half-armed, and in a haze of doubt because of a divided nation behind them; may they never have cause for belief that their country sent them to foreign battlefields through subterfuge and indirection."[9]

Despite Richards' plea, the president's supporters eked out a narrow victory. Shortly before the congressmen cast their votes, administration-backer United States Representative Sam Rayburn (Democrat of Texas), the House Speaker, read a letter from Roosevelt arguing that rejection of his request would "cause rejoicing in the

Axis Nations" and would "bolster aggressive steps and intentions in Germany." FDR's supporters predicted victory by seventy-five votes. Representative Fish, Richards' ally on the issue, dismissed this optimistic assessment as "pure bunk." When the roll was called, Fish's vote prediction proved more accurate as the president squeezed by 212 to 194.[10]

Richards was the only member of the South Carolina delegation to desert President Roosevelt that November day. The five other House members from the state voted for revision of the Neutrality Act. As Professor George Brown Tindall has shown, most southern congressmen had abandoned their "lip service to neutrality and non-involvement" the year before. Among the southerners who voted with the president in November was Representative Carl Thomas Durham, a North Carolinian who served in the House from 1939 to 1961.[11]

Durham made his position for arming merchant ships known during the spring of 1941. As debate intensified, Durham wrote a constituent in late September, "I believe that we should be permitted to arm our merchant vessels and maintain the rights of the freedom of the seas." He considered the existing Neutrality Act to which Richards so vigorously clung "a waste of time." Backing the president, Representative Durham said that revision of the act was "necessary for the English speaking races to stand together in the common cause."[12] Durham's constituents, however, were far from convinced that their congressman was right on this issue. Letters in the Durham Papers on this subject were split fifty-fifty on allowing American ships to sail into the war zone.

Among Representative Richards' constituents there was also much debate over the legislator's November vote. Approximately 150 letters and telegrams in the Richards papers supported his position whereas fifty criticized him. This ratio concurs favorably with the research of diplomatic historian Thomas Paterson, who estimates that in September 1941 an overwhelming 80 percent of the American public opposed the national drift toward war and away from neutrality. Public opinion polls published that autumn confirm that this decisive margin held firm until the eve of Pearl Harbor.[13]

Fellow Democratic congressman Charles A. Eaton of New Jersey, a supporter of the president's position, wrote Richards, "I want to express my heartfelt admiration and affection for you in the noble spirited stand you took in defense of your convictions during the neutrality debate." Other House members were similarly impressed with Richards' impassioned neutrality speech. Representative Robert E. Chiperfield of Illinois wrote, "We were all proud of you on that day." Ohio's Frances T. Bolton concurred and predicted, "There will come the moment when the country will turn to such as you, when only truth and honesty will be sought."[14]

Pro-neutrality Republican Representative Karl Mundt took to the air waves to defend the South Carolinian. Mundt told his South Dakota constituents, "Probably the most impressive speech of the debate was given by Congressman Jim Richards." Mundt noted, "at the conclusion of his argument, every member on both sides of the aisle stood in tribute to a brave man fighting a valiant fight." Continuing his praise of Richards, Mundt added that he was thankful for lawmakers "who put patriotism above politics, who serve their conscience as they read its insistent plea, and who dare to speak out against tremendous pressure urging them to hold their peace."[15]

A Georgetown University professor wrote Richards, "As I sat in the House gallery and looked down upon the closing hours of that debate, nothing it seemed to me, stood out so magnificently in those closing hours as those strong, sincere and eloquent words which you there expressed." A soldier on maneuvers in South Carolina agreed and confided to Richards, "Let me say that the applause was not limited to the House chamber but welled up over all the Carolinas from three hundred thousand voiceless young men."[16]

Not all the reaction was as complimentary. The commander of South Carolina's American Legion lambasted the congressman. Richards replied that he regretted that he had disappointed the veteran, and "I am sure that we both, as well as the overwhelming majority of the members of the American Legion, are willing, should the call come, to die for our country." A constituent agreed with the legionnaires and urged Richards to reverse his position and vigorously combat the Nazis, who the constituent called "a bunch of International outlaws." Another resident of the fifth district, criticizing Richards' alliance with Representative Fish, inquired, "Does the Republican Party look good to you?" Scribbled across that letter was Richards' response, "*Don't answer this fool.*" One York County constituent warned, "I heard so many people in here giving you H— this A.M." Ominously, an anonymous postcard warned "Chesterfield County is surprised."[17]

Among the people giving the congressman "H —" was his old University of South Carolina law professor, J. Nelson Frierson. Writing to his former student, Frierson lectured Richards about America's historic and cultural ties to Great Britain. Frierson rebuked him, "You have made a great mistake in voting as you did." The professor then questioned Richards' alliance with Representative Fish by commenting that the New Yorker was being investigated by the House for possible violation of franking privileges. Stung by this reproach from Professor Frierson, Richards replied, "I have great admiration for the British Government and the British people, but I owe no allegiance to the Crown. America comes first with me."[18]

By and large, Richards received praise for his neutrality position. One Kershaw County citizen told him, "I and thousands of loyal South Carolinians endorse your stand as true Americanism." Complimenting the congressman for his courage, a Chester County businessman wrote, "I can have very little respect for a Government which wages an undeclared war." A Lancaster minister scribbled only one line on his letter "the vote of a man." Richards told a Camden physician, "I have received hundreds of telegrams and letters commending my position."[19]

The Washington correspondent of the Spartanburg, South Carolina *Herald-Journal* defended Richards and his brief alliance with Representative Fish. Reporter Howard Suttle wrote the newspaper's editor, "I have concluded that to join hands with this Republican was somewhat of a bitter dose for him." Suttle noted, "[T]he entire house membership, with possibly a few exceptions, rose and applauded him." Analyzing Richards' loyalty to President Roosevelt, Suttle said, "his voice against neutrality act repeal is the only vote on foreign policy which has been anti-administration." Suttle added, "He honestly believes that repeal of the act means war."[20]

Other South Carolina newspapers agreed that Richards was usually a Roosevelt supporter. The *State* wrote in an editorial that Richards was "a rather steadfast administration adherent." The editorial did not endorse the congressman's neutrality position, but the newspaper published an edited version of his speech. The paper observed, "he was aware of the fact that he was differing from the majority opinion in his home state." House Speaker Rayburn was quoted as saying, "I was glad to see the ovation given him." The newspaper reported that Richards' speech had been given "in a voice which was described as shaking with emotion."[21]

A district newspaper published a front-page editorial about Richards. The *Chester News* complimented Richards' break from the administration, commenting, "We have often felt that if the Hall of Congress were to be filled with nothing but me-tooers, then we had just as well abolish our Congress and let the Administration run the show." Speaking of Richards, the newspaper said, "we want to tip our hat to him." The town's other newspaper, however, criticized Richards' vote and likened the congressman's neutrality posture "to a boxer's entering the ring with Joe Louis with his arms dangling by his side."[22]

How would Richards' position effect his political career? He confided to a Lancaster friend, "A great many of my friends may possibly stray away because it is always easy to go along with the crowd; but as [Apostle] Paul said, 'I will meet them at Philippi.'" Richards' concern for his political future and all the words of praise and condemnation were swept aside three weeks later when Japan attacked America's naval base at Pearl Harbor. One of the last letters to reach the congressman before the December 7, 1941 surprise attack was from a University of South Carolina law student who commended the congressman for defending neutrality and included a copy of a poem written after World War I:

> Here dead we lie,
> Because we did not wish to shame the land
> from which we sprung.
> Life's nothing much to lose 'tis sure
> But young men think it is
> And we were Young.[23]

Thus, we find Congressman Richards at the end of 1941 disheartened by the reality of a war he had struggled to stall and bruised by his break with the commander in chief. Richards' neutrality was founded both on his memory of the devastating previous war and its young casualties, and on his conviction that the United States, still weak from the effects of the Great Depression, was not prepared to battle the Axis powers. He had resisted the president's "through the back door" war, which now was upon the United States with all its predicted fury. The voices from the trenches of World War I would return a generation later. The climax of James P. Richards' early political career was his sincere but unsuccessful attempt to gain for America a few more precious months to, as he had told his congressional colleagues during his November 12 speech, "clear our decks at home."

After the war, the representative steadily accumulated congressional power. By the early 1950s, the seniority system rewarded the South Carolinian by making him chair of the House Foreign Affairs Committee, a position he held for four years. Bipartisan, Richards worked closely with President Dwight Eisenhower and Secretary of State John Foster Dulles to resist Soviet encroachment in the oil-rich Middle East. Fifteen years after his clash with Franklin D. Roosevelt, Richards worked in harmony with another commander in chief to win the early rounds of the cold war.[24]

NOTES

1. Since little research has been published on Congressman Richards, the best place to gain an understanding of the man and his times is my dissertation, "'America Comes First With Me': The Political Career of Congressman James P. Richards, 1932–1957" (University of South Carolina, 1987); Jack Irby Hayes Jr., "South Carolina and the New Deal, 1932–1938," Ph.D. dissertation (University of South Carolina, 1972), p. 150; Richards to R.E. Wylie, June 15, 1933, James P. Richards Papers, University of South Carolina, Caroliniana Library (hereafter referred to as Richards Papers); *Congressional Record*, 76th Congress, 1st session, pp. 2273–74; the fifth congressional district throughout Richards' tenure consisted of seven rural counties, Cherokee, Chester, Chesterfield, Kershaw, Lancaster, Fairfield, and York; Richards' uncle, John G. Richards, was the state's governor (1927–1931) and his father, Norman Richards, had been a state legislator.

2. *Congressional Record*, 77th Congress, 1st session, p. 8771.

3. Ibid.

4. Ibid.

5. Ibid.

6. Ibid.

7. Ibid., p. 8773.

8. Ibid.

9. Ibid.

10. The *State*, (Columbia, SC) November 14, 1941; ibid., November 11, 1941; ibid., November 14, 1941; James MacGregor Burns, *Roosevelt: The Soldier of Freedom* (New York: McGraw-Hill, 1970), pp. 147–148.

11. *Chester News* (SC), November 18, 1941; George Brown Tindall, *The Emergence of the New South 1913–1945* (Baton Rouge: Louisiana State University Press, 1967), p. 690.

12. Carl Thomas Durham to Allan H. Gilbert, September 29, 1941, Carl Thomas Durham Papers, Southern Historical Collection, Chapel Hill; Durham to John Dalzell, October 17, 1941, Durham Papers; Durham to Cecil Johnson, November 14, 1941, Durham Papers.

13. Thomas G. Paterson, J. Garry Clifford, and Kenneth J. Hagan, eds., *American Foreign Policy: A History* (Lexington: D.C. Heath, 1977), pp. 382–383; *New York Times*, November 22, 1941.

14. Charles A. Eaton to Richards, November 14, 1941, Richards Papers; Robert B. Chiperfield to Richards, November 15, 1941, Richards Papers; Frances T. Bolton to Richards, November 13, 1941, Richards Papers.

15. Transcript of radio broadcast by Karl Mundt, November 20, 1941, copy in Richards Papers.

16. Charles L. Coolan to Richards, November 17, 1941, Richards Papers; James P. Ready to Richards, November 18, 1941, Richards Papers.

17. Richards to R.F. Fairly, November 15, 1941, Richards Papers; W.W. Crawford to Richards, November 18, 1941, Richards Papers; Dave Moore to Richards, November 18, 1941, Richards Papers; R.W. Boulware to Richards, November 17, 1941, Richards Papers; anonymous to Richards, November 16, 1941, Richards Papers.

18. J. Nelson Frierson, November 18, 1941, Richards Papers; Richards to Frierson, November 24, 1941, Richards Papers; former University of South Carolina history professor Daniel W. Hollis states that Frierson, an Anglophile, often called upon students from the fifth district to contact Richards to lobby for aid for Great Britain prior to Pearl Harbor; interview with Daniel W. Hollis, March 1, 1986, Florence.

19. H.L. McPherson to Richards, November 13, 1941, Richards Papers; George M. Wright to Richards, November 17, 1941, Richards Papers; R. Carl Griffith to Richards, November 17, 1941, Richards Papers; Richards to Maurice Clarke, November 26, 1941, Richards Papers.

20. Howard Suttle to S.C. Wallace, Jr., November 27, 1941, copy in Richards Papers.

21. The *State*, November 15, 1941.

22. The *Chester News*, November 18, 1941; The *Chester Reporter*, November 17, 1941.

23. Richards to R.W. Jopling, November 29, 1941, Richards Papers; Tom Abbott to Richards, December 3, 1941, Richards Papers.

24. Richards survived a vigorous challenge to his House seat in 1942. In mid-March 1943, forty-eight-year-old Richards attempted unsuccessfully to persuade Secretary of War Henry Stimson to allow him to serve in the military, Richards to Stimson, March 15, 1943, Richards Papers. Ironically, he became, later as chairman of the House Foreign Affairs Committee, a champion of America's global responsibilities. In 1957, President Dwight D. Eisenhower selected Richards to tour the Middle East in an attempt to solidify that region's support for what Richards labeled "the American Doctrine" or what most of us refer to as the "Eisenhower Doctrine."

III

**Looking at the Record
Fifty Years Later**

CHAPTER EIGHT

The 1938 Purge: A Re-Examination

Thomas Phillip Wolf

Unlike sports contests, political events and social actions in general tend not to be clear cut. People prefer to view events as open or shut, black or white, win or lose, but life is rarely so definitive. This absolutism is a central factor in the bewilderment of many in assessing political situations and explains why politicians are often held in disrepute. Society is more tolerant when assessing fault or cause-and-effect in other social situations such as divorce (Who was at fault? The villain? Was there a villain?) or adolescent misbehavior (Were the parents responsible? The school? The child? The child's friends?)

There is an inclination to blame politicians for not living up to their word, which ignores their lack of complete control over decision-making processes and their responsibility to react to change in situations. For example, criticism of President George Bush for back-tracking on his 1988 "No new taxes" campaign pledge was misdirected; his error was in making the pledge, not in reneging on it. No one can predict the need for taxes four years in advance. Similarly, then-Governor Bill Clinton's promise early in his campaign of a middle class tax cut was unwise. To have honored his campaign pledge would have been irresponsible when, once in office, he found the budget deficit to be worse than any presidential candidate had asserted in the 1992 campaign.

Moreover, an executive or legislator in a democracy cannot enact a major policy without the cooperation of others, usually legislators. And, generally, to get that cooperation requires compromise. Thus, much criticism of elected officials is illogical. Such criticism is often generated by other elected officers seeking personal gain or partisan advantage. This seems obvious, but conversation and other commentary customarily ignore it.

The upshot of this rumination is to accentuate the complexity of political situations and the complications involved in assessing them. Whether a course of action, such as the "Purge of 1938" was effective depends, in the first place, upon how one conceptualizes "effective." If it is entirely a matter of whether all targets— or no targets—of the purge were defeated, assessment is straightforward. But like other aspects of life, politics is not usually simple. Since there are so many factors impinging on most political actions, one should not expect an all-or-nothing outcome.

A second factor in determining the effectiveness of the purge depends on how one defines the 1938 effort to influence elections: Should it refer only to those congressional candidates of the president's party that Franklin Roosevelt sought to replace with other Democrats? Should it encompass all congressional contests that year in which the president intervened? In other word, should the situation be defined as "intervention," rather than "purge"? Finally, should it be extended to other electoral contests, such as gubernatorial races? That is to say, should the White House actions in 1938 be conceived as an effort to "purify" the Democratic party—not just in Congress, but across the nation—which might either destroy the Republican party or lead to a partisan realignment?

A further difficulty with the "purge" is the very use of that term. In 1938, that word was most commonly associated with Joseph Stalin's persecutions, even murders, of thousands of Communist party members, including high-ranking officials in the government and the military. And before the Soviet atrocities, Adolf Hitler had conducted a less sweeping but bloody purge of Ernst Röhm and his associates within the Nazi party. Certainly, Franklin Roosevelt's efforts to influence the 1938 elections were not on the scale of the Stalinist or Nazi actions in any sense. Nor were the operations and ideology of the Democratic party comparable to those of the two totalitarian parties. This pejorative term is not warranted for the 1938 congressional elections. Yet, the persistent use of "purge" to refer to FDR's efforts leaves no choice but to use it.

Another consideration is to put the purge within the context of the period within which it occurred. Just as with the 1995 controversy about the correctness of Harry Truman's decision to use the atomic bomb, often the key contextual factors pertinent to the purge are ignored. Most commentary on the events of 1938 divorce them from the political background of that era, applying to FDR's situation criteria that would not be used to assess other presidents in similar situations. More about that subsequently.

Before examining the details of the 1938 purge, it is essential to consider the accepted, conventional posture of presidents toward congressional elections. In general, presidents try not to become openly involved in such matters. Why? Because to do so is to encounter risks that are not beneficial to the president. Obviously, if more than one candidate is seeking the nomination of the president's party, the candidate or candidates who do not receive the presidential blessing resent the interference of the White House. And if the president's preferred choice does not gain the nomination, the unendorsed nominee will be less sympathetic to the president than he would have been if the latter had not intervened.

Since by 1938 the direct primary was used in nearly every state to nominate candidates, a campaign to influence a congressional nomination involved many more actors (voters) than in the days of the caucus, which consisted mainly of party officials. Where patronage might be sufficient to persuade a caucus, it would be relatively ineffective in influencing a substantial segment of an electorate participating in a primary.

Whether using the caucus or the primary, party officials and other opinion leaders in a state are likely to be offended by outside interference in that state's internal matters. The separation of powers and the division of powers (federalism) carry powerful emotional impact even for persons unfamiliar with exactly what those terms mean. An appeal that an outsider, i.e., the president, is meddling in the affairs of a state will engender opposition to the outsider whether the opposition is informed or not.

State party officials also have their own agenda, and although they may support a president in national matters, they are likely to be offended by presidential efforts to intrude in matters traditionally the province of the state parties. That was more likely to be true before the New Deal, which eliminated most of the traditional spoils that parties could dispense, and with the rise of the direct primary, which was intended to and succeeded in undermining the ability of party leaders to control nominations. But in 1938 these processes were in transitional stages. It was not until the 1960s that wealthy candidates could essentially buy a nomination through the use of television spots and there was a concomitant decline in the power of state party officials to affect nominations.

Caution warns that more important than the resentment of either a nonfavored candidate or the voters and party officials in a state is the damage to a president's image as an influential leader if the attempt to influence a congressional nomination is unsuccessful. Since media analysts make much of such failure, it assumes national, not merely statewide or regional, consequences.

The case for presidential intervention in congressional nominations has more drawbacks than advantages. Even if the president's announced choice prevails, that success may be explained away by factors other than the presidential blessing. To borrow an analogy from football, in attempting a pass only one favorable result—completion—can occur, but various negative results—incompletion, interception, quarterback sack—are possible.[1] The likely negative consequences of presidential intervention in congressional contests outweigh the only hoped for positive consequence. Presidents, therefore, generally have taken one of two postures: either publicly maintain public silence about congressional nominations or support the choice of the president's party once that choice has been made.[2]

Five persons are usually listed as the prime targets of FDR's purge: Senators Walter George of Georgia, Guy Gillette of Iowa, Ellison DuRant "Cotton Ed" Smith of South Carolina, and Millard Tydings of Maryland; and in the House, John O'Connor of New York. Only O'Connor was defeated in 1938.

Walter George was involved in the most renowned instance in which Roosevelt sought to remove an incumbent of his own party. After a stop at Warm Springs, Georgia, where the president had often vacationed for more than a decade to exercise his polio stricken legs in the waters, he travelled by his special train to Barnstable, Georgia. There on August 11, 1938, he shared a campaign platform with Senator George. After commenting at some length on the success and setbacks of the New Deal, he urged the crowd, estimated at 50,000, to support liberal candidates. He added that his "old friend, the senior Senator from this State" (i.e., Walter George) could not be classified as a liberal. Then FDR directed his remarks to two others on the platform. He briefly condemned former governor Eugene Talmadge, George's main rival for renomination, before lauding United States Attorney Lawrence Camp, a former state legislator and the administration's chosen candidate. As Roosevelt left the podium, George shook his hand and announced that he accepted the president's challenge.[3] This was the only face-to-face confrontation between any of the purge targets and FDR on the campaign trail and is often mentioned, probably because of its obvious drama. Camp came in third in the Democratic primary, trailing Talmadge and George, who was easily renominated and elected.

While a case can be made for FDR's opposition to the renomination of Walter George, it strains reason to justify White House opposition to Guy Gillette. Vernon Allen Fagin has aptly characterized the effort to unseat the freshman senator from Iowa as "the wrong campaign...with the wrong challenger against the wrong incumbent."[4] Gillette's voting record was very similar to that of the challenger chosen to oppose him, Congressman Otha Wearin. The main flaws in Gillette's record were his opposition to the administration's wages and hours bill and the litmus-test issue, the court-packing bill.

To be successful, it was crucial that Wearin have the visible support of prominent Iowa Democrats. Yet, by the time he was chosen to be the challenger, key Iowa Democrats, such as the senior Senator Clyde Herring and Governor Nelson Kraschel, had already publicly endorsed Gillette. Both indicated they would have backed Wearin if asked to do so sooner.[5]

Support for Wearin from within the national administration was even more muddled. Despite direct pressure from the White House, Henry A. Wallace, Secretary of Agriculture and the most influential Iowan in the administration, declined to endorse Wearin.[6] Another native Iowan, Harry Hopkins, head of the Works Progress Administration (WPA), openly praised Wearin, but Hopkins had left Iowa promptly after graduating from its distinguished liberal arts institution, Grinnell College, and had never registered to vote in the state. His endorsement was inconsequential compared to the absence of one by Wallace, not only the son of a former Agriculture Secretary and heir to an influential farm journal, but also a distinguished agronomist in his own right.[7]

Compounding this situation, Wearin was not an inspirational campaigner. Given this set of circumstances, it is no wonder that Gillette easily defeated Wearin, as a prelude to reelection in November.

In Maryland, the administration anointed Congressman David J. Lewis, almost assured of reelection to the House and long-time advocate of what became the Social Security Act, to oppose Millard Tydings. Lewis had better prospects than Wearin in Iowa, but Tydings refused to discuss his stance on the New Deal. Instead he focused on the matter of outside interference in Maryland politics. And despite a half dozen Labor Day weekend speeches by FDR in Maryland, including one broadcast nationwide, just over a week later Tydings crushed Lewis in the Maryland primary.[8] (Among other charges, Tydings implied the attack on him smacked of communism. Ironically, twelve years later he would suffer defeat as a target of Wisconsin Senator Joseph McCarthy's anticommunist tirade.)

In South Carolina, the White House seemed to have a strong chance of prevailing. Its target was the openly racist and longest serving member of the Senate, Ellison

D. Smith, who was seeking a sixth term. The national administration's candidate to oppose him was the young governor of the state, Olin Johnston, who early in the primary election campaign appeared to be an excellent choice to defeat Smith.

But the political situation in South Carolina was complex. When a third candidate, state senator Edgar Brown, entered the race, he announced his backing for the New Deal. A bitter foe of Johnston, Brown was aided by the efforts of the state's other U.S. Senator, James F. Byrnes, who sought to keep Roosevelt from openly endorsing Johnston. Byrnes was concerned that a Johnston victory would obstruct his plan to dominate South Carolina's political apparatus when the aging "Cotton Ed" Smith passed on. While Byrnes would have welcomed warm words from FDR about Charleston mayor Burnett Maybank, Byrnes' choice for governor, Byrnes advised the president not to visit the state, apparently apprehensive that the president might take that occasion to praise Johnston.

A few days before the primary, Brown announced his withdrawal and Smith won renomination (and subsequent reelection), defeating Johnston by 40,000 of 313,000 votes cast for the two.[9]

The one clear success of the purge had an ironic twist. Representative John J. O'Connor of New York, Chairman of the House Rules Committee, was the brother of Basil "Doc" O'Connor, a former law partner of President Roosevelt and the head of the March of Dimes, a national organization created in honor of FDR to find a cure for the poliomyelitis that had stricken him. O'Connor represented the Sixteenth Congressional District, known as New York City's Silk Stocking District. The administration persuaded a reluctant James H. Fay to oppose O'Connor. Fay was a member of Ed Flynn's Democratic organization in the Bronx,[10] not to be confused with the city's Tammany Hall, which FDR had opposed since the earliest days of his political career. Most observers thought Fay was behind throughout the primary campaign, but he narrowly defeated O'Connor.[11] The struggle for the seat was not over: O'Connor, who had filed in the primaries of both parties took the Republican nomination, but ultimately lost again to Fay in November.[12]

Some general trends emerge from these attempts to influence primary races: Despite FDR's obvious desire to unseat these Democrats, they refrained from criticizing President Roosevelt. Instead, they blamed the opposition to their renominations as coming from the president's advisers, such as Thomas Corcoran and Secretary of the Interior Harold Ickes. Where it could be done, the administration sought to establish a local tie to the states involved in order to mute the charge of carpet bagging. Thus, FDR could claim that he was not an outsider in his home state of New York and that, given his visits to Warm Springs over many years, Georgia was like his second home. A weaker case was Iowa, where Hopkins, although a native of the state, had no strong ties there in his adult years. In Maryland and South Carolina, no local connection was asserted.

If the focus in 1938 is expanded beyond the incumbent Democrats that FDR sought to unseat to other efforts to influence the composition of Congress, a different mix of success and failure emerges.

The administration contemplated purges in several other states. Senatorial contests involving Democratic incumbents such as Bennett Champ Clark in Missouri, Augustine Lonergan in Connecticut, Frederick Van Nuys in Indiana, and William H. Dieterich in Illinois were scrutinized. In these cases, the White House decided not to take sides for various reasons: the incumbent seemed invincible, no suitable opponent could be recruited, there were irreconcilable factions within the Democratic party in the state, the incumbent demonstrated an increased affinity for New Deal legislation, or a combination of these factors.[13] These potential purges never materialized, indicating that the decisions to purge were based on the prospects of succeeding.

The intervention campaign began with a contest in which there was no incumbent. That occurred in a January 1938 primary to fill a Senate seat vacated when Hugo Black was appointed to the U. S. Supreme Court. In this Alabama contest, the White House initially worked behind the scene to persuade Governor Bibb Graves to switch his support from former Congressman J. Thomas Heflin, an avowed racist, to Congressman Lister Hill. Ultimately, FDR made a widely publicized train trip through Alabama with Hill, who easily won the primary, assuring victory in November.[14] Hill's victory, along with that of Claude Pepper, was seen as instrumental in moving New Deal legislation, particularly the wages and hours bill, through Congress.

In other senatorial contests, the administration intervened to bolster a Democratic incumbent who had been loyal to the New Deal and faced a seemingly strong challenge for renomination. Among the notable examples were Alben Barkley of Kentucky and Claude Pepper of Florida. Pepper, the most dedicated New Dealer from the South, was opposed for renomination by Congressman Mark Wilcox and former governor David Sholtz, along with two other minor figures. Wilcox, the main foe, had opposed many White House legislative proposals.

At a press conference in Florida the president's eldest son and aide, James Roosevelt, indicated the administration's appreciation for Pepper's loyalty. Shortly thereafter, in response to a question about that seeming endorsement of Pepper, the president humorously gave only an oblique reply. When Pepper was renominated with 60 percent of the primary vote in May, there was an immediate upsurge for New Deal proposals in Congress.[15]

Alben W. Barkley, who became Senate Majority Leader only with the assistance of the administration, was opposed for renomination by Kentucky Governor Albert B. Chandler, known throughout his career as "Happy." Chandler was a formidable challenger, and if Barkley did not return to the Senate, his leadership post would almost certainly be filled by the arch conservative Pat Harrison of Mississippi, who had narrowly lost that office to Barkley. It was this position that determined the White House posture, as there was little ideological difference between Barkley and Chandler.

From the outset of the Barkley renomination campaign, the administration manifested its support for him. The capstone of the White House campaign for Barkley came in July when FDR visited Kentucky aboard the Presidential Special train and spoke on Barkley's behalf while Chandler frantically sought to position himself physically next to the president. There were charges, some confirmed, that both the governor and the senator had abused patronage to garner votes, but the August primary gave Barkley victory and assured his reelection.[16]

In Alabama, Florida, and Kentucky, White House intervention had immediate and significant positive consequences for bolstering the administration's influence with Congress. Roosevelt also backed the renomination of Robert Bulkley in Ohio, Hattie Caraway of Arkansas, and Elmer Thomas of Oklahoma to the Senate, and Lyndon Johnson of Texas to the House. All won renomination and all but Bulkley were re-elected.[17] By focusing only on those contests in which the administration sought to replace a disfavored incumbent, it is possible to miss these successful efforts. There were other elections in 1938, including gubernatorial ones, which the administration sought to influence, but those are not central to this chapter.[18]

There are issues that either have not been addressed or have been addressed only tangentially, despite the lengthy bibliography dealing with the 1938 elections. These can be listed as a series of questions: How have previous studies of the purge assessed its impact? What is the public's view, as far as it has one, about the purge? And what is that of politicians? Was there a common motivation that probably played a role in the position that various New Dealers assumed toward the purge? Was FDR influenced by Woodrow Wilson's similar efforts in 1918? What structural obstacles offered by the electoral cycles impair presidential efforts to exploit their coattails? What outcome should have been expected in 1938 if the White House had made no attempt to influence congressional elections?

Scholarly evaluations of the purge are mixed. But one of the earliest, which may well have had an impact at least on the views of the public and political figures, was that of journalist Raymond Clapper. He concluded that the purge was a failure.[19] His article is cited in nearly every study of these events. Yet as Fagin notes, Clapper was hardly a disinterested observer. He was a journalist with close ties to political conservatives, particularly the chairman of the Republican National Committee.[20] Fagin, while balanced generally, sees the 1938 purge as unsuccessful, as does Sidney M. Milkis.[21] In contrast, John E. Hopper, lacking the extended commentary of Fagin, concludes that the purge was a success, as did E.E. Schnattschneider when evaluating it in 1942.[22] Sean Savage, after summarizing the evaluations of several prior studies, finds the purge campaign to have positive results.[23] His analysis is the most informed and instructive to this point.

Of course, most citizens and politicians are not and were not familiar with these scholarly studies. Why then did these groups deem the purge a failure? Probably, because of the fashion in which it was covered by the media. The media, then consisting of newspapers, magazines, and radio, played up the purge. It was an ideal media event: Much of its effort had to be conducted in the open in order to achieve the desired influence of public opinion within the targeted states. In contrast to the typical administrative action, which could be shielded from public view, much purge activity had to be visible if it was to be effective. Voters had to be informed by some public mechanism if sufficient numbers of them were to be persuaded to back administration candidates. And the purge was an ideal issue for assessment, subjectively or objectively, by pundits.

In the aftermath of the first televised presidential debates in 1960, politicians and their advisors concluded that a candidate who was ahead in the polls should not agree to debate opponents, although a careful examination of public opinion data from the first of the "Great Debates" did not support that conclusion. The 1938 efforts of the White House to influence congressional contests has had a similar impact on presidential behavior: Don't interfere in those electoral battles. The evidence from the events of 1938 is more complex than that pertaining to the 1960 debates, but the conclusion may be comparably faulty.

In spite of the media's fascination with it, apparently the purge effort did not command a high priority in the White House. It was of a secondary or tertiary order, as indicated by comments in personal and official papers of those in the administration as well as in biographic works on those individuals. Lack of direct presidential involvement shows it was not a top priority. If it had been, the President would have made a greater effort to appeal to the nation as a whole than the single fireside chat broadcast in June in which he issued a call to his radio audience to support liberal candidates across the nation.

What was a common motivation of key administration persons in their stance toward the 1938 elections? Simply, it was that many of them hoped to succeed FDR as the Democratic party nominee for president in 1940. That does not fully explain their posture in 1938 but it had an impact. Postmaster General James A. Farley, who refused to be involved in the purge, was clearly looking toward his own prospects for 1940, although as Democratic National Chairman, he was always more sensitive to the desirability of being tactful with the state parties than other administration figures such as Corcoran or Ickes. Hopkins was also thought of as a contender for the 1940 nomination, perhaps as Roosevelt's chosen heir. Wallace also had presidential aspirations, which he knew could be damaged if he misspoke or misstepped, particularly in his home state of Iowa. And others could be added to this short list of presidential hopefuls. Presidential aspiration probably was not the determining factor for any of these individuals' attitudes toward the purge, but it was a consideration.

Was Roosevelt inspired by the efforts of previous presidents to rid themselves of obstreperous members of Congress? In particular was he consciously emulating Woodrow Wilson's campaign in 1918 to unseat certain Democrats in Congress? One might presume that to be the case as Franklin Roosevelt obviously admired Wilson and had been a member of the Wilson administration, serving as assistant secretary of the Navy. But at the Franklin Roosevelt Library the papers of those closest to the purge do not indicate any influence of Wilson's 1918 efforts. Nor does that appear in any of the biographies about Roosevelt or other studies of the 1938 campaign.

Is there an explanation for that? It seems puzzling, as FDR was clearly a close observer of political machinations and as a member of the Wilson administration might have been expected to be particularly attentive to Wilson's unusual venture.

But in 1918, Roosevelt was preoccupied with other matters. First, he was under sustained pressure to seek the Democratic nomination for governor of New York. Despite repeated inquiries, as reflected in letters to him throughout the spring and summer of 1918, he declined to pursue the office.[24] Second, that reluctance was based upon his repeated assertion that he could best serve the public by concentrating on his duties with the Department of the Navy, which had greatly increased with the entrance of the United States into World War I in 1917. In conjunction with those obligations, he made an extensive trip to Europe, departing by ship on July 9, 1918 and returning in mid-September. Upon landing in New York City, he was rushed to his mother's home to recuperate from double pneumonia and influenza. When he returned to Washington, D.C. to resume his duties at the Navy in the middle of October, he was still pale from his illness.[25] And it was during this illness that Eleanor Roosevelt found the letters revealing her husband's love affair with Lucy Mercer that nearly ended the Roosevelt marriage.[26] Thus, FDR was too preoccupied with other concerns to have the time or strength to follow closely Wilson's campaign to dispose of certain congressional Democrats.

What about the structural effects of the electoral cycles? One obstacle to effective presidential intervention in congressional elections is the fact that the House, the Senate, and the president follow different election cycles: two years, six years, and four years, respectively.[27] A consequence is that it is difficult for a president to exploit his popularity or "coattails." In addition, since presidents now are restricted to eight years in office, they have only a limited period in which to influence congressional nominations and elections. (There will be more about the eight-year term in reference to FDR later.) But Smith was defeated for renomination in 1944 and Gillette lost his reelection bid that year. Can anyone doubt that the purge efforts of 1938 weakened the chances of both six years later? We can assume that 1938 did have an effect, even though Smith's failing health was probably a factor; he died after the 1944 South Carolina primary. Three of the five principal purge targets were gone by the time the next election cycle for their offices expired. It took another round before Millard Tydings lost, a victim of the McCarthyite campaigns of the late 1940s and early 1950s. Thus, the purge may not have brought immediate benefits to FDR, but its long-term consequence may have helped his successor.

What should we have expected in 1938, given the circumstances of that time? For example, Franklin Roosevelt is the only president who served more than two terms, but in 1938, he was a lame duck in the parlance of presidential–congressional relations. We now know that he successfully sought reelection in 1940, but that was not a foregone conclusion in 1938, and much of the maneuvering in 1938 was predicated on who would be his successor as the nominee of the Democratic Party in 1940. While much has been made of the lame-duck status of presidents in the postwar era, there is literally no mention of that by those who have evaluated the purge. Moreover, it was not with the purge that FDR became a lame duck, but with his 1936 reelection victory. Lame duck presidents customarily have difficulty not only in their relations with Congress but in maintaining their party's strength in Congress.

Certainly, the president regarded his second term to be his last.[28] In late 1937 and into 1938, he sought to promote Hopkins as his successor, despite the latter's dual handicaps of ill health and a divorce. But FDR clearly preferred Hopkins to Farley.[29] Many, perhaps most, scholars specializing in the New Deal era are convinced that it was not until the president determined that war was unavoidable that he reluctantly decided to seek a third term. That decision crystallized in the spring of 1940 when Germany's victory in Europe seemed inevitable.

Students of legislative behavior are also aware that parties with large legislative majorities such as the Democrats had after the 1936 elections are inclined to factionalism: After all, dissent will affect the party's majority only at the margins, not threaten its control of legislative power, i.e., in the American context, particularly the command of committee chairmanships and other key legislative posts. In fact, the Democratic congressional majorities were without precedent, having an advantage of a 333 to 89 in the House and 75 to 17 in the Senate.

If the trend of the previous four congressional elections had continued, the Republican Party would have nearly disappeared from the national political scene. One would have to return to the Reconstruction era to find either party with as little strength in Congress, and in that period the proportionate share—there were fewer seats in each chamber—of the minor party (then the Democrats) was larger than that of the GOP after the 1936 elections. From the high mark of 1928 through the 1936 elections, the number of Republican seats in each congressional chamber had continuously declined by totals of 178 House seats and 39 in the Senate. If that trend persisted through the 1938 elections, the GOP would have had fewer than 50 U.S. representatives and fewer than a dozen senators.

Unless the electoral pattern of the previous century of partisanship was at an end, it should have been expected that in 1938 there would be a swing in the direction of increased Republican support. More remarkable than the 1938 Democratic losses were the 1934 Democratic increases of nine House seats and ten in the Senate. It was the only time in this century (and back into the nineteenth century) that a president's party had added congressional seats in an off-year election. Much has been made of the 1938 Republican gains in the House (80 seats), but they were in the range of the Democratic increase in 1922 (75).[30] And the 1938 increases were added to a much smaller base of seats held by the Republicans.

In the Senate, Democrats could not expect to gain seats since of the 34 at stake, only 3 were held by Republicans. Of the 31 Democratic Senators, 10 were conservative or unreliable, and the administration would have liked to remove them.[31] As noted, the administration took direct action against only half of those.

It can be assumed that if the White House had done nothing to influence the 1938 elections, Republican strength would have increased in Congress. On the average, the minority party could expect 36 more House and 2 more Senate seats, based on off-year elections from 1914 (the first in which all Senators were elected) through 1936. If the "aberrant" elections, when the president's party atypically gained seats, are discarded, the expected gains are 43 House and 7 Senate seats. On that basis, the GOP did slightly worse than should have been anticipated in the Senate by adding only 6 new Senators in 1938.

To characterize the 1938 purge as a failure is again to lose historical perspective. If John Kennedy could have defeated the House Rules Committee Chairman, "Judge" Howard Smith of Virginia, in the 1962 nominating processes, it would have been hailed as a monumental victory. Smith was a major obstacle to Kennedy's program and a leader in the conservative coalition of Republicans and Southern Democrats. Franklin Roosevelt in 1938 did unseat the House Rules Committee Chairman, John O'Connor of New York, retaining O'Connor's seat for the Democrats, but FDR's overall effort was deemed a failure.

Retroactively applying the criteria of the 1960s to 1938, the defeat of O'Connor was a remarkable success. Applying the standards of the typical off-year congressional elections, it was also successful. And, had there had been no Republican gains in 1938, it is doubtful that the Republican Party would have survived. From that standpoint, i.e., the survival of the two-party system, it is well that purge was not more effective.

In recent decades, there are two generalizations widely accepted by regular observers of congressional elections and the presidency. One is that the incumbent president's party will lose seats in the off-year congressional races. There are only two exceptions to that in the twentieth century: 1934 and 1998. The second generalization is that as lame ducks, second-term presidents will be less effective in influencing Congress and the public. In 1938, Franklin Roosevelt was a lame duck. Despite these two time-proven generalizations, the executive branch's attempts to affect congressional elections that year are deemed to have been failures.

President Roosevelt's own assessment of the failure to be successful in more Democratic primaries was taken as sour grapes or, at least, self-serving. Ted Morgan says that FDR "rationalized his blunder by saying that .... it was not the general public that had voted but only the enrolled Democrats."[32] Again, if knowledge of electoral behavior that social scientists have developed since World War II is applied, FDR's statement is prescient: numerous studies have demonstrated that it is not a typical cross-section of the public that votes in primary elections or in off-year congressional elections. The president did not have such studies in 1938 on which to base his assertion.

The late William Riker and his student William Bast examined cases of presidential intervention from 1913 to 1956, as reported in the *New York Times*. They recommended that presidents (1) seek to influence congressional nominations; (2) not endorse incumbents; and (3) endorse a candidate only when that candidate has a reasonable chance of winning.[33] They note that a principal reason that presidents have not intervened in such contests is that the efforts of the Roosevelt administration in 1938 are considered a failure. Presidents and their political advisers have interpreted those efforts incorrectly, according to Riker and Bast.[34]

This chapter confirms their reservations about the conventional wisdom about the events of 1938. If one insists on a simple test of all or nothing for the 1938 purge, it was a failure. Or if one assumes that a partisan realignment should have been the goal of administration actions in 1938, that did not occur either. If one is more realistic in assessing these actions by the Roosevelt administration, the purge has to be considered, at least partially, successful. That is a particularly sound conclusion when the events of 1938 are put in historical perspective. Without the intervention effort, one might have expected the congressional situation after 1938 for FDR to be considerably less promising. As with so many matters, success or failure depends upon whether one sees the glass as "half full or half empty."

NOTES

1. Football fans will recognize my debt here to the late legendary Woody Hayes, long-time gridiron coach at Ohio State University.

2. For a general assessment that unfortunately has many factual errors, see William H. Riker and William Bast, "Presidential Action in Congressional Nominations," pp. 250–267 in Aaron Wildavsky, ed. *The Presidency* (Boston: Little, Brown, 1969).

3. Kenneth S. Davies, *FDR: Into the Storm 1937–1940, A History* (New York: Random House, 1993), pp. 277–280.

4. Vernon A. Fagin, "Franklin D. Roosevelt, Liberalism in the Democratic Party, and the 1938 Congressional Elections: The Urge to Purge," (Los Angeles: University of California, unpublished Ph. D. dissertation in history, 1979), pp. 136.

5. Ibid., pp. 137–141.

6. Ibid., p. 144.

7. Even Hopkins' endorsement had its conflicting aspects. He did not immediately reply when Wearin said that Hopkins would confirm Wearin's White House support. When Hopkins did state that if in Iowa he would vote for Wearin, Roosevelt at a subsequent press conference responded to a question on the matter, off the record, noting that whatever a president said in such cases would be misconstrued. Then he added that he did not approve of Hopkins' action; Henry H. Adams, *Harry Hopkins: A Biography,* (New York: G.P. Putnam's Sons, 1979), p. 134.

8. Davies, *FDR: Into the Storm,* pp. 281, 291–293.

9. John Edward Hopper, "The Purge: Franklin Roosevelt and the 1938 Nominations," (Chicago: University of Chicago unpublished Ph.D. dissertation in history, 1966), pp. 179–192.

10. Ibid., p. 294.

11. Ibid., p. 295.

12. Sean J. Savage, *Roosevelt, The Party Leader: 1932–1945,* (Lexington: University of Kentucky Press, 1991), p. 153.

13. Hopper, "The Purge," pp. 14–31.

14. Savage, *Roosevelt, The Party Leader*, pp. 131–132.

15. Hopper, "The Purge," pp. 53–62.

16. Ibid., pp. 96–114.

17. David L. Porter, "'Purge' of 1938," in Otis L. Graham Jr., and Meghan Robinson Wander, eds. *Franklin D. Roosevelt: His Life and Times: An Encyclopedic View,* (Boston: G.K. Hall, 1985), pp. 338–339.

18. For the additional contests within the states, see the Fagin and Hopper dissertations.

19. Raymond Clapper, "Roosevelt Tries the Primaries," *Current History*, 159, no. 2 (October 1938), pp. 16–19.

20. Fagin, "Franklin D. Roosevelt," p. 54 at fn. 28 & p. 89.

21. Fagin, "Franklin D. Roosevelt," pp. 330–366. Sidney M. Milkis, "Presidents and Party Purges: With Special Emphasis on the Lessons of 1938," pp. 151–175, esp. pp. 166–170 in Robert Harmel, ed. *Presidents and Their Parties: Leadership or Neglect?* (New York: Praeger, 1984).

22. Hopper, "The Purge," pp. 220–222, and E.E. Schnattschneider, *Party Government,* (New York: Holt, Rinehart and Winston, 1942), pp. 163–169.

23. Savage, *Roosevelt, The Party Leader*, pp. 154–158.

24. "Papers as Assistant Secretary of the Navy, 1913–1920," Franklin D. Roosevelt Library.

25. Davis, *FDR: Into the Storm* pp. 516–530.

26. Frank Friedel, *Franklin Delano Roosevelt: A Rendezvous with Destiny,* (Boston: Little, Brown, 1990 pb. ed.), pp. 33–37.

27. Charles O. Jones points out the problems of linking these election cycles and how those ties obstruct changing the terms for the House of Representatives: *Every Second Year: Congressional Behavior and the Two-Year Term,* (Washington: Brookings, 1967).

28. William E. Leuchtenberg notes that Roosevelt "was not expected to run again in 1940..." and on the same page he cites Raymond Clapper stating, "that President Roosevelt could not run for a third term even if he so desired." *Franklin D. Roosevelt and the New Deal,* (New York: Harper Torchbooks, 1963), 272. Of course, Clapper was writing *after* the 1938 elections and Leuchtenberg's observation is about the post-election situation in 1938.

29. George McJimsey, *Harry Hopkins: Ally of the Poor and Defender of Democracy,* (Cambridge: Harvard University, 1987), pp. 120–121.

30. The figures cited in the text are from *Congressional Quarterly's Guide to U.S. Elections,* (Washington, DC, 3rd ed., 1944), p. 1344. The amount of Republican gains vary slightly in other sources, e.g., James S. Olson states 75 House and 7 Senate seats, "Election of 1938" pp. 140–141 in James S. Olson, ed. *Historical Dictionary of the New Deal: From Inauguration to Preparation for War,* (Westport: Greenwood, 1985); Patrick Maney gives 82 House and 7 Senate seats, *The Roosevelt Presence: A Biography of Franklin Delano Roosevelt,* (New York: Twayne, Twayne's 20th Century American Biography Series, No. 13, 1992), p. 106; Russell D. Buhite and David W. Levy report 80 House and 8 Senate seats in the "Introduction" of their edition of *FDR's Fireside Chats,* (Norman: University of Oklahoma, 1992); Ted Morgan offers 82 House and 8 Senate seats, *FDR: A Biography,* (New York: Simon and Schuster, 1985), p. 496; George McJimsey reports 81 House and 8 seats, Adams, *Harry Hopkins,* p. 122.

31. James T. Patterson, *Congressional Conservatism and the New Deal: The Growth of the Conservative Coalition in Congress, 1933–1939* (Lexington: University of Kentucky Press, 1967), p. 263 and fn. 42.

32. Morgan, *FDR: A Biography,* p. 496.

33. Riker and Bast, "Presidential Action," pp. 263–264. Their study had its origins in an honors thesis that Bast wrote and Riker supervised at Lawrence College.

34. See especially their footnote 3 on p. 246.

CHAPTER NINE

The Realignment Theory After Fifty Years

STEFANO LUCONI

In the analysis of United States voting behavior, the term "realignment" refers to fundamental turnabouts in the existing power relationships between the two major political parties. These radical transformations of the party system either strengthen the governing party or produce a new majority party. Generally, they also cause sharp alterations in the political agenda. In particular, realignments arise from the persistence of a massive shift of partisan allegiance concomitant with an unusual intensity in political conflict as well as a relevant increase in voter turnout.[1]

The realignment theory implies a cyclical interpretation of election outcomes according to which periods of relative stability in one-party dominance in the political system are followed by elections that abruptly change the lines of partisan cleavage among voters. Scholars usually divide the history of American elections into at least five eras: a pre-party phase before the birth of mass parties in the 1820s; the Jacksonian age, which lasted until the emergence of slavery as a paramount electoral issue caused the dissolution of the Whig party; the Civil War system, spanning the rise of the new Republican party to William J. Bryan's defeat in 1896; a subsequent Republican era that ended with the election of Franklin D. Roosevelt to the White House; and the New Deal period.[2]

This chapter seeks to show that the dynamics of both the formation and the persistence of the Roosevelt coalition provided scholars with a framework to elaborate the realignment theory. It also aims to evaluate the extent to which that model is still useful for understanding American voter behavior fifty years after Roosevelt. Therefore, this chapter places the New Deal in a broad historical perspective and compares the party system of those years to contemporary developments of American politics.

The traditional pre-New Deal interpretation of the course of American electoral history stressed the substantial continuity of the American party system. On the eve of the economic depression, Charles A. Beard summarized that view in *The American Party Battle*, a study that portrayed partisan competition in the United States as a continuing struggle between "the Hamilton-Webster-McKinley-Coolidge party" and "the frank alignment of agricultural interests made by Jefferson, continued by Jackson (who added an army of mechanics), solidified by the slave-owning planters, and marshalled anew by Bryan after division in the Civil War."[3]

Only after Franklin D. Roosevelt became president was the term "realignment" added to the vocabulary of political science. In 1938, for instance, in a brief comment on the outcome of the 1936 presidential contest, Arthur Holcombe argued that Roosevelt's reelection could determine a "realignment" of Southern Democrats toward the Republican party matched by a secular "realignment" of progressive Republicans toward the Democratic party. Two years later, emphasizing the importance of the election of Roosevelt for the ensuing radical changes in the American party system, Cortez Ewing stated that "the 1932 election represented a major realignment of party membership." The introduction to Basil Rauch's 1944 overview of the New Deal years offered an interpretation of United States politics in terms of cycles of election outcomes. Attempting to place Roosevelt's legislation within the development of the American democratic tradition and to confute charges that the President was a communist in disguise, Rauch argued that the New Deal represented the latest of five relevant discontinuities—or, as he called them, "peaceful revolutions"—that marked the course of United States history and had been "made by voting into power new administrations which abandon the policies of their predecessors and turn the nation toward new goals."[4]

The elaboration of a theory that highlights the key role of some elections as turning points in the developments of United States political history began a decade later, in 1955, when V. O. Key proposed a comprehensive theory of these watershed elections. Key called them "critical" and argued that they were characterized by at least four factors: intense partisan conflict, high voter turnout, "a sharp alteration of the pre-existing cleavage within the electorate," and the durability of the new party alignment in the following elections.[5]

To illustrate his theory, Key pointed to the 1928 presidential contest as the critical pre-New Deal election in New England because Alfred Smith's majority in Massachusetts and Rhode Island, as well as a sizable increase in the Democratic vote in Maine, New Hampshire, and Vermont foretold Roosevelt's capture of the White House in 1932. Key's views of the dynamics of the American party system reflected the legacy of the New Deal. These years encompassed all four factors associated with the realignment model. From the harsh partisan conflict that resulted from the Great Depression and spurred an increase in voter turnout, Roosevelt managed to forge a stable electoral coalition that ended three consecutive Republican terms in the White House and marked the beginning of twenty years of Democratic control over the presidency.

In the 1940s when the majority of the American electorate demonstrated its Democratic preference by rejecting Republican Thomas E. Dewey's bid for the White House twice, Key shared Beard's analysis. In the first edition of his *Politics, Parties, and Pressure Groups*, Key held that the United States' electoral history could be divided into different periods on the basis of changes in the names of the two major parties that dominated the political system. In his opinion, however, variations in partisan labels did not imply relevant discontinuities in policies and electoral support because each new party relied primarily upon the same cohorts of voters of its predecessor and represented similar interests.[6]

Harry Truman's election in 1948 demonstrated the persistent cohesion of the New Deal Democratic majority that supported the realignment thesis. Indeed, it was the durability of the Roosevelt coalition at least through 1948 that best exemplified the concept of the long-term stability of voters' party allegiance. The 1948 election was particularly revealing for the concept of the entrenchment of partisan identifications of the realignment theory. On that occasion, the Democrats demonstrated that they had managed to translate Roosevelt's personal popularity into enduring support for their party.

Key's seminal 1955 article loosened a flood of commentary on electoral realignment in American political history. With the Lyndon B. Johnson presidency, that interpretation of voting behavior faced escalating skepticism. Given Johnson's inability to revitalize the Roosevelt coalition under the pressure of the Vietnam war and civil rights issues in the late 1960s, was the realignment thesis valid?[7]

A sizable decline in partisanship since the 1970s impaired one principle of the realignment theory, which assumes strong party identification by American voters. The existence of durable partisan loyalties validates the electorate's new orientation after a critical election. Yet this supposition did not reflect the American public's posture toward political parties after the 1964 presidential contest. Indeed, the ratio of voters who identified themselves with any party dropped from 75 percent in 1960 to 61 percent in 1992. In those years, the portion of voters who split their tickets rose from 14 to 36 percent between presidential and House candidates and increased from 9 to 25 percent between senatorial and House candidates.[8]

The progressive weakening of voters' ties to parties was only one indication of growing dissatisfaction with institutional politics. That attitude was also expressed in a dramatic slump in turnout in the three decades before the 1992 presidential election. From a high of 62.8 percent in 1960, voting participation in 1988 dropped to 50.2 percent of the eligible population, its lowest level in presidential races since 1924. In congressional elections turnout declined from 47.5 percent in 1962 to 36.4 percent in 1990.[9]

The realignment model has been further undermined by a lack of evidence showing a clearly recognizable postwar realignment. Prior to the New Deal, realignments occurred approximately every thirty to forty years. A post-New Deal turnabout in partisan orientation and the entrenchment of a new polarization of voters were expected for the late 1960s, or the early 1970s at the latest. Kevin Phillips hailed the 1968 election of Republican presidential candidate Richard Nixon as the birth of a new conservative majority—made up primarily of religious traditionalists and white Southerners eager to avenge themselves on Democrats for the achievements of the civil rights movement—that had replaced the New Deal coalition and its later revitalization.[10]

Yet, with only 43.4 percent of the 1968 popular vote, Nixon was a minority president, and his putative majority subsequently proved to be unstable. Following Phillips' reasoning, Nixon's "Southern strategy" of wooing the 1968 breakaway Democrats who had bolted to segregationist George Wallace should have contributed to consolidation of the new cleavage of United States voters in 1972. Nonetheless, in spite of Nixon's landslide reelection, the Democratic party retained its hold on Congress. Four years later the Watergate scandal helped elect the Democratic presidential candidate and, ironically in terms of Phillips' hypothesis, put the born-again Christian Southerner Jimmy Carter into office, halting the rising Republican cycle.

Although the Democratic success of 1976 was brief and the GOP controlled the presidency through the 1980s until the election of Bill Clinton, the increase in ticket-splitting prevented the Republican party from attaining congressional dominance. The GOP was a Senate majority only from 1981 through 1986, and the House of Representatives remained in Democratic hands. The Reagan and Bush presidencies witnessed a marked deterioration of Republican fortunes in state elections and, consequently, a sharp decline in the number of state legislatures controlled by the GOP after a short-lived increase between 1976 and 1980.[11]

Similarly, despite the hasty claims of some commentators that the 1992 presidential election marked the beginning of a new Democratic era,[12] Clinton was a minority President, like Nixon in 1968, and his own following turned out to be extremely volatile. A dramatic slump in consensus for the president accompanied the success of the Republican candidates in most major 1993 state and local contests. Dissatisfaction with Clinton gained even more momentum a year later, when the GOP won a House of Representatives majority for the first time since 1954, recaptured the Senate, extended its control to eighteen additional state legislatures, and attained a majority of the governorships.[13]

The collapse of voter turnout, the shifts in party preferences from one election to the other, and the divided government were factors at odds with the realignment perspective of the New Deal era. After a steady decline in voter participation from the late nineteenth century, with lows of 48.9 percent in the 1924 presidential contests in 1924 and of 35.2 percent in mid-term elections in 1926, turnout increased for presidential elections from 56.9 percent in 1928 to 62.5 percent in 1940 and rose from 39.4 percent in 1930 to 48.7 percent in 1938 in off-year elections.[14] During the New Deal there was also a relative persistence in partisan voting. The Democratic party controlled both chambers of Congress as well as the White House throughout the Roosevelt presidency. State and local contests came to follow national electoral patterns. After 1932, former Republican strongholds such as Pennsylvania gradually followed the Democratic trend in local contests. In particular, as James Sundquist has pointed out, the establishment of the New Deal party system took two stages in most northern states that had been Republican strongholds before the economic depression: Democratic victories in state elections followed Democratic majorities in presidential races after a number of years.[15]

Although today's political scenario differs markedly from the realignment thesis, a few scholars have tried to rescue that model of voting behavior. On the one hand, it has been argued that the American party system saw a "split-level" realignment characterized by pro-Republican changes in presidential contests and the persistence of voters' orientation toward the Democratic party in congressional elections.[16] On the other hand, it has been suggested that, in fact, a realignment did occur between the late 1960s and the early 1970s. Yet, in contrast to Key's classic thesis, this latter realignment was "non-partisan-channeled." In other words, its main feature in terms of systemic transformations of the political geography of the

United States was not a reshuffling of traditional party allegiances with the appearance of a new majority party but the very demise of partisanship itself.[17]

Nonetheless, while the Democratic candidate won the 1992 presidential race, a Republican Congress emerged from the 1994 midterm elections. Moreover, lack of partisan identification among the eligible voters did not necessarily imply that the participating electorate failed to cast ballots along party lines. After all, despite at least twenty-five years of prognostications of the end of political parties, the most successful independent presidential candidate in eight decades, Ross Perot, managed to win only 19 percent of the total popular vote in 1992. In addition, an analysis of political behavior between 1952 and 1992 showed that nearly two-thirds of the self-proclaimed independents had some partisan leanings and that the latter did play a role as voting cues.[18]

Therefore, in the face of both the current disengagement of voters from long-time party affiliations and the ensuing fluidity of partisan cleavage even in consecutive elections, a dealignment thesis has replaced the realignment synthesis as a more reliable conceptualization to describe recent developments in American politics. While the realignment theory presumes the existence of strong partisan attachments, vanishing party loyalties—but not necessarily vanishing party voting, at least in presidential races—are at the core of the dealignment model. In this perspective, the evaluation of officeholders' performances is the main determinant of party choices rather than partisan allegiance. According to the dealignment theorists, the outcome of presidential elections does not reflect traditional patterns of voting behavior. Rather, it is the result of a sort of highly transitory referendum on the public record of the incumbent administration, isolated from previous and future votes.[19]

Of course, some referendum-like elections characterized the New Deal years, too. Roosevelt himself acknowledged that he was the main issue in the 1936 presidential race.[20] Local Democratic officials often endeavored to cash in on the growing popular consensus for the president during his first term, portraying support for Democratic candidates in municipal contests in those years as a vote of confidence in Roosevelt. Such attempts were often so extensive that on the eve of the 1933 mayoralty elections, the *New York Times* remarked ironically that "the proverbial man from Mars might indeed get the notion that it is Mr. Roosevelt who is running for Mayor of Pittsburgh."[21] The dynamics of the party competition have changed so much in the fifty years since Roosevelt's death that the model of voting behavior of the New Deal years is obsolete. Still, the realignment theorists have tried to apply it to the subsequent course of United States electoral history.

Roosevelt won his largest plurality in 1936 after a divisive campaign that split the American electorate along class lines with the entrenchment of business interests in the Republican party and the President's emotional welcome of the hatred of "organized money" in defense of the New Deal legislation. The 1932 protest upheaval that sent the Democratic party to the White House cut across class divisions in the American electorate, and some of the early measures of the new administration, like the National Recovery Act, met the approval of industrial trade associations. Nonetheless, in launching the Second New Deal, Roosevelt declined to appease business any longer, enacting legislation to regulate public utility companies, increase income taxes, encourage industrial unionism, and raise wage rates. This offended conservative Democrats, who began to defect to the Republican party.

The GOP followed a similar path of radicalization. Kansas governor Alfred Landon, the Republican presidential candidate, started his campaign by promising a more efficient and less extravagant version of the New Deal but ended up by harshly criticizing the core philosophy of Roosevelt's programs. Both major parties refused to move toward the center in 1936 and target the moderate voters. Therefore, realignment came to a climax as the political system underwent a high degree of ideological polarization.[22]

Roosevelt's share of the popular vote in 1936 (60.8 percent) was not exceeded until Lyndon Johnson beat Barry Goldwater (61.1 percent) in 1964. That margin was exceeded again eight years later, when Richard Nixon defeated George McGovern by a 61.8 percent landslide. These two latter presidential campaigns witnessed a sharp division in the policy alternatives facing the American electorate. On the one hand, Goldwater wanted Americans to make a clear-cut decision about the role of the federal government in their lives and sought to offer voters "a choice, not an echo" by campaigning against Johnson's Civil Rights Act and welfare programs. On the other hand, McGovern placed himself on the far left of the average Democratic voter by calling for withdrawal from Vietnam.[23]

The resounding defeats of Goldwater and McGovern seemed to prove that radicalism did not pay at the polls, and both major parties began to retreat toward the center of the political spectrum. That attitude gained momentum in the 1980s and early 1990s when the support of the "Reagan Democrats" became pivotal to election outcomes. Parties began to target primarily the white middle-class switchers who had gone over to the GOP because they thought that the Democratic party had neglected their needs in order to benefit minorities and the poor. Consequently, while Democrats distanced themselves from liberalism and the governmental-interventionist policies that Roosevelt had legitimized, even Reagan refused to dismantle New Deal programs like Social Security, which, according to Hugh Heclo, ultimately conserved the core of the welfare state.[24]

The 1992 presidential campaign was the pinnacle of the centrist campaign strategy. Bush's economic program, the "Agenda for American Renewal," celebrated small business and "an entrepreneurial capitalism that grows from the bottom up, not the top down" as the way out of the national recession. Meanwhile, Clinton lashed out at an allegedly overgrown and impersonal federal bureaucracy, criticized big government, pledged to "end welfare as we know it," and announced his support for capital punishment. Campaign oratory demonstrated that the Democrats had abandoned polarizing appeals to embrace a pacifying rhetoric designed to appeal to the suburban voters. In contrast to FDR, who addressed the concerns of "the forgotten man at the bottom of the economic pyramid" during his 1932 campaign, Clinton accepted the 1992 Democratic nomination in the name of "our forgotten middle class," promising this cohort of voters that "when I am President you will be forgotten no more."[25]

However, it is racial policy that highlights the search for middle ground by both parties. In 1969 Kevin Phillips pointed to southern backlash to Democrats' advocacy of civil rights legislation as the leading issue contributing to 1968 Republican success. Two decades later the GOP played on racial fears of white voters, as the race-tinged themes of Bush's 1988 Willie Horton ads and Senator Jesse Helms' 1990 reelection commercials demonstrated. Nevertheless, the party never embraced white supremacy officially even in local contests in the South. For instance in 1989, when former Ku Klux Klan Grand Wizard David Duke ran as a Republican for the Louisiana House of Representatives, President Bush, former President Ronald Reagan, and the state GOP leadership disavowed him and endorsed his opponent. In addition, African American demands sometimes found champions in GOP advocates in municipal elections, as happened when Republican W. Thatcher Longstreth opposed Democratic Frank Rizzo for mayor of Philadelphia in 1971. However, while Republicans prevented racial conservatism in their ranks from becoming blatant segregationism, Democrats restrained their racial liberalism. Commitments to affirmative action or racial justice, previously paramount issues in the Democratic platforms, were conspicuously missing in Clinton's 1992 agenda.[26]

FDR also had dampened more progressive stands on race within the Democratic ranks. He refused to push an antilynching bill, and a number of the New Deal programs discriminated against African Americans. Roosevelt was concerned less about the votes of the conservative Democratic electorate than about the support of the southern congressmen who could jeopardize his whole legislative agenda in retaliation. Moreover, in times of economic depression, racial politics was not so divisive an issue as it became in the post-New Deal party system, that is, after the 1960s.[27]

The curb on political radicalism in the late 1980s and early 1990s undermined the realignment thesis because scholars stressed the sharp ideological cleavage between the Republicans and the Democrats during the New Deal years as contributing to intense political conflict, high voter participation, and strong party allegiances after a critical election. Apparently, blurring ideological differences weakened partisan identities and made it easier for voters to cross party lines. This reduced the number of policy options and, thereby, depressed turnout: eligible voters no longer felt represented by the candidates and their platforms.

Abstention primarily affected the traditional cohorts of the Democratic electoral coalition of the New Deal years, namely ethnic minorities and the poor. For example, 8.3 million African Americans, or 10.5 percent of the participating electorate, cast their ballots in the 1988 presidential contest. These figures dropped to 8.1 million and 8 percent, respectively, four years later when Clinton's campaign ignored traditional liberal issues. Roosevelt's class-conscious liberalism and his interventionist administration managed to forge a stable coalition of voters by accommodating the needs of organized labor and the hyphenated Americans who were swelling the ranks of the eligible electorate in the Depression years. In contrast, Clinton retreated from the distinguishing features of the New Deal. That inhibited the mobilization of the urban underclass, African Americans and other minorities. George Wallace in 1968 and, more recently, David Duke, in recruiting support from partisan nonidentifiers and previous nonvoters, demonstrated the existence of potential reservoirs of rightist votes waiting for the appeals of extremist candidates to be mobilized.[28]

Even the Republican sweep in the 1994 midterm elections failed to revitalize the realignment thesis. The shift of the GOP toward a more conservative agenda, as epitomized by Newt Gingrich's "Contract with America," and the ensuing Republican landslide persuaded a number of commentators to hail the election of that year as the onset of a Republican Age in American politics. In particular, Grover Norquist offered an interpretation of the forging of the alleged new Republican majority that is the mirror image of the dynamics that created the Roosevelt electoral coalition, according to the realignment perspective. As the New Deal majority made inroads below the presidential level in the years after its appearance in the 1932 race for the White House, in Norquist's opinion the conservative coalition that first surfaced in the outcome of the 1968 presidential election had been consolidating since that year, until it was established also in congressional and state contests in 1994.[29]

The Republican party emphasized its further rightward trend by launching a crusade for family values at its 1992 convention in Houston.[30] In addition, Gingrich's "Contract" was less a platform than a device to nationalize the congressional races and transform each of them into a referendum on the Clinton administration.[31] Therefore, far from reflecting a radicalization of the conservative stand of the bulk of the United States electorate, the 1994 Republican sweep capitalized on the anti-incumbent mood of the American people and thereby exploited the volatility of voters in the post-New Deal party system.

Finally, contrary to the realignment model, the last few years failed to produce a sharp polarization of policy alternatives. Indeed, while the GOP became more conservative, the Democratic party and President Clinton followed suit and shifted to the center in search of the moderate votes of white middle-class America to counteract the Republican appeal. For instance, on the eve of the 1993 elections, as Republicans were warming up for a welfare counterrevolution, the federal government allowed Wisconsin to impose a two-year limit on benefits for indigent families with children. This implemented Clinton's 1992 campaign pledge. After the Democratic defeats in the major 1993 races, Clinton placed welfare reform among his top priorities in the 1994 State of the Union speech that endorsed the "three-strikes-and-you-are-out" policy, enabling Democrats to compete with the GOP on tough crime legislation and seeking to minimize the predicted Democratic losses in the 1994 midterm elections. When those losses greatly surpassed forecasts, Clinton departed further from his party's traditional liberalism. His 1995 State of the Union address embraced such customarily conservative claims as limited and cheaper government, tax cuts, and reduction in regulations. This program aligned the presidential agenda with the needs and aspirations of white-middle class voters.[32]

In conclusion, the end of the New Deal system not only meant rolling back the tide of liberal policies but also involved a sharp alteration in the mechanics of party competition. The harsh partisan conflict, the increase in voter turnout, and the long-term persistence of party allegiance resulting from the radical polarization of policy alternatives in the Roosevelt years provided the foundations of the realignment theory. That structure of voting behavior, however, is no longer a viable model for interpreting election outcomes in contemporary American politics. The pursuit of the same cohort of white middle-class voters by both the Republicans and the Democrats has produced a scenario at odds with the framework of the realignment perspective, as the present dynamics of the political system tend to subdue sharp differences between the two major parties, to inhibit political participation, and to encourage voter volatility.

NOTES

1. For an overview of the huge realignment literature, see Harold F. Bass, Jr., "Background to Debate: A Reader's Guide and Bibliography," in Byron E. Shafer, ed., *The End of Realignment? Interpreting American Electoral Eras*, (Madison: University of Wisconsin Press, 1991), pp. 141–178.

2. Paul Kleppner, Walter Dean Burnham, Ronald P. Formisano, Samuel P. Hays, Richard Jensen and William G. Shade, *The Evolution of the American Electoral Systems*, (Westport: Greenwood Press, 1981).

3. Charles A. Beard, *The American Party Battle*, (New York: Macmillan, 1928), pp. 140, 135–136.

4. Arthur N. Holcombe, "The Changing Outlook for a Realignment of Parties," in Edward B. Logan, ed., *The American Political Scene*, rev. ed., (New York: Harper, 1938), pp. 278–288; Cortez A. M. Ewing, *Presidential Elections*, (Norman: University of Oklahoma Press, 1940), p. 41; Basil Rauch, *The History of the New Deal, 1933–1938*, (New York: Creative Age, 1944), p. 3.

5. V. O. Key Jr., "A Theory of Critical Elections," *Journal of Politics* 17, no. 1 (February 1955), pp. 3–18 (quote p. 4).

6. ———. *Politics, Parties, and Pressure Groups*, (New York: Thomas Y. Crowell, 1942), pp. 263, 270–272.

7. Allan J. Lichtman, "The End of Realignment Theory? Toward a New Research Program for American Political History," *Historical Methods* 15, no. 4 (Fall 1982): pp. 170–188; Everette C. Ladd, "Like Waiting for Godot: The Uselessness of Realignment for Understanding Change in Contemporary American Politics," in *The End of Realignment?*, pp. 24–36.

8. Martin P. Wattenberg, *The Decline of American Political Parties, 1952–1992* (Cambridge: Harvard University Press, 1994), p. 174.

9. Ruy A. Teixeira, *The Disappearing American Voter,* (Washington: Brookings Institution, 1992), p. 6.

10. Walter Dean Burnham, "Party Systems and the Political Process," in William N. Chambers and Walter Dean Burnham, eds., *The American Party Systems: Stages of Political Development,* (New York: Oxford University Press, 1967), pp. 287–288; Kevin Phillips, *The Emerging Republican Majority,* (New Rochelle: Arlington House, 1969).

11. Morris P. Fiorina, *Divided Government* (New York: Macmillan, 1992).

12. Laurence I. Barrett, "A New Coalition for the 1990s," *Time,* November 16, 1992, pp. 47–48; Lars-Erik Nelson, "Clinton's Moderate Shield Could Deflect a GOP Challenge for Years," *Denver Post,* November 22, 1992, p. D4.

13. Tim Hames, "The US Mid-term Election of 1994," *Electoral Studies* 14, no. 2 (June 1995), pp. 222–26.

14. Walter Dean Burnham, "The Turnout Problem," in A. James Reichley, ed., *Elections American Style,* (Washington: Brookings Institution, 1987), pp. 113–114. *Dynamics of the Party Systems: Alignment and Realignment of Political Parties in the United States,* rev. ed. (Washington: Brookings Institution, 1983), pp. 240–268.

15. Edwin B. Bronner, "The New Deal Comes to Pennsylvania: The Gubernatorial Election of 1934," *Pennsylvania History* 27, no. 1 (January 1960), pp. 44–68; James L. Sundquist, *Dynamics of the Party Systems: Alignment and Realignment of Political Parties in the United States,* rev. ed. (Washington: Brookings Institution, 1983), pp. 240–268.

16. Paul R. Abramson, John H. Aldrich and David W. Rohde, *Change and Continuity in the 1984 Elections,* rev. ed., (Washington: CQ Press, 1987), p. 287; James Ceaser and Andrew Busch, *Upside Down and Inside Out: The 1992 Elections and American Politics,* (Lanham, MD: Rowman and Littlefield, 1993), p. 174.

17. Walter Dean Burnham, "Critical Realignment: Dead or Alive," in *The End of Realignment?,* pp. 106–7, 115–116, 125–127 (quote p. 116).

18. Walter Dean Burnham, "The End of American Party Politics," *Trans-Action* 7, no. 2 (December 1969), pp. 12–22; Bruce E. Keith, David B. Magleby, Candice J. Nelson, Elizabeth Orr, Mark C. Westlye and Raymond E. Wolfinger, *The Myth of the Independent Voter,* (Berkeley: University of California Press, 1992).

19. Everett Carll Ladd, "The Brittle Mandate: Electoral Dealignment and the 1980 Presidential Election," *Political Science Quarterly* 96, no. 1 (Spring 1981), pp. 1–25; Morris P. Fiorina, *Retrospective Voting in American National Elections,* (New Haven: Yale University Press, 1981); Edward G. Carmines, John P. McIver, and James A. Stimson, "Unrealized Partnership: A Theory of Dealignment," *Journal of Politics* 49, no. 2 (May 1987), pp. 376–400.

20. James MacGregor Burns, *Roosevelt: The Lion and the Fox,* (New York: Harcourt Brace and Co., 1956), p. 287.

21. As quoted in Anthony J. Badger, *The New Deal: The Depression Years, 1933–40,* (London: Macmillan, 1989), p. 250.

22. Edward G. Benson and Paul Perry, "Analysis of Democratic-Republican Strength by Population Groups," *Public Opinion Quarterly* 4, no. 3 (September 1940), pp. 464–473; Burns, *Roosevelt,* pp. 282–283; William E. Leuchtenburg, "Election of 1936," in Arthur M. Schlesinger, Jr. and Fred L. Israel, eds., *History of American Presidential Elections,* 9 vols., (New York: Chelsea, 1985), vol. 7, pp. 2812–2821; Clyde P. Weed, "What Happened to the Republicans in the 1930s: Minority Party Dynamics During Political Realignment," *Polity* 22, no. 1 (Fall 1989), pp. 5–23.

23. John Bartlow Martin, "Election of 1964," in *History of American Presidential Elections,* vol. 9, pp. 3588–3589; Arthur H. Miller and Warren H. Miller, "Issues, Candidates and Partisan Divisions in the 1972 American Presidential Election," *British Journal of Political Science* 5, no. 4 (October 1975) pp. 395–400.

24. Peter Brown, *Minority Party: Why Democrats Face Defeat in 1992 and Beyond,* (Washington: Regency Gateway, 1991); Thomas Byrne Edsall and Mary D. Edsall, *Chain Reaction: The Impact of Race, Rights, and Taxes on American Politics,* (New York: Norton, 1991); Randall Rothenberg, *The Neoliberals: Creating the New American Politics,* (New York: Simon and Schuster, 1984); David Stockman, *The Triumph of Politics: The Inside Story of the Reagan Revolution,* (New York: Harper and Row, 1986); Hugh Heclo, "Reaganism and the Search for a Public Philosophy," in John L. Palmer, ed., *Perspectives on the Reagan Years,* (Washington: The Urban Institute, 1986), p. 60.

25. George Bush, "Agenda for American Renewal," p. 2, as quoted in Stanley B. Greenberg, *Middle Class Dreams: The Politics and Power of the New American Majority* (New York: Times Books, 1995), p. 229; Basil Rauch, ed., *The Roosevelt Reader: Selected Speeches, Messages, Press Conferences, and Letters of Franklin D. Roosevelt,* (New York: Rinehart, 1957), p. 66; Bill Clinton and Al Gore, *Putting People First: How Can We All Change America* (New York: Times Books, 1992), quotes pp. 165, 217.

26. Phillips, *The Emerging Republican Majority*, pp. 468–473; William C. Berman, *America's Right Turn: From Nixon to Bush* (Baltimore: Johns Hopkins University Press, 1994), pp. 140, 142, 152; Lawrence N. Powell, "Slouching Toward Baton Rouge: The 1989 Legislative Election of David Duke," in Douglas D. Rose, ed., *The Emergence of David Duke and the Politics of Race*, (Chapel Hill: University of North Carolina Press, 1992), pp. 26–27; S.A. Paolantonia, *Frank Rizzo: The Last Big Man in Big City America* (Philadelphia: Camino, 1993), pp. 117, 120–121; Clinton and Gore, *Putting People First*, pp. 63–66.

27. Robert L. Zangrando, *The NAACP Crusade Against Lynching, 1909–1950*, (Philadelphia: Temple University Press, 1980), pp. 98–165; Raymond Wolters, *Negroes and the Great Depression: The Problem of Economic Recovery*, (Westport: Greenwood Press, 1970); John A. Salmond, *The Civilian Conservation Corps*, (Durham: Duke University Press, 1967), pp. 88–101; Edward G. Carmines and James A. Stimson, *Issue Evolution: Race and the Transformation of American Politics*, (Princeton: Princeton University Press, 1989).

28. Frances Fox Piven and Richard A. Cloward, *Why Americans Don't Vote*, (New York: Pantheon Books, 1989, 2nd ed.), pp. xi, 160–164, pp. 204–205; Sydney Verba, Kay Lehman Scholzman, Henry Brady, and Norman H. Nie, "Race, Ethnicity and Political Resources: Participation in the United States," *British Journal of Political Science* 23, no. 4 (October 1993), pp. 461–463; F. Christopher Arterton, "Campaign '92: Strategies and Tactics of the Candidates," in Gerald M. Pomper, ed., *The Election of 1992*, (Chatham: Chatham House, 1993), p. 102; John M. Allswang, *The New Deal and American Politics: A Study in Political Change*, (New York: Wiley, 1978); Richard Jensen, "The Cities Re-elect Roosevelt: Ethnicity, Religion, and Class in 1940," *Ethnicity* 8, no. 2 (June 1981), pp. 189–195; Steve Fraser and Gary Gerstle, "Epilogue," in Fraser and Gerstle, eds., *The Rise and Fall of the New Deal Order, 1930–1980*, (Princeton: Princeton University Press, 1989), pp. 294–298; Roland Inglehart and Avram Hochstein, "Alignment and Dealignment of the Electorate in France and the United States," *Comparative Political Studies* 5, no. 3 (October 1972), p. 369; Powell, "Slouching Toward Baton Rouge," p. 28.

29. Dan Goodgame, "Right Makes Might," *Time*, November 21, 1994, p. 28; Steven V. Roberts, "Sea of Change," *U.S. News and World Report*, November 21, 1994, p. 39; Harvey C. Mansfield, "Real Change in the USA," *Government and Opposition* 30, no 1 (Winter 1995), pp. 36–37; Grover Norquist, *Rock the House* (New York: Vytis, 1995).

30. Gary Wills, "The Born-Again Republicans," *New York Review of Books*, September 24, 1992, pp. 9–14.

31. James Fallows, "The Republican Promise," *New York Times Review of Books*, January 12, 1995, p. 3.

32. Jason DeParle, "Clinton Allows State to Limit Aid to Indigent," *New York Times*, November 2, 1993, pp. A1, B9; Ann Devroy, "Clinton vows to Veto Any Nonuniversal Health Plan," *International Herald Tribune*, January 27, 1994, pp. 1, 4; Elizabeth Drew, *On the Edge: The Clinton Presidency* (New York: Simon and Schuster, 1994), pp. 416–417; Ann Devroy, "Clinton, Bowing to Political Reality, Models a More Centrist Presidency," *International Herald Tribune*, January 26, 1995, p. 3.

CHAPTER TEN

Cutting the Deck: New Deal, Fair Deal, and the Employment Act of 1946: Problems of Study and Interpretation

ARTHUR R. WILLIAMS, KARL F. JOHNSON
AND MICHAEL P. BARRETT

The Employment Act of 1946 offered a broad—but vague—promise to Americans that their government would pursue "*maximum* employment, production, and purchasing power."[1] It did not indicate how it would accomplish these objectives. Although the legislation preceding and leading to the act was viewed by its supporters in 1944–1946 as a culmination of New Deal pledges to assure full employment through a guarantee of jobs for all, improve economic conditions, and promote a rational, planned use of resources—a "rebuilding of the Commonwealth" in Franklin Roosevelt's words—the act was never implemented to achieve its objectives. Despite the specific exclusion by the Congress of an employment guarantee from the act, and the failure of subsequent administrations to develop an incomes and employment policy, the Act of 1946 still can be found referenced as the "*Full Employment Act.*"[2]

Both Franklin Roosevelt and Harry Truman vigorously supported several full-employment bills that were grist for the congressional mill between 1944 and 1946. Each contained strong guarantees of jobs for those seeking but unable to find work, as well as comprehensive national economic planning to assure full employment. The New Deal work-relief model of job creation was embedded within these bills.[3] If necessary, the federal government was directed to provide jobs to assure full employment; however, these and related provisions that would have made government the employer of last resort were eliminated from the act by Congress.

This chapter focuses on the reason that such a guarantee was eliminated, particularly since both the public and most politicians believed that job creation would be required during the impending postwar demobilization and reconversion. Every advanced industrialized country except the United States instituted some form of income and employment policy after World War II.[4]

Documents produced between the demise or "legislative execution" of the National Resources Planning Board (NRPB) in 1943 and the first economic report of a president to Congress on January 8, 1947, were examined to determine the effects of the transition, Roosevelt to Truman, on the drafting, passage, and implementation of this important but neglected act.[5] By this process, an effort was made to shed light on forces awakened by this transition that defined the limited role now taken by the national government in maintaining adequate levels of employment.

The Employment Act of 1946 and its implications received scant mention, less than three sentences, in recent commentary about Roosevelt or Truman.[6] Such neglect may be justified in that the act became a statement of aspiration rather than a commitment to full employment and growth. During those presidencies, however, the employment pledge in the bills leading to the act was among the highest priorities of the executive branch. Indeed, the pledge embedded in these bills remains the only attempt in American history to assure full participation by all citizens in the economy through work, by means of direct government action for employment creation.[7]

Postwar "reconversion" was one of the foremost domestic topics of the time. As early as 1940, FDR directed the NRPB to study problems of postwar reconversion, particularly unemployment.[8] Despite constant attention to what was euphemistically referred to as the employment problem, the Employment Act of 1946 was the only piece of legislation directed toward fighting unemployment to emerge from the 79th Congress, the last Congress serving with FDR and first with Truman.

Stephen K. Bailey's *Congress Makes a Law*, published in 1950, is the only book-length examination of the origins and passage of the act.[9] While acknowledged as a political science classic, the need for follow-up studies has long been recognized.[10] Bailey, focusing primarily on the internal workings of Congress, stimulated further examination of the committee structure of both houses. However, his book only superficially explored factors outside Congress that influenced legislation, particularly the organization and impact of coalitions.

Unfortunately, pursuit of an adequate description and understanding of coalition structures by studying a piece of key legislation spanning both the New Deal and Fair Deal proved more difficult than anticipated for three reasons. First, the depth of secondary material that scholars rely on to minimize lengthy, expensive archival drudgery is sparse. General studies of domestic policy during the World War II are scarce. Scholars have more or less taken at face value FDR's pronouncement that the administration in 1941 changed from "Dr. New Deal to Dr. Win the War."[11] Until recently, the best scholarly works on domestic policy during the war remained the succinct but useful 1972 study by Polenberg and one by Blum four years later.[12] Perhaps Doris Kearns Goodwin's 1994 Pulitzer Prize winner will encourage additional research on domestic policy during World War II.[13]

By the 1990s, several monographs touching on aspects of the home front under total war, were published, but these materials primarily address specialist concerns. In contrast, recent memoirs and documentaries are clouded by nostalgia. In summary, one can wade through an enormous amount of material for little information, most of which is not relevant to domestic policy making. For example, the Employment Act of 1946 is rarely indexed in recent publications surveying the period or covering the Roosevelt–Truman presidencies. Even when mentioned, the act is merely noted without description, interpretation, or critique.

A second set of difficulties stemmed from an apparently incorrect or at least misleading premise. This premise was that the passage of the act and its content were shaped by the decline of New Deal coalition structures and the emergence of a new, less liberal Fair Deal coalition. Truman apparently preferred to associate with less radical persons than FDR, but, as suggested below, this may have been due more to inherent anti-intellectualism than to policy differences. Yet, research indicates that no probable realignment of political coalitions in 1945 or 1946 could have saved the guaranteed full employment provisions of the act.

Third, the omission of these provisions was the consequence of a hidden agenda. The legislative outcome was decisively defined by racism. There may have been other forces that impinged upon the legislative process. As examples, further analysis should evaluate the reemergence of big business after its New Deal eclipse, the decline of domestic radicalism—particularly that of socialist and communist influences, and the restructuring of the economy during and after the war. Nevertheless, the influence of racism on legislation in and of itself offers a sufficient explanation for the limited provisions that survived in the Employment Act of 1946.

This chapter can be viewed as a report on problems of study and interpretation. Despite its preliminary nature and the thin support that can be provided for some of the assertions contained herein, this chapter serves to reshape thinking about the transition from the Roosevelt to the Truman administration. It compelled perusal of works about the status of African Americans during and immediately following the war, including a rereading of Gunnar Myrdal's *An American Dilemma*.[14]

The next section summarizes the development and passage of the Employment Act of 1946. (Readers wishing more detail should consult Stephen Bailey's book, *Congress Makes a Law*.) After that section, four possible explanations for the elimination of guaranteed full employment provisions in the act are assessed. The final section contains general observations about this study, as well as its lessons for analyzing factors affecting legislation.

As with any legislation, the Employment Act of 1946 went through a number of changes from inception to bills in the Senate and House to Public Law 304 signed by President Truman on February 20, 1946. The principles embedded in the law were under extensive examination for almost three years prior to the signing of the act; however, the origins of the act go back, if somewhat arbitrarily, to the New Deal's inception.

Allusions by FDR to government-guaranteed full employment appeared as early as 1933, with more frequent references after the Reorganization Act of 1939 and with conspicuous presidential statements during the 1944 campaign. Throughout the war, especially during campaign periods, FDR took ample opportunity to talk about freedom from want and the need for a guarantee of employment to all citizens. Efforts by the administration to engage in dialogue about postwar "reconversion" kept employment concerns and the need for a planned postwar economic order before the public even while casualties mounted in the Pacific and North Africa. After successes in those theaters, the administration's attention to reconversion intensified. This was prompted by the nearly unanimous belief of economists and probably at least 68 percent of the general public that some form of guaranteed full employment would be required to avoid massive postwar unemployment.[15]

Formally, the origins of the Employment Act can be dated to the March 10, 1943, NRPB report entitled "Security, Work, and Relief Policies." The report called for a system of planned economic management during reconversion and employment creation by the federal government when necessary to secure full employment.

Eight months after the NRPB report, Senator Harley Kilgore (Democrat of West Virginia) began work on an omnibus reconversion bill and picked up a number of cosponsors, including Harry Truman (Democrat of Missouri). The Kilgore Reconversion Bill (S. 1823) introduced on March 29, 1944, offered a comprehensive framework for postwar economic planning and work relief funded by the federal government.

However, after a series of complex maneuvers, Walter F. George (Democrat of Georgia), Chairman of the powerful Senate Finance Committee and of the Committee on Postwar Economic Policy and Planning, succeeded in placing his own bill on the calendar ahead of S. 1823. FDR signed the George bill into law in October, 1944. It eliminated the employment provisions and planning measures in the Kilgore bill, but it did provide for limited unemployment compensation payments to be paid and administered through the states.

The George bill satisfied no one concerned about reconversion policy. On January 22, 1945, S. 380, called the Full Employment Bill, was introduced in the Senate. Section 2(b) of this bill stated "it is the policy of the United States to assure the existence at all times of sufficient employment opportunities." Section 2(c) added that "it is essential that continuing full employment be maintained in the United States." The bill also required the President to submit annually a National Production and Employment Budget that would implement provisions of the bill.

Complementary legislation was introduced in the House (H.R. 2202) by Wright Patman (Democrat of Texas). After legislative maneuvering, the bill was not sent to the important Banking or Labor committees but to the Committee on Expenditures in the Executive Department, one of the most conservative House committees. Senior Democratic members of this committee came from rural southern districts. Chairman Carter Manasco (Democrat of Alabama) represented one of the poorest districts in the country, but "his voting record was almost consistently conservative on domestic issues."[16]

Between the February 15, 1945, introduction of H.R. 2202, and the end of conference committee action on the House and Senate bills on February 2, 1946, a number of intricate legislative maneuvers were invoked by the opposition. These are well described in Bailey's book. At this stage, S. 380's full-employment and economic-planning provisions remained intact despite a vigorous assault in committee hearings and the full Senate.

Meanwhile, H.R. 2202 encountered strong opposition within committees. Two of the three Democrats on the drafting subcommittee, Manasco and Will Whittington (Democrat of Mississippi), were on record as opposed to federally guaranteed full employment; both also were allies of Senator George.

Of the two Republicans on the subcommittee, George Bender (Republican of Ohio) had a liberal record, but Clare Hoffman (Republican of Michigan) had one of the most conservative in the House. Hoffman was described by Bailey as "anti-union, anti-liberal, and xenophobic."[17] Hoffman's closest friend in the House was John Rankin (Democrat of Mississippi), a racial demagogue.[18] Ultimately, Hoffman and Rankin would vote against the conference committee report, despite both the substantial dilution of the original bill and Hoffman's presence on both the drafting subcommittee and conference committee.

The presence of Hoffman, Manasco, and Whittington, three of five members of the House drafting subcommittee, was sufficient to assure that liberal provisions would not remain in any legislation forwarded to a Senate–House conference committee. While such provisions theoretically could have been reinserted into the bill by the full committee on Expenditures in the Executive Department or by the House in session, this would require overriding Manasco, chair of both the drafting subcommittee and the full Committee. Such an override would be contrary to customary House practice.

By early February, 1946, it was obvious that the conference-committee report would fail to maintain the full-employment-guarantee provisions of S. 380. Not surprisingly, the bowdlerized conference-committee report, based on the Senate bill with its employment provisions excluded, passed the House by a vote of 320 to 84. It passed the Senate without opposition; in fact, Robert A. Taft (Republican of Ohio), the conservative Republican leader, endorsed the report.

The act, signed by Truman as Public Law 304, had a statement of support by the federal government for "maximum employment, production, and purchasing power" with the proviso that this be done in a manner to "promote free competitive enterprise." The extensive planning elements of earlier legislation were reduced to an annual Economic Report of the President, a Council of Economic Advisors (CEA) reporting to the President, and the establishment of a joint Congressional Committee on the Economic Report. No broad-gauged planning apparatus was established, and the appropriation to implement the legislation was limited to no more than $50,000, a paltry sum even in the 1940s.

Despite the exclusion of guaranteed full employment and comprehensive economic planning provisions from P.L. 304, the Truman administration attempted to put the best spin on the remainder. In his "Annual Economic Report of 1947", the first under the new law, Truman emphasized the commitment to economic planning implicit, according to him, in P.L. 304. Richard Neustadt, who served on Truman's White House staff, later praised the Employment Act which bound "personal responsibility for gauging and for guiding the American economy" to the presidency.[19] Nevertheless, New Deal liberals viewed the passage of the act as a severe defeat for Truman and a betrayal of FDR's policies. The act lacked the crucial guarantee that the government would serve as an employer of last resort in times of deficient aggregate demand. Truman was accused of failing to vigorously support the full employment "planks" of the bill.[20]

Five explanations may be offered for the failure of the act to be signed into law with its original New Deal employment and planning planks intact: (1) An explanation subscribed to by many New Deal liberals is that Truman's incompetence foreordained defeat; (2) a current conservative argument is that full employment is an impractical even utopian objective; (3) the assertion that the American public desired a return to normalcy after the war is an obvious seeking of parallels with World War I; (4) Stephen K. Bailey's explanation—that the legislative process itself was too complex, cumbersome, and failed to represent the will of the majority—has considerable merit, but ignores a fifth, more cogent, explanation; (5) a fresh explanation offered in this chapter is that racism assured the defeat of full employment and other more liberal provisions of the act.

Truman's alleged incompetence

As noted, Truman supported full employment in both the Kilgore Bill and S. 380 even before assuming the presidency. Less than five months after becoming president, Truman delivered a twenty-one-point message to Congress in which dedication to full employment and a planned, rational use of economic resources were declared to be administration policy. There can be little doubt that Truman was genuinely committed to full-employment legislation and economic planning. The effectiveness of his leadership on domestic issues, however, has been a matter of controversy for fifty years.

Favorable evaluations of Truman emphasized the degree to which he held enough of the New Deal coalition together to pass modest progressive legislation as well as protect social security and other liberal initiatives.[21] Critical evaluations placed part of the blame for coalition disintegration on Truman himself.[22] However, such criticisms should be tempered by the fact the New Deal coalition began cracking as early as 1938 with disintegration continuing during the 1942 congressional campaign. Therefore, criticisms of Truman's leadership more properly focus on whether the earlier coalition could have been rebuilt and whether anyone could have succeeded in this effort.

Recent research suggests that by 1943, at least, Roosevelt was seeking ways to build a different, more effective party coalition around New Dealers, liberal Republicans, and various minor parties. Sean Savage maintains that the construction of a national liberal party was Roosevelt's goal as early as the 1920s.[23] The immediate issue confronting FDR was how to do this, win the upcoming 1944 election, and better manage the Democratic party in both houses of Congress.

Truman emerged as the vice presidential candidate because being from a border state he was acceptable to the South, yet unlikely to be anathema to liberals on the race issue, and was acceptable to moderate members of the Senate and House.[24] Based on his previous record, Truman could function effectively as congressional liaison, which Vice President Wallace could not, while Roosevelt explored the construction of a new liberal party with Wendell Willkie.[25] In addition, Truman's previous record of support for the administration and pragmatic politics made him unlikely to object to a party realignment, a case that could not be made for any other candidate.

Unfortunately for FDR's plans, Willkie, the most promising bridge between liberal Democrats and Republicans, died suddenly in October 1944, about one month before the Democratic electoral victory. His death and Roosevelt's the following spring ended any hope of a liberal coalition developing between 1944 and 1948. FDR's death increased the likelihood of Republican success in the off-year elections of 1946 and the 1948 presidential election. With improved probability of Republican victory, a revival of liberal fusion discussions, initiated by FDR and to which Truman was not privy, was unlikely.

If Truman can be faulted, it is for trying to *maintain* a New Deal coalition, which FDR knew needed reconstruction. Truman, however, was a quick study, and the defeat of key provisions in the Employment Act was part of that learning.

Certain criticisms of Truman's leadership are hard to fathom. For example, both Harvard Sitkoff and Barton Bernstein cite Bailey as evidence supporting Truman's "unwillingness to struggle" for the act as having "doomed" it.[26] Bailey, however, absolves Truman of any blame in the last chapter of his book: "President Truman cannot be held responsible. ... He attempted to provide political leadership through his messages to Congress, his radio appeals to the public, the testimony of members of his cabinet before the Senate and House committees, his conversations with key Congressional leaders, and his appointment of a cabinet committee under Fred Vinson to press for passage of a strong bill. ... The forces which shaped and modified the legislation were far beyond his control."[27]

Even authors favorably predisposed to Truman convey his incompetence with statements such as "the comprehensiveness of Truman's lack of preparation [for the presidency] would be hard to duplicate."[28] In fact, Truman's preparation for the presidency exceeded that of many others. His ten years as a local government official and almost eleven years in the Senate constitute more years of elective public service than were served by Lincoln, Theodore Roosevelt, Wilson, or FDR prior to their assuming the presidency.

If intended to mean that Truman was less prepared by education to assume the office of president, then it must be conceded that of all twentieth century presidents, he was the least prepared. He never went beyond high school,[29] and, more important, he possessed personal characteristics that alienated the more intellectually inclined, better educated New Dealers. These characteristics and prejudices cannot be explored here, but a number are relevant to the topic under review. For whatever reasons, personal hostility existed between Truman and many New Dealers.

For example, Harold Ickes, who had built an earlier career on Progressive municipal reform could never reconcile himself to Truman's Pendergast associations. On the other side of the issue, Truman's anti-intellectualism and hostility to Eastern college men made his communication with the more cerebral colleagues of FDR extremely difficult, Dean Acheson being a notable exception.

Truman was not skilled in working with ideas. He had the characteristics of a Babbitt or man on Main Street. Anti-intellectualism and feelings of inadequacy often led him to frame issues in terms of personal experience, exhibiting a glaring failure to consider other forms of knowledge and denigrating expert opinion or advice.[30] Such actions contributed to the appearance of cronyism early in his administration, although most observers now agree that policies of his administration were not influenced by Truman's friends.[31]

On the other hand, the response of many New Dealers to Truman showed considerable intolerance and even elitist arrogance. Despite his shortcomings, recent biographies show that he possessed an essential characteristic of a great president, a capacity for growth in office.[32]

The more relevant issue here is: Did Truman's actions contribute to the defeat of the full employment provisions of S. 380 and H.R. 2202? The above quotation from Bailey indicates that Truman provided leadership on this issue. Recently published materials do not identify any feasible strategy that offered greater likely success.

Full Employment Is Not Practicable

An objection to guaranteed full employment is its alleged utopianism; however, this is more an objection of the late twentieth century than one relevant in 1946. Modern economists claim to have identified trade-offs between employment and inflation: the lower the rate of unemployment, the higher the rate of inflation. Even though evidence for the existence of such trade-offs is ambiguous and contingent upon debatable assumptions, this statistical relationship, known as the Phillips curve, has guided economic policy in the United States since the 1960s. Indeed, one economist has called the modern view of labor markets the Sargasso Sea of Economic Shipwrecks, since empirically observed behavior fits prevailing economic models so poorly.[33]

These models were developed after the New Deal/Fair Deal period. Nevertheless, they are so entrenched in public consciousness that they may lead to dismissal of a position in favor of guaranteed full employment as being theoretically and practically untenable. Such beliefs may explain why there is so little study of a perceived *bad* idea—full-employment guarantees in the act of 1946—but they cannot be used to explain reactions to proposed legislation in 1945–1946.

The conservative assault on the Employment Act rarely used any inflation argument. The bill was attacked on ideological grounds: its "totalitarian" and "un-American" implications, such as the possible dominance of government over free enterprise via planning. Despite later assertions by prominent economists, such as Herbert Stein,[34] there is little evidence that Keynesian or any other system of economic thought had significant impact in shaping the resistance to bills proceeding the act or the dropping of full employment provisions from P.L. 304.

By 1945, some form of government-mandated postwar planning and employment policy seemed imminent.[35] Public sentiment favored this in the United States, as did postwar policy in other advanced industrialized countries. The 1942 Beveridge Report in Britain and later social partnership agreements that emerged in Britain, the Scandinavian countries, Austria, and more generally throughout Western Europe demonstrated that the war produced sentiment in favor of expanding government participation in the economy and society.[36] If one were concerned about the impracticality of full-employment legislation, one would have to explain why the United States followed an exceptional course compared to other developed countries.

While avoiding a detailed discussion of differences between the United States and other countries, a single crucial difference can be noted: During the war, large-scale business in the United States not only survived but thrived on government contracts, cost-plus delivery of goods and services, and growing prosperity and its expanding influence in the war effort. In fact, compliance with government rules and regulations, including cooperation in procurement between public and private sector managers, promoted a weakening of shareholder control over corporations and a strengthening of management.

The United States Chamber of Commerce, the National Association of Manufacturers, and organized business in general emerged from the war in strong political positions. Their coffers were full, and executives of major corporations controlled not only critical information about their industries and operations but possessed considerable access to insider information about government through well-placed "dollar-a-year" men on loan to Washington agencies and departments while they remained on corporate payrolls.[37]

Bailey emphasized the important "indirect" influence of business interests on the defeat of the full-employment bills.[38] This influence, according to him, was exerted through control and manipulation of "word-symbols," and spreading the belief that "What is good for business is good for America." Bailey argued that the "conditioned climate of values" indirectly influenced congressmen. Yet, his discussions of the personalities of congressmen provided little evidence that key players' opinions could have been shaped by any hastily organized business lobbying effort or by a prevailing "climate of values." Each of his personality vignettes emphasized the shaping of political opinions and beliefs of congressmen prior to 1938, particularly by experiences in their home districts.

At most, the educational effort of business could have helped legitimate stands taken by opponents of the act for a variety of reasons. The business lobby, in fact, did not focus its attention on the impractical economics of full-employment or even on the specifics of legislation. Perhaps the apparent groundswell in favor of full-employment policies "for our boys in uniform" frightened business into pursuing an aggressive, emotive, and hastily contrived lobbying campaign as opposed to a more directed education effort.[39] Of course, Democrats had the votes to pass full-employment legislation. Little was said during debates about economic theory that could have swayed the Democratic majorities in the House and Senate, neither of which at that time was pro-business.

The Desire For Return to Normalcy

Was it a desire to return to normalcy that made it difficult or impossible to pass social-welfare legislation after the war? This explanation for defeat of the Employment Act of 1946 has an uncomfortable parallelism with the failure of progressivism at the close of World War I—uncomfortable, because the scope of American participation in the two wars was very different. Not only was the American involvement more extensive in deployment of men and material in World War II, but also the demographic and economic effects at home were substantially different.

To a considerable degree, World War I reinforced historic American economic patterns by stimulating agricultural prosperity and growth of traditional industries, such as the production of agricultural machinery, in villages and towns. These patterns reinforced what was then primarily a rural, small-town economy. In this respect, demobilization as a return to normalcy may accurately describe 1919 to 1921.

In contrast, the demographic and social changes in the United States between 1941 and 1946 are mind-boggling. For example, estimates that up to one-third of the United States population changed residence during this period would make this the largest migration in American history. Twenty percent of the labor force relocated to different states. Personal income and wages grew faster than at any other time in modern history, and the recorded share of labor in personal income grew for the first and only time in that history. Even as relative returns to capital declined, some of the largest industrial combinations since the turn of the century emerged. The new economic and political power of large-scale industry and commerce, combined with the desire of labor to maintain and expand wartime gains raised concerns about postwar economic instability.[40]

Minorities, especially African Americans, and women entered the paid labor force in large numbers, and openings occurred for these groups among skilled labor and the professions. Of the millions of males and thousands of females who served in the military, many received health care, training, and higher social status for the first time. These changes were accompanied by new social problems as well as new manifestations of old ones, not the least of which was whether previously excluded groups, particularly African Americans, would return to prewar places in the social and economic order.[41]

Post-World War II America confronted a world of change, and faced the new world of large-scale organization and technology with anxiety. The death of FDR, who had been in office as long as many young adults could remember, did little to assuage concerns. By comparison, Harry Truman, "the Man from Pendergast," seemed a bench jockey, representing the contradictory impulses of decaying urban political machines and a fading agrarian populism.

The public mood at the end of the war was one of fear, or at least anxiety, rather than exhilaration, a marked difference from the end of World War I. The mass media reflected a lack of both the confidence and the drive to return to normalcy observed at the close of the previous world war. For example, the special V-E (Victory in Europe) Day issue of *Time* (May 14, 1945) described public opinion as "somber" and noted that 59 percent of Americans expected a future war. The letters-to-the-editor column exuded anxiety, and one feature story described the difficulties of bringing the "boys" home from Europe—the lack of transport for large numbers was a major point.

A careful examination of the media after World War II suggests that the public mood was shaped by a loss of confidence brought on by the Great Depression and uncertainty arising from dislocations created by the war. The public anticipated a different world, and it was ambivalent about the new one. Opinion polls through 1945 found respondents anticipating postwar economic planning and federal job creation. The popular image seems to have been that of a postwar New Deal, arising not from nostalgia but rather from the belief that the economy would fail to absorb increased numbers during demobilization. Few periods in American history appear on the surface to have been as fertile and well-prepared sociologically for changes in the structure of economy and society.

The Cumbersome Legislative Process

The culprit responsible for the failure of economic-planning and full-employment provisions to remain in the act, according to Bailey, was the "complex" and "cumbersome" legislative process,[42] already described. Bailey contends that legislative rules offered few opportunities for the majority to prevail over a Will Whittington or Walter George. Retrospectively, Bailey's conclusion sounds like a 1940s version of gridlock. His prescription also sounds familiar: Strengthen the presidency and national political parties to build a Congress more responsive to the people.

His well-written and fascinating description of congressional politics illustrates that authority can reside in committees and the rules of an institution. Yet, his analysis and prescription largely ignore the possibility that the structure of Congress and its rules may be shaped to sustain powerful vested interests that obstruct democratizing changes. Deficiencies in description and prescription appear to arise from lack of fit between his analytical framework or paradigm and the analysis presented herein. The paradigm used by Bailey is a liberal democratic one. It normatively presupposes that the legislative process largely rests upon decisions arrived at openly through reasoned analysis, discussion, and debate, which results in law that approximates majority opinion. Using this paradigm as a map, Bailey follows the Employment Act and related bills through the halls of both houses, and discovers that Congress does not conform to his paradigm.

He concludes that strengthening familiar institutions (the presidency and national political parties) might make Congress do so. He fails to consider the possibility that the system within which Congress functions and the Congress itself might be organized around another paradigm.

A Hidden Agenda and "Non-Decision:" Racism and Segregation

Criticisms of Bailey's work, nevertheless, should not be unduly harsh. Predispositions of American political scientists to use liberal democratic paradigms analytically are so common in the professional mainstream that it is not unusual for critical insight to be impeded. Even after reviewing forty-five years of additional scholarly research, this study began with a similar paradigm or map, causing the authors to become lost in unfamiliar terrain.

Only after following Bailey's trail for some distance was it apparent that his discussion of how Congress made a law was predicated upon a defective mapping of undemocratic territory. Since the most significant portion of the *actual* legislative agenda was unstated in provisions of the full-employment bills, Bailey's description of the making of a law also conformed poorly to Webster's definition of legislation: "The exercise of power and function of making rules (as laws) that have the force of authority by *virtue of their promulgation* by an official organ of state or other organization."[43] Within Bailey's narrative, democratic vistas are marred by hidden agendas and nondecisions analogous to washed out bridges and unmarked roads on a map. These obstacles have an intentionality about them; they are not acts of God or force majeure inducing complexity and confusion.

A nondecision is a consensus built by powerful political players that *no* decision will be made on an issue; the status quo is at least acceptable. In the case of a hidden agenda, the intent or motives behind action or inaction are not openly discussed. A policy that is shaped by both a nondecision and a hidden agenda is by definition difficult to identify, since its essence is that nothing happens and little is directly observed.[44] Political arenas are structured in such a manner that fundamental concerns are excluded from debate and open decision making.

None of the sources initially examined included any mention of race as an issue during debates of the Employment Act of 1946, nor did the publicly available speeches on the bills, such as those in the *Congressional Record*.[45] Bailey's book index has only one item under "Negro support for the bill." None appear under racism, segregation, or other related terms.[46] No black faces appear on the score card; not even that of A. Philip Randolph.[47] African Americans are invisible in the examination of the act.

A key to linkage between the formulation of the act and segregation was that consistent opposition to its original employment and planning provisions within the majority party came from the South, from its most demagogic and race-baiting elements. Although the House vote on the conference committee report of S. 380 on February 6, 1946, essentially counted for little due to the deletion of its most offensive provisions, and passage of the act was certain, the intransigent "nay" votes cast are revealing. Of the seventeen Democratic nays, all but one came from the deep South; that one was cast by a rural Maryland Democrat.[48] Bailey lumps these oppositionists together with conservative Republicans.[49]

These legislators and others from the South, who later voted with the majority, had exceptional influence in the Congress due to their seniority, positions on key committees, and knowledge of parliamentary procedure arising from length of service, dominance of the Rules Committee, and control of congressional staffing. They were key voters, since their votes in the 78th and 79th Congress were required for a Democratic majority. Extra majorities common on votes on rules and committee activities were impossible without their support. Moreover, cooperation between House and Senate southerners was common.

The introduction of the original full-employment bill in the Senate as an amendment to the Budget and Accounting Act of 1921 by Senator George and friends was deliberate, taking full advantage of bicameral coordination among Southern legislators. This action doomed H.R. 2202 by justifying its referral to the conservatively packed Committee on Expenditure in the Executive Department rather than the more liberal banking or labor committees.

Explorations of the segregationist opposition to the act are just underway. Thus far, the evidence strongly suggests that opposition—not persistent economic conservatism—was part of a broad assault on any federal program that might weaken the pattern of segregation in the South. Changes in society provoked by the need to fight a total war had clear and disturbing implications for race relations in the Old South.

In his 1949 study, *Southern Politics in State and Nation*, V. O. Key Jr. observed that while a number of factors contributed to southern politics its "peculiarities...come from the impact of the black race."[50] In comments throughout his book, Key also noted that the politics of race (segregation) contributed to the unusual solidarity of southern delegations in both the House and Senate.[51] This solidarity applied to both liberals and conservatives in these delegations. Evidence of this is found in split votes within delegations, which are found on many economic issues, but on few matters that were deemed to alter race relations. Indeed, the New Deal and the fighting of total war released forces of economic and social change that threatened segregation and thereby stimulated solidarity within the southern bloc against economic legislation that previously would have been seen as having few racial consequences.

The attempted purge of southern congressmen by FDR in 1938 was based upon a fundamental misunderstanding of the underlying socio-psychological strength of segregations, which would bring diverse interests in the South together to resist any appearance of federal intervention. Like many liberals, FDR believed that the race issue would be resolved harmoniously as economic growth and development proceeded. Why not intervene to eliminate southern economic reactionaries?

FDR was too confident in his belief that as a result of his Warm Springs experiences, he knew the South and the causes of its economic backwardness. He failed to understand that the race issue was fundamentally one of psychology and socialization not one of economics or livelihood. While racial domination could and did manifest itself through economic exploitation, fundamentally racism was a matter of deeply held belief in white superiority that southerners were willing to maintain even at considerable economic cost to many whites. Or, as Howard Odum put it in 1943, within the South "[t]he Negro is a Negro, and nothing more."[52]

During the Great Depression, the South was literally knocked to its knees. The region was primarily agricultural with a few cities acting as entrepôt and service providers in a sea of tenancy. The price of cotton, still the main cash crop, dropped to less than five cents a pound, extending an agricultural crisis that began in 1927. Already faced with a low standard of living, a substantial portion of the population was pushed below the subsistence level by the events following November 1929.

Southerners voted heavily for the New Deal in 1932 and 1936. Under the threat of starvation and the security of the apparent states'-rights leanings of Governor Roosevelt, few were concerned about abstract meanings of economic liberalism. In the campaign of 1936, the southern vote was overwhelmingly Democratic despite dissatisfaction with the elimination of the 104-year-old two-thirds rule at the Democratic National Convention that year. This rule had been used by southern delegates to block the nomination of presidential candidates who might jeopardize the racial status quo.

In 1935, the year preceding the convention, a battle for white supremacy was won in a unanimous Supreme Court decision sustaining the legality of the white primary in Texas. Despite this victory, the courts became the arena for a concerted attack on segregation by African Americans and their liberal allies. During 1936 and 1937, Southern anxiety was further heightened as "the Supreme Court's responsiveness to black litigants wanting the full protection promised by the Fourteenth and Fifteenth amendments quickened perceptively."[53]

Fear concerning winds of black change had consequences in the organization of the House and Senate. According to Representative Richard Bolling, the resurgence of conservatism in Congress began immediately after the 1936 election with the return of a near two-thirds Democratic majority in the House. Bolling believed that the forces of "conservatism" focused on control of the powerful Rules Committee, which "became transformed from a cockpit of the majority leadership into a slaughterhouse for legislative programs."[54]

He also observed that "the inside story of these years has not yet been told....If the Supreme Court was never packed by F.D.R., someone saw to it that Rules was packed with Southern Democrats."[55] From the 1930s on, southern Democrats equaled or outnumbered members of the Rules Committee from all other regions of the country. Control of the Committee facilitated the placement of allies on committees, subcommittees, and important positions within the Congress.

Roosevelt was aware of the undue power of the South in Congress. Walter White, director of the NAACP, recorded a conversation with the President in 1934 during which FDR said:

> Southerners, by reason of the seniority rule in Congress,
> are chairmen or occupy strategic places on most of the
> Senate and House committees. If I come out for the anti-
> lynching bill now, they will block every bill I ask Congress
> to pass to keep America from collapsing."[56]

Of course, as the Democratic majority eroded in 1938 and, particularly, in 1942, the power of southern legislators increased both on the floor and in committee.

Despite astute forecasts by some southern leaders that racial change was an inevitable consequence of the New Deal, white southern masses continued to vote in large numbers for that complex of programs throughout the Depression crisis.[57] By 1938, the positive economic impact of the New Deal was clearer in the South than in other parts of the nation. The price of cotton doubled, personal incomes were close to those of 1929, and improvements in roads, bridges, water control, and electrification stimulated economic development, employment, and personal security. Yet, by 1938, many southern politicians had not only abandoned but actively turned against the New Deal. Why?

As suggested above, one explanation may be that the FDR court-packing scheme, coming on the heels of action by the federal courts on civil rights and federal programs, such as the Works Progress Administration and the National Youth Administration that allegedly promoted negrophilia, alerted members of southern delegations to incipient legal and administrative challenges to segregation. An interesting case in point is that of Maury Maverick (Democrat of Texas), leader of the "liberal" Congressional bloc known as "Maury's Mavericks." He wrote at the time that attempts in Congress to introduce civil rights legislation in 1937 and 1938 demonstrated "wide divergence" of opinion about the degree to which the Fourteenth Amendment provided the federal government with powers to intervene in state legislation such as the white primary. He said that "extremists" wanted to "write a law which invites the colored cotton pickers into white people's drawing rooms."[58] Of course, Maury and his liberal mavericks voted with southern conservatives to resist such legislation.

Much written about the politics of the late New Deal (1938—1945) tends to assume that southern congressional opposition and conservative Republican resistance to the New Deal coalesced around a shared economic conservatism. Key, however, labelled this belief a "canard," since his observations of voting behavior inside Congress on roll calls and outside among the populace at the polls found numerous exceptions to such a proposition. For example, southern liberals tended to vote for the New Deal on economic issues, but with the opposition as a solid front against anti-lynching, voting, and any economic legislation that implied even the possibility of federal intervention.[59]

On the other hand, James T. Patterson, in a noteworthy study of Congress and the New Deal, argued that an alliance of economic conservatives began developing as early as 1934.[60] Nevertheless, of these two explanations, the evidence favors Key. While economic conservatism existed within southern delegations, its more prominent manifestations could be found among a few senators, most notably Democrats Carter Glass (Virginia), Walter George (Georgia), Josiah Bailey (North Carolina), and Harry Byrd (Virginia). Economic conservatism within these delegations has been considerably exaggerated as Key correctly noted[61]. Evidence used by Patterson to support the existence of a coalition based on economic conservatism, in fact, raises questions about whether such a coalition existed and its substantive importance.

The appendix to Patterson's book *Congressional Conservatism and the New Deal* provides a breakdown of roll-call voting for or against the New Deal by the "most conservative" Democratic Senators and Representatives.[62] The exhibit shows that 32 percent of the Democrats from the South in the House could be considered "most conservative" and 46 percent in the Senate. In the House, this percentage was 1.5 to 3.0 times the percentages from the eastern, midwestern, western, and border states. In the Senate, the percentage of "most conservative" among the southern Democrats was actually slightly exceeded by those in the border, eastern, and midwestern states. Using Patterson's method, House Democrats were classified "most conservative" if they voted 25 percent or more against the administration; Senators only 12 percent or more! Such standards hardly seem to represent intransigence or even effective opposition.[63]

Of note in Patterson's count is that only 38 of the 128 southern Representatives and 10 of the 22 Senators could be classified among the most conservative Congressmen. These are small numbers, particularly in the House, since the southern voting bloc on many issues was a solid 80 or more from the 75th through 79th Congresses. Therefore, the number of more liberal (or less conservative) southerners voting within a bloc against any one New Deal initiative must have exceeded the number of the most conservative southerners so voting. This finding is particularly striking when a loose standard is used to classify Democratic legislators as "most conservative."

For example, only five southern Democrats in the House voted against the New Deal in 50 percent or more roll calls. Will Whittington, who played a significant role in the legislation examined in this chapter, voted *with* the New Deal on two-thirds of the roll calls. Although Manasco did not enter the House until after the period included in Patterson's study, he was secretary to Will Bankhead, and upon Bankhead's death succeeded to his seat. Bankhead is not on Patterson's list.

Moreover, Patterson's list included some of the more ardent racists in the House of Representatives such as John Rankin, who was considered an *economic liberal* by most observers until the 1940s. Rankin voted with the administration in almost three-fourths of the roll calls used by Patterson.

In the other house, the classification used by Patterson seems no more reliable. The list of most conservative senators included James Byrnes (Democrat of South Carolina), who later entered the administration after having voted with the New Deal 86 percent of the time; Pat Harrison (Democrat of Mississippi), who voted with the administration 88 percent of the time, Richard Russell (Democrat of Georgia) with the administration on 75 percent of the roll calls; and, last but not least, Walter George, who voted with the New Deal on two-thirds of the roll calls. In terms of both personality and political careers, this is quite a heterogeneous group.

This legislative mix cannot be painted with an economic conservative brush, but it can be painted black. The hypothesis of our analysis is that black is the color missing in the mosaic. It explains why southerners turned away from the New Deal between 1938 and 1945. Southern congressmen, whether liberal or conservative, could *not* vote for legislation that would appear to facilitate federal intervention in the South.[64] Segregation was a way of life or "folkway" to use Odum's term.[65]

Many believed that would end with the extension of federal programs to the South. Perhaps Roosevelt believed this too. In any event, the opposition of Glass and Byrd to New Deal economics reflected prescient insight and a strong commitment to racial separation. Perhaps this commitment was stronger even than their commitment to fundamentalist economic ideology, particularly in the case of Byrd.

Correspondence of these two senators shows consistent and early opposition to the New Deal, based upon beliefs that federal programs would threaten segregation. This belief rested upon speculation about the posture of federal courts; likely legislative provisions; administrative rulings mandating equal employment opportunities; rumors that pervaded Washington (to which they were continually exposed through the proximity of their home state); as well as an abiding bigotry, which led them to dwell upon fantastic illusions.[66] Glass leads Patterson's list of most conservative Democratic senators with 81 percent opposition to the New Deal; Byrd follows at fourth on the list with 65 percent anti-administration voting.

Southern liberals were in an embarrassing position, especially as the warnings of Glass and Byrd were fulfilled during the war.[67] Southern legislative districts had been and still were among the poorest in the nation. Federal assistance was needed and wanted by constituents, but, as assistance came—and it came to the South in greater amounts than to other regions—the local economy improved and race relations often deteriorated, at least from the viewpoint of many whites.

Unfortunately, linkages between events in congressional districts and behavior in Congress have not been studied closely. The most revealing general survey to date remains James T. Patterson, *The New Deal and the States*, which should be read in conjunction with his *Congressional Conservatism and the New Deal*.[68] In the former book, Patterson observed that a definitive study would require decades of hard work with state documents and local newspapers. He then noted that a state-by-state approach to developments in states and Congress would lose the forest for the trees.

While Patterson may be correct, no other approach seems consistent with the testing of the hypothesis of this analysis: that the economic and social changes embedded in the New Deal and World War II threatened segregation and led to reaction in the South that made the passage of any liberal domestic legislation nearly impossible by 1946. Two prominent students of southern politics and history, V. O. Key and George B. Tindall, suggested that linked local–national studies are needed, although exceptionally difficult to accomplish.[69]

To confirm the hypothesis of this chapter would require a demonstration that the extraordinary influence that southern congressional delegations exercised on the national political agenda through bloc voting was tied to fears that changes produced by federal government programs threatened the existing racial order. Plenty of evidence exists that the racial motive was a strong one, but its influence on policy outside the area of civil rights is debatable. Selected evidence has been cited in this chapter that supports the plausibility of the hypothesis presented.

Further evidence should be examined. With this hypothesis case studies of southern localities are suggestive. For example, in 1938, while doing fieldwork in a southern town, John Dollard found that resistance to federal work relief was linked to black participation. The major tensions in the town were those between the white middle-class ("strainers") and Negro entrepreneurs who wanted to share in the local economy.[70] "Strainers," of course, dominated the electorate and campaign resources. Evidence from case studies should be supplemented by that from other sources, local histories, and biographies of the southern political elite. In addition, improvements in archives facilitate data examination. A National Endowment for the Humanities project provides pertinent information on the home districts of many congressmen of the period through the United States Newspaper Program.[71]

The approach used in this analysis may be helpful to other students of Congress. A case study not obviously connected to race or civil rights may reveal the importance of a racial connection. Research on that finding in the legislative process needs to be linked to collateral examination of local influences within a number of legislative districts. This combined approach would alleviate the obstacles to information sources that James T. Patterson finds to be burdensome.

Until such studies are done, none of the other explanations for the defeat of the full-employment provisions of the Employment Act of 1946 seems to fit the facts as well as that of the apprehension aroused by prospective federal involvement in race relations in the South. If this hypothesis is correct, racism offers both a necessary and sufficient explanation for the elimination of potentially intrusive provisions such as guaranteed full employment from the act. This provision clearly had the aura of work relief of the WPA about it. National economic planning provisions in the bills threatened to continue economic development in a manner that might cause "difficulties" in southern localities.[72]

The fate of the Employment Act was an essential part of Truman's education in the complexities of southern obstructionism. What often is overlooked is that the employment and planning provisions of the act went down to defeat at virtually the same time as Truman's fair employment practices legislation was killed in another committee. Bailey does not mention the other legislation in his discussion of the act, nor does William Berman note the act in his discussion of fair employment practices legislation.[73] Yet, the two were linked in Truman's mind and in that of southern obstructionists. An angry Truman returned to Independence to make certain that a Kansas City Democrat member of the offending committee was not renominated in the 1946 primary. This purge was successful!

The race issue "came out of the bag slowly,"[74] and infuriated a hot-tempered, yet fair-minded man like Truman. After all, he entered the vice presidency as a bridge between the New Deal and the South. The improbability of any president acting as a southern bridge over troubled waters and meeting his constitutional obligations in a modernizing, industrializing America was a lesson Truman learned quickly, perhaps, more quickly than FDR. Moreover, he met this obligation without regard to personal belief; Truman was a white supremacist in the context of the last quarter of the twentieth century, as were most Caucasian Americans of his generation.[75]

Commentary on the "walkout" at the 1948 Democratic national convention has emphasized the abrupt schism in the party. That schism came from the accumulating economic and social consequence of changes due to the New Deal, war mobilization, and Fair Deal.[76] The Roosevelt–Truman legacies were crutches carved from similar political stuff on which an ailing America hobbled across the mid-twentieth century.

If these conclusions are correct, Truman assumes heroic or Jacksonian stature in his fight for a Fair Deal. Pundits criticized him for failure to pass domestic legislation. Yet, he could have produced much more legislation by abandoning his stand on fair treatment for African Americans. That he did not produce a battery of legislation has been attributed to his stubbornness, ineptness, or lack of intelligence. The cost of such legislation to a fair-minded man like Truman was exorbitant and impossible in a modern America. Looking at Truman and Roosevelt retrospectively, a dangerous preoccupation in any historical analysis, it may be concluded that the time for FDR's "first class temperament" had passed and an irascible man from Main Street was needed.[77]

Acknowledgment

Valuable research assistance on this project was rendered by Diane Dauz Williams, Kansas State University. The authors appreciate assistance given by the staff of the Harry S. Truman Library, Independence, Missouri.

NOTES

1. Section 2, Employment Act of 1946, otherwise known as Public Law 304. Emphasis added.

2. See, for example, Thomas D. Lynch, *Public Budgeting in America,* 4th ed. (Englewood Cliffs: Prentice Hall, 1995), p. 42, which incorrectly refers to the "Full Employment Act of 1946." Emphasis added.

3. For a brief discussion of the close association of "work relief" with New Deal employment policies see June Hopkins, "The American Way to Welfare: Harry Hopkins and New Deal Work Relief," paper presented at the conference Franklin D. Roosevelt After 50 Years: The Politics and Culture of the 1930s and 1940s, September 14–16, 1995, Louisiana State University in Shreveport. Clearly, the intent of legislation between 1944 and 1946 was to use work relief as part of government economic stabilization policy.

4. See, for example, Frederic L. Pryor, *Economic Evolution and Structure* (New York: Cambridge University, 1996); Frederic L. Pryor, *Public Expenditures in Communist and Capitalist Nations* (Homewood: Irwin, 1968); and Charles L. Lindblom, *Politics and Markets* (New York: Basic Books, 1977).

5. The term "legislative execution" were used in John D. Millett, *The Process and Organization of Government Planning* (New York: Columbia University, 1947), p. 6.

6. Doris Kearns Goodwin, *No Ordinary Time: Franklin and Eleanor Roosevelt on the Home Front* (New York: Simon and Schuster, 1994); David McCullough, *Truman* (New York: Simon and Schuster, 1992); Stephen Skowronek, *The Politics Presidents Make* (Cambridge: Harvard University, 1993); and Bruce Miroff, *Icons of Democracy* (New York: Basic Books, 1993). The act is discussed in John M. Blum, *V Was for Victory* (New York: Harcourt Brace Jovanovich, 1976), pp. 329–332, and Alan Brinkley, *The End of Reform* (New York: Alfred Knopf, 1995), pp. 227–264. Both Brinkley and Blum give too much weight to Keynesian theory in the promul-

gation of the legislation. Neither the bills put before Congress nor debate within Congress engaged in any lengthy presentation of compensatory economic policy; emphasis is given to the kind of role, if any, that government should play in employment creation. The biography by Alonzo L. Hamby, *Man of the People: A Life of Harry S. Truman* (New York: Oxford University, 1995) is excellent, but offers little information on the Employment Act.

7. This statement assumes that efforts in the middle 1990s to change the welfare system in the United States by instituting "workfare" will not use government employment to create jobs, even if temporary ones. In any case, the debate on this suggests that if job creation is employed it may be in the states not at the national level. This turnabout in employment creation ("work relief") from a liberal to a conservative policy is one of numerous paradoxes in American history. While paradoxes make for interesting reading, one should be concerned about their implications for social stability, economic growth, international competitiveness and the quality of life.

8. Millett, *Process and Organization*, pp. 48ff. Reconversion from an "Arsenal for Democracy" was the issue, since the United States was not yet in World War II.

9. Stephen K. Bailey, *Congress Makes A Law: The Story Behind the Employment Act of 1946* (New York: Columbia, 1950). A second book, Edward S. Flash, *Economic Advice and Presidential Leadership: The Council of Economic Advisors* (New York: Columbia University, 1965), has a brief discussion of the origins of the Employment Act, but, as its subtitle suggests, focuses on the Council of Economic Advisors. The act provided for the formation of a council to study economic issues and assist the President in his preparation of an annual economic report.

10. Richard S. Kirkendall, "Opportunities for Research," in Richard S. Kirkendall, ed., *The Truman Period As A Research Field* (Columbia, MO: University of Missouri, 1967). And, Alonzo L. Hamby, "The Clash of Perspectives and the Need for New Synthesis," in Richard S. Kirkendall, ed., *The Truman Period As A Research Field: A Reappraisal, 1972* (Columbia: University of Missouri, 1974).

11. An exception is Richard O. Davies, "Social Welfare Policies" in Kirkendall), *The Truman Period*, pp. 156–157. "The entire scope of domestic political activity during World War II should provide many scholars with exciting and significant research topics, and not until we have sufficient monographic publications in this area can we fully understand the social welfare policies of the Truman Administration."

12. Richard Polenberg, *War and Society: The United States 1941–1945,* (Philadelphia: J. B. Lippincott, 1972). Blum, *V was for Victory.*

13. Goodwin, *No Ordinary Time.*

14. Gunnar Myrdal, *An American Dilemma: The Negro Problem and Modern Democracy*, (New York: Harper and Brothers, 1944).

15. Bailey, *Congress Makes a Law*, p. 9, cites an October 30, 1944, poll by the Washington *Evening Star*. Studies were also done by the NRPB and other federal government agencies.

16. Bailey, p. 153.

17. Bailey, p. 198.

18. Harvard Sitkoff, *A New Deal For Blacks*, (New York: Oxford University, 1978), p. 112.

19. Richard E. Neustadt, *Presidential Power*, (New York; John Wiley, 1960), p.19.

20. James Wechsler, "Did Truman Scuttle Liberalism?" *Commentary*, vol. 3, no. 3, March 1947, p. 226.

21. A position taken in Eric F. Goldman, *The Crucial Decade and After, America 1945–1960*, (New York: Vintage, 1960).

22. Harvard Sitkoff, "Years of the Locust: Interpretations of the Truman Presidency Since 1945," in Kirkendall, *The Truman Period As A Research Field* (1974).

23. Sean J. Savage, *Roosevelt: The Party Leader*, (Lexington: University of Kentucky, 1991).

24. Robert H. Ferrell, *Choosing Truman: The Democratic Convention of 1944*, (Columbia: University of Missouri, 1994).

25. Goodwin, *No Ordinary Time*, pp. 525–526.

26. Sitkoff, "Years of the Locust" in Kirkendall, *The Truman Period as a Research Field*, pp. 87–88; Barton J. Bernstein, "Economic Policies," in Kirkendall, *The Truman Period as a Research Field*.

27. Bailey, *Congress Makes a Law*, p. 237.

28. Elmer E. Cornwell, Jr., "The Truman Presidency," in Kirkendall, *The Truman Period as a Research Field*, p. 220.

29. Truman did take courses at a business school in Kansas City and later at Kansas City School of Law, but he never completed any degree or credential beyond his high school diploma. See Hamby, *A Man of the People*, pp. 18, 117, 135.

30. A brief, relatively unbiased description of the personality or mind-set of Harry Truman is Alonzo L. Hamby, "The Mind and Character of Harry S. Truman," in Michael J. Lacey, ed., *The Truman Presidency,* (New York: Cambridge University, 1989).

31. McCullough, *Truman*, pp. 605ff, offers only one example of the possible influence of a Kansas City friend on any policy decision. This was the personal appeal of Eddie Jacobson, Truman's former haberdashery partner, for U.S. support for the partitioning of Palestine and the establishment of the state of Israel. However, McCullough also notes the many diverse influences pressing Truman for a decision in favor of a Jewish state at the time.

32. McCullough, *Truman*, pp. 991–992.

33. Lester C. Thurow, *Dangerous Currents: The State of Economics,* (New York: Random House, 1983), pp. 173ff. See also the more recent, David Card and Alan B. Krueger, *Myth and Measurement: The New Economics of the Minimum Wage,* (Princeton: Princeton University, 1995).

34. Herbert Stein, *The Fiscal Revolution in America,* (Chicago: University of Chicago, 1969).

35. Millett, *Process and Organization*, p. 175.

36. Alan T. Peacock and Jack Wiseman, *The Growth of Public Expenditure in the United Kingdom* (Princeton: National Bureau of Economic Research and Princeton University, 1961). Theodor Tomandl and Karl Fuerboeck, *Social Partnership: The Austrian System of Industrial Relations and Social Insurance* (Ithaca: ILR Press, Cornell University, 1986).

37. See Grant McConnell, *Private Power and American Democracy,* (New York: Vintage, 1970), pp. 261ff.

38. Bailey, *Congress Makes a Law,* pp. 148–149; chapter 10, pp. 188–219.

39. The hatred of some businessmen for the New Deal and FDR in particular should not be underestimated as a force underlying ideological histrionics. Goodwin, *No Ordinary Time*, pp. 53–54, and Miroff, *Icons of Democracy*, pp. 257–272.

40. William H. Chafe, "Postwar American Society: Dissent and Social Reform," in Lacey, *The Truman Presidency*, pp. 158. Also, excellent on changes under total war is Goodwin, *No Ordinary Time*, and Polenberg, *War and Society*.

41. Myrdal, *An American Dilemma*; Sitkoff, *A New Deal for Blacks*; and Polenberg, *War and Society*, pp. 99ff.

42. Bailey, *Congress Makes a Law*, p. 236.

43. *Webster's Ninth New Collegiate Dictionary,* (Springfield: Merriam Webster, 1990). Emphasis added.

44. The classic statement on this subject is Peter Bachrach and Morton S. Baratz, "Decisions and Nondecisions: An Analytical Framework," *American Political Science Review*, vol. 57, no. 3, September 1963.

45. An interesting case in point is the speech of May 29, 1945, by Butler Hare (D-SC), which was placed in the *Congressional Record*. The speech mentions racial separation but only in the context of the rumor of Fair Employment Practices Commission legislation which was to be killed in committee when submitted some nine months later.

46. Bailey, *Congress Makes a Law*, p. 87. This is a brief, informational reference to Judge William Hastie and NAACP support for the bill.

47. Randolph was the most successful advocate of African American rights between 1930 and 1950. In fact, increased militancy and consequent later gains in civil rights may owe more to Randolph than to anyone else. Every student of the period attributes FDR's important Executive Order 8802 officially ending segregation in many federal programs to Randolph's efforts. See, among others, Harvard Sitkoff, *A New Deal for Blacks*, pp. 320–325, and Goodwin, *No Ordinary Time*, pp. 247–252. Moreover, Randolph was among the most important labor leaders and organizers in American history, a contribution often unappreciated. If Randolph had not been a black socialist and, at an advanced age, an outspoken critic of the Vietnam War, public recognition might not have been so long delayed. Perhaps belated recognition reflects an understanding that he was correct and prescient on issues rather than just "left."

48. Bailey, *Congress Makes a Law*, pp. 253–256.

49. Bailey, *Congress Makes a Law*, pp. 124–125.

50. V. O. Key Jr., *Southern Politics in State and Nation,* (New York: Alfred Knopf, 1949), p. 665. Myrdal, *An American Dilemma*, correctly noted five years earlier that the problem of race in American was primarily the white man's problem.

51. Key, *Southern Politics in State and Nation*, p. 667.

52. Howard W. Odum, *Race and Rumors of Race,* (Chapel Hill: University of North Carolina, 1943), p. 22. This phrase follows a chapter entitled "The Rising Tide of Tension."

53. Sitkoff, *A New Deal for Blacks*, p. 229. In 1944, the white primary was held unconstitutional in *Smith v. Allwright*, another Texas case.

54. Richard Bolling, *Power in the House,* (New York: E. P. Dutton, 1968), pp. 135–136.

55. Bolling, *Power in the House*, pp. 136, 137.

56. Cited from Walter White's memoirs in Frank Freidel, *F.D.R. and the South,* (Baton Rouge: Louisiana State University, 1965), p. 86.

57. John S. Ezell, *The South Since 1865,* (New York: Macmillan, 1963), pp. 431–432. Ezell notes the willingness of the masses even to try radical reforms such as the WPA.

58. Richard B. Henderson, *Maury Maverick* (Austin: University of Texas, 1970), pp. 110–112.

59. V. O. Key Jr., *Southern Politics*, pp. 350ff.

60. James T. Patterson, *Congressional Conservatism and the New Deal,* (Lexington: University of Kentucky, 1967).

61. Key, *Southern Politics*, pp. 355–359.

62. Patterson, *Congressional Conservativism and the New Deal*, pp. 339–352.

63. Effective opposition may be more relevantly assessed by understanding what was killed in committees and subcommittees than in appraisal of roll calls. For this reason, we have also noted the pattern of committee assignments and actions.

64. This is a point repeatedly emphasized by V. O. Key Jr, *Southern Politics*, pp. 315–316, 358, 667, and numerous other places in his text. "It must be conceded that there is one, and only one, real basis for southern unity: the Negro." (p. 315)

65. Odum, *Race and Rumors*, pp. 13ff. Although somewhat dated, the classic discussion of segregation as a social-psychological event remains C. Vann Woodward, *The Strange Career of Jim Crow,* 2nd ed., (New York: Oxford University, 1966).

66. Freidel, *FDR and the South*, pp. 72ff. Excellent and illustrative vignettes that vividly picture the racial know-nothingism of Glass and Byrd are peppered throughout Sitkoff, *A New Deal for Blacks*.

67. Interesting examples in relationship to the Byrd machine can be found in James R. Sweeney, "Sheep Without a Shepherd: Virginia's Liberals During the New Deal Era," paper presented at the conference Franklin D. Roosevelt After 50 Years: The Politics and Culture of the 1930s and 1940s, September 14–16, 1995, Louisiana State University in Shreveport.

68. James T. Patterson, *The New Deal and the States,* (Princeton: Princeton University, 1969), p. vii.

69. Key, *Southern Politics;* George B. Tindall, *The Emergence of the New South,* (Baton Rouge: Louisiana State University, 1967).

70. John Dollard, *Caste and Class in a Southern Town,* 3rd ed., (New York: Doubleday, 1949), pp. 119–120; 125–133.

71. To find the location of a state's collection, write the USNP Coordinator, Serial Records Division—Lm515, Library of Congress, Washington, DC, 20504.

72. This term was used to describe changes arising from New Deal programs and economic improvements after 1938 in James Codling Starkville, "FDR's Economic Policy in Mississippi," paper presented at the conference Franklin D. Roosevelt After 50 Years: The Politics and Culture of the 1930s and 1940s, September 14–16, 1995, Louisiana State University in Shreveport.

73. William C. Berman, *The Politics of Civil Rights in the Truman Administration* (Columbus: Ohio State University, 1970).

74. Sitkoff, *A New Deal for Blacks*, p. 105.

75. It is useful to distinguish attitudes held by the majority toward racial minorities in the United States. Most Americans historically have been white supremacists. The belief that whites somehow share characteristics that make them superior to other racial groups has been widespread. However, the white supremacist also can believe that other racial groups should be treated fairly; that is, these groups share a common humanity with whites. On the other hand, the bigot would deny minorities all elemental human characteristics. At this extreme, slavery, lynching, and other abuses can be justified. Between these two extremes, each of which might be labelled "racism," there are various levels of recognition of a common humanness.

76. One should not neglect to note that it was also a consequence of increasingly focused African American militancy on obtaining constitutionally guaranteed rights. Nevertheless, economic and social changes brought about by the New Deal, the total war, and the Fair Deal established an environment in which African American leaders could have some of the success that eluded them after World War I.

77. Geoffrey C. Ward, *A First Class Temperament: The Emergence of Franklin Roosevelt,* (New York: Harper and Row, 1989).

Appendix

Congressional Mavericks

Identifying the "Mavericks" is not a simple task. At various times newspaper and magazine articles identified a host of congressmen who obviously were not ideological cohorts. Journalists mistakenly associated individuals who may have momentarily agreed with or supported a "Maverick" position as belonging to the bloc. These journalistic references include:

New York Times, March 10, 1935, p. 1, which covered the group's organizational meeting.

New York Times, March 17, 1935, p. 33, which listed the congressmen who signed the first position paper.

Jonathon Mitchell, "Front-Fighters in Congress," *New Republic*, Vol. 83, June 19, 1935, pp. 156-157, in which the author presented his list of group members.

TRB, "Washington Notes," *New Republic*, Vol. 86, April 29, 1936, p. 343 and Vol. 90, February 10, 1937, pp. 17-18, in which the famous Washington insider gave his list of members.

Stanley High, "The Neo-New Dealers," *Saturday Evening Post*, Vol. 209, May 22, 1937, pp. 10-11, 105-109, in which the author presented his list of group members following the 1936 election.

Philadelphia *Record*, June 24, 1937; the article identified Democrats associated with the "Mavericks."

Philadelphia *Record*, February 8, 1938; the article identified congressmen who met with FDR to try to gain his support for the "Maverick" platform.

More reliable are congressional records demanding a public proclamation of support for the "Maverick" platforms. These sources include:

Congressional Record, Vol 81, Part 9, Appendix, March 9, 1937, pp. 485-486. This is a signed "round robin" initiated by H. Jerry Voorhis.

Congressional Record, Vol. 81, Part 9, Appendix, April 6, 1937, pp. 725-726. This is a signed policy statement.

Congressional Record, Vol. 83, Part II, Appendix, June 11, 1938, pp. 2584-2585. This is a signed policy statement.

A final source, albeit one which does not include supporters from the 74th Congress defeated for reelection in 1936, is an attendance sheet for a Mavericks meeting held May 1, 1938, given to the author by H. Jerry Voorhis. He evaluated the level of participation of each person on the list, but could not speak in reference to the 74th Congress, of which he was not a member.

On the basis of the materials evaluated, the bona fide Mavericks included:

Democrats
Robert Allen, PA
Herbert Bigelow, OH
Charles Binderup, NE
Michael Bradley, PA
John Coffee, WA
Matthew Dunn, PA
Charles Eckert, PA
Edward Eicher, IA
Frank Freis, IL
Fred Hildebrandt, SD
Knute Hill, WA
John Hoeppel, CA
John Houston, KS
Edouard Izac, CA
Lyndon Johnson, TX
Kent Keller, IL
John Luecke, MO
William McFarlane, TX
John Martin, CO
Samuel Massingale, OK
Maury Maverick, TX
Jerry O'Connell, MT
Byron Scott, CA
H. Jerry Voorhis, CA
Marion Zioncheck, WA

Minnesota Farmer-Labor
John Bernard
Richard Buckler
Dewey Johnson
Paul Kvale
Ernest Lundeen
Henry Teigan

Wisconsin Progressives
Thomas Amlie
Gerald Boileau
Bernard Gehrmann
Merlin Hull
Harry Sauthoff
George Schneider
Gardner Withrow

Republicans
Usher Burdick, ND
Vito Marcantonio, NY

Chronology

January 1882 Born Hyde Park, New York

June 1903 Received B.A. from Harvard University

March 1905 Married Anna Eleanor Roosevelt

November 1910 Elected to New York Senate

November 1912 Reelected to New York Senate

July 1920 Nominated as Vice President candidate of Democratic Party

November 1920 Defeated with Democratic Presidential Nominee James N. Cox

August 1921 Stricken with polio

November 1928 Elected governor of New York

November 1930 Reelected governor of New York

November 1932 Elected president

March 1933 Inaugurated as 32nd president

Economy Act—required balanced budget, cut veterans' bonus and wages of Federal employees.

May 1933 Federal Emergency Relief Act—required virtually all private welfare programs to be turned over to federal agencies

Tennessee Valley Authority Act—created three-man board of directors authorized to develop hydro-electric generation and conservation programs in the Tennessee Valley region

April 1934 Debt Default Act—forbid U.S. loans to nations in default on debts to the United States, aka the (Hiram) Johnson Act, linked to the Neutrality Acts

June	1934	Securities and Exchange Act—created five-member Securities and Exchange Commission (SEC) with staggered five-year terms. This Act, the Securities Act (1933), Bankruptcy Act (1939) and the Investment Act (1940) gave the SEC power to monitor securities and commodities transactions, and insure that corporations made full disclosure when issuing bonds or stock. Investment dealers were to register and abide by stringent rules.
		Reciprocal Trade Act—authorized executive branch to negotiate bi-lateral trade agreements of which twenty-two were made by the end of 1940
August	1935	War Pension Act—enacted over FDR's veto, this restored the veterans' bonus that was cut two years before, aka Bonus Act
		Public Utility Holding Company Act—gave the SEC power to regulate public utilities, including their mode of operations, finances and organization
		First Neutrality Act—this, along with three other Neutrality Acts (2/29/36, 5/1/37, 11/4/39) collectively, prohibited loans to belligerents, embargoed direct and indirect shipments of munitions or weapons to them, and banned Americans from traveling on ships of belligerents. (See Debt Default Act and Lend Lease Act)
February	1936	Second Neutrality Act
August	1936	Social Security Act—created a federal-state program of Old Age Assistance (OAO) that initially covered about 60 percent of the work force, who paid a percentage of their wages. Created unemployment insurance and benefits for dependent mothers and children
November	1936	FDR reelected president
March	1937	Court 'Packing' Bill introduced—would give president authority to appoint additional members to lower federal and Supreme courts for sitting judges over seventy years old
May	1937	Third Neutrality Act

June   1938   Fair Labor Standards Act—established minimum wage of 25
                    cents/hour and put restrictions on hiring of persons under age
                    sixteen, aka Wage and Hour Act

September 1939   War officially began in Europe

November 1939   Fourth Neutrality Act

September 1940   Selective Training and Service Act—required registration of
                    males ages twenty-one to thirty-six and created local draft
                    boards

November 1940   FDR reelected president—unprecedented third term

March   1941   Lend Lease Act—gave president broad discretion to sell, lend,
                    lease or otherwise dispose of" articles to any nation that was
                    vital to the security of the United States (See Debt Default Act
                    and Neutrality Acts.)

December 1941   Japanese bombed Pearl Harbor

                    Selective Service Training Act—extended military service from
                    one year to seventeen months and lowered draft age to
                    eighteen.

November 1944   FDR reelected president—unprecedented fourth term

April   1945   Died at Warm Springs, Georgia

Biographical Digest

A

Allen, Robert Gray (1902–1963). D-PA. House 1937-1941.
Amlie, Thomas R. (1897–1973). R-WI. House 1931–1933.

B

Bailey, Joseph Weldon (1862–1929). D-TX. House 1891–1901. Senate 1901–1913.
Bailey, Josiah William (1873–1946) D-NC. Senate 1931–1946.
Bankhead, William Brockman (1874–1940). D-AL. House 1917–1940 (majority leader
    1935–1937, Speaker 1936–1940). Father of actress Tallulah Bankhead.
Barbour, W. Warren (1888–1943). R-NJ. Senate 1931–1937.
Barkley, Alben William (1877–1956). D-KY. House 1913–1927; Senate 1927–1949,
    1955–1956 (Senate majority leader 1937–1947, minority leader
    1947–1948); U.S. vice president 1949–1953.
Beard, Charles A. (1874–1948). American historian, perhaps best known for his
    An Economic Interpretation of the Constitution of the United States.
    One of the few to have been president of both the American Historical
    Association and the American Political Science Association. Leader in
    several controversial organizations and movements, along with his wife,
    Mary, also a distinguished historian. An isolationist opponent of FDR.
Bender, George H. (1896–1961). R-OH. House 1939–1949, 1951–1954. Senate
    1954–1957. Went to Senate upon the death of Robert A. Taft.
Binderup, Charles Gustave (1873–1950). D-NB. House 1935–1939.
Black, Hugo Lafayette (1886–1971). D-AL. Senate 1927–1937. Associate Justice
    U.S. Supreme Court 1937–1971.
Blaine, John James (1875–1934). R-WI. Senate 1927–1933. Governor WI
    1921–1927.
Boileau, Gerald John (1900–1981). R-WI House 1931–1935; Progressive.
    House 1935–1939.
Bolling, Richard Walker (1916–1991). D-MO. House 1949–1983. Chair, Rules
    Committee, 1978–1983. Expected by many to be Rayburn's successor
    as Speaker, but he did not attain that position. His book *House Out of*
    Order urged reform of House practices.
Bolton, Frances Payne (1885–1977). R-OH. House 1940–1969; First woman
    appointed as congressional delegate to the U.N. General Assembly.
Bone, Homer (1883–1970). D-WA. Senate 1933–1944. Washington State House of
    Representatives 1923–1924.
Borah, William Edgar (1869–1940). R-ID. Senate 1907–1940.
Brookhart, Smith Wildman (1869–1944). Progressive Republican-IA. Senate
    1922–1926, 1927–1933.

Bryan, William Jennings (1860–1925). D-NE. Senate 1891–1895. Democratic
     presidential nominee, 1896, 1900. Secretary of State 1913–1915.
Buchanan, James Paul (1867–1937). D-TX. House 1913–1937.
Bulkley, Robert Johns (1880–1965). D-OH. House 1911–1915; Senate 1930–1939.
Burdick, Usher Lloyd (1879–1960). R-ND. House 1935–1945, 1949–1959.
Byrnes, James Francis ("Jimmy") (1879–1972). D-SC. House 1911–1925; Senate
     1931–1941; Associate Justice U.S. Supreme Court 1941–1942; U.S.
     Secretary of State 1945–1947; Governor South Carolina 1951–1955.
Byrns, Joseph Wellington (Sr.) (1869–1936). D-TN. House 1909–1936, majority
     leader 1933–1935, Speaker 1935–1937.

C

Cannon, Joseph Gurney ("Joe") (1836–1926). R-IL. House 1873–1891, 1893–1913,
     1915–1923, Speaker 1903–1911.
Caraway, Hattie Wyatt (1878–1950). D-AR. Senate 1931–1945.
Chandler, Albert Benjamin ("Happy") (1898–1991). D-KY. Senate 1939–1945;
     Governor KY 1935–1939, 1955–1959; Commissioner of organized
     baseball 1945–1950.
Chavez, Dennis (1888–1962). D-NM. House 1931–1935; Senate 1935–1962.
Chiperfield, Robert Bruce (1899–1971). R-IL. House 1939–1963.
Clark, Joel Bennett ("Champ") (1890–1954). D-MO. House 1913–1917. Senate
     1933–1945.
Coffee, John Main (1897–). D-WA. House 1937–1947.
Collier, John (1884–1968). Commissioner of Indian Affairs 1935–1945.
Connally, Thomas Terry ("Tom") (1877–1963). D-TX. House 1917–1929; Senate
     1929–1953.
Corcoran, Thomas Gardiner (1900–1981) "Tommy the Cork," a protégé of Felix
     Frankfurter at Harvard Law School, law clerk for Oliver Wendell Holmes,
     served on legal staff of President Hoover's Reconstruction Finance
     Corporation. Most important role was as an adviser to FDR for whom he
     took a leading role in organizing the drive that led to FDR's seeking a
     third term. By 1941, Corcoran's actions had become so controversial
     that he resigned from the RFC to enter private law practice.
Costigan, Edward Prentiss (1874–1939). D-CO. Senate 1931–1937.
Cullen, Thomas Henry ("Tom") (1868–1944). D-NY. House 1919–1944.
Cutting, Bronson Murray (1888–1935). R-NM. Senate 1927–1928, 1929–1935. Died
     in an airplane crash. Succeeded in Senate by Dennis Chavez.

D

Davis, James Harvey ("Cyclone") (1853–1940). D-TX. House 1915–1917.
Davis, John W. (1873–1955). D-WV. Senate 1911–1913. Ambassador to Great
     Britain 1918–1921. Democratic candidate for president 1924.

Dewey, Thomas E. (1902–1971). Republican Governor of New York 1943–1955. Unsuccessful Republican candidate for president, 1944, 1948, despite public opinion polls that indicated he would win the latter election.

Dieterich, William Henry (1876–1940). D-IL. House 1931–1933; Senate 1933–1939.

Dulles, John Foster (1888–1959). R-NY. Senate 1949–1949; U.S. Secretary of State 1953–1959.

Dunn, Matthew Anthony (1886–1942). D-PA. House 1933–1941.

Durham, Carl Thomas (1892–1974). D-NC. House 1939–1961.

E

Early, Stephen Tyree (1889–1951). Journalist. Met FDR in 1912, worked as his advance man in 1920 election campaign, returned to Associated Press after that campaign loss. In 1927, became Washington representative for Paramount News. Appointed FDR's assistant secretary of press relations in 1933. In 1937, became press secretary. After FDR's death Early became vice president of the Pullman Company. Returned to government service in 1949.

Eaton, Charles Aubrey (1868–1952). R-NJ. House 1925–1953.

F

Farley, James A. (1888–1976). Chair, Democratic National Committee 1932–1940. A principal strategist in FDR's 1932 and 1936 campaigns. U.S. Postmaster General 1933–1940. "Mr. Democrat" and "Gentleman Jim." Broke with FDR over issue of third presidential term.

Fay, James Herbert (1899–1948). D-NY. House 1939–1941, 1943–1945.

Fish, Hamilton, Jr. (1888–1991). R-NY. House 1920–1945.

Frazier, Lynn Joseph (1874–1947). R-ND. Senate 1923–1941; Governor ND 1917–1921.

G

Garner, John Nance (1868–1967). D-TX. House 1903–1933, minority leader 1929–1931, Speaker 1931–1933; U.S. vice president 1933–1941.

George, Walter Franklin (1878–1957). D-GA. Georgia State Supreme Court, 1919–1922. Senate, 1922–1957, president pro tempore, 1955–1957.

Gilchrist, Fred Cramer (1868–1950). R-IA. House, 1931–1945.

Gillette, Guy Mark (1879–1973). D-IA. House 1933–1936. Senate, 1936–1945, 1949–1955.

Glass, Carter (1858–1946). D-VA. House 1902–1918; Senate 1920–1946; U.S. Secretary of the Treasury 1918–1920.

Gore, Thomas Pryor (1870–1949). D-OK. Senate, 1908–1921, 1931–1937. Unsuccessful candidate for re-nomination in 1920 and 1936.

Guffy, Joseph F. ("Joe") (1870–1959). D-PA. Senate, 1935–1947.

H

Hare, Butler B. (1875–1967). D-SC. Served in U.S. Department of Agriculture
1911–1924. House 1925–1933, 1939–1947.

Harrison, Byron Patrick ("Pat") (1881–1941). D-MS. House, 1911–1919; Senate
1919–1941, president pro tempore 1941.

Hearst, William Randolf (1863–1951). D-NY. House 1903–1907. Publisher of major
chain of U.S. newspapers.

Heflin, James Thomas (1869–1951). D-AL. House 1904–1920; Senate 1920–1931.

Herring, Clyde LaVerne (1879–1952). D-IA. Senate 1937–1943. Governor IA
1933–1937.

Hill, (Joseph) Lister (1894–1984). D-AL. House 1923–1938; Senate 1938–1969.

Hoeppel, John Henry (1881–1976). D-CA. House 1933–1937.

Hoffman, Clare E. (1875–1967). R-MI 1935–1963.

Hopkins, Harry Lloyd (1890–1946). Roosevelt's advisor, head of the Federal
Emergency Relief Administration 1933, and the Works Progress
Administration 1935, U.S. secretary of commerce 1938–1940, lend-lease
administrator 1941.

Huddleston, George (1869–1960). D-AL. House 1915–1937.

Hull, Cordell (1862–1948). D-TN. House 1907–1921, 1923–1931; Senate 1931–1933;
Secretary of State 1933–1944.

I

Ickes, Harold (1874–1952). Secretary of the Interior, 1933–1946, Ickes was known
for his independence of thought and strong-handed administrative
style. Before joining the New Deal, he was active in several Progressive
campaigns from his base in Chicago, where he practiced law. He took on
several special tasks for FDR, and was a voice for civil liberties and
minority rights within the administration. His *Secret Diaries of Harold
Ickes* (3 volumes) is a detailed account of his activities through 1940. He
was a less prominent figure during World War II.

J

Johnson, Lyndon Baines (1908–1973). D-TX. House 1937–1949; Senate 1949–1961,
majority whip 1951–1953, minority leader 1953–1955, majority leader
1955–1961; U.S. vice president 1961–1963; U.S. President, 1963–1969.

Johnson, Hiram Warren (1866–1945). R-CA. Senate 1917–1945. Governor CA
1911–1917.

Jones, Jesse Holman (1874–1956). Businessman and administrative official.
Declined Woodrow Wilson's offer to become Secretary of Commerce.
Executive, American Red Cross Military Relief Section in World War I.
After serving as finance chair, Democratic National Committee, Jones
was appointed as Democratic member of the Reconstruction Finance
Corporation board of directors. In 1939, appointed first administrator of
the Federal Loan Agency, an office he continued to hold when

appointed Secretary of Commerce in 1940. Increasingly at odds with FDR during the early 1940s, Jones resigned from the RFC and Commerce in January 1945 when FDR wished to appoint Henry A. Wallace to head Commerce, having dropped Wallace from the vice-presidential spot on the 1944 ticket.

K

Keller, Kent Ellsworth (1867–1954). D-IL. House 1931–1941.

Kvale, (Paul) John (1896–1960). Farmer-Laborite-MN. House 1929–1939.

L

LaFollette, Robert Marion Jr. (1895–1953). Progressive Republican-WI. Senate 1925–1947.

LaFollette, Robert Marion Sr. (1865–1925). R-WI. House 1885–1891; Senate 1906–1925. Governor Wisconsin 1901–1906. Progressive Party presidential nominee, 1924

La Guardia, Fiorello Henry (1882–1947). NY. Republican House 1917–1919,1923–1925; Socialist House 1925–1927; Republican Progressive House 1927–1933. Mayor New York City 1934–1945.

Landon, Alfrend Mossman (1887-1987). Governor Kansas 1935-36. Republican candidate for president, 1936. Father of Nancy Landon Kassebaum, R-KS, Senate, 1978-1997.

LeHand, Marguerite "Missy" (1898–1944). Longtime executive secretary to FDR, she worked for the Democratic National Committee in 1920. After his unsuccessful campaign as the party's vice-presidential candidate, FDR hired LeHand. As a result she was among those who worked for him as he recovered from polio. LeHand served as hostess in his Warm Springs Georgia home, a site that Eleanor Roosevelt disliked. LeHand became one of FDR's closest confidants. In 1941 she suffered a stroke that left her an invalid until her death.

Lemke, William (1878–1950). ND. Nonpartison (Republican ticket) 1933–1941; Republican 1943–1950.

Lewis, David John (1869–1952). D-MD. House 1911–1917, 1931–1939.

Lonergan, Augustine (1863–1947). D-CT. House 1913–1915, 1917–1921, 1931–1933; Senate 1933–1939.

Long, Huey Pierce ("The Kingfish") (1893–1935). D-LA. Governor LA 1928–1932. Senate, 1932–1935. Assassinated.

Lundeen, Ernest (1878–1940). MN. Republican House 1917–1919; Farmer-Labor House 1933–1937, Senate 1937–1940.

M

Maas, Melvin Joseph (1898–1964). R-MN. House 1927–1933, 1935–1945.

Manasco, Carter (1902–1992). D-AL House 1941–1949. First Hoover Commission 1947–1949.

Mann, James Robert (1856–1922). R-IL. House 1897–1922 (minority leader 1911–1917).

Marcantonio, Vito (1902–1954). NY. Republican House 1935–1937; American Laborite House 1939–1951.

Maverick, (Fontaine) Maury (1895–1954). D-TX. House 1935–1939.

McCarthy, Joseph Raymond (1908–1957). R-WI. Senate 1947–1957.

McCormack, John William (1891–1980). D-MA. House 1928–1971, majority floor leader 1940–1947, 1949–1953, 1955–1961; minority whip 1947–1949, 1953–1955; Speaker 1962–1971.

McDuffie, John (1883–1950). D-AL. House 1919–1935.

McIntyre, Marvin "Mac" Hunter (1878–1943). Met FDR in 1917 while serving as press relations head for the Navy Department; handled press relations for FDR in the 1920 vice presidential and 1932 presidential campaigns. Served as secretary to FDR in White House until McIntyre's death.

McKellar, Kenneth Douglas (1869–1957). D-TN. House, 1911–1917; Senate 1917–1953, president pro tempore 1945–1947, 1949–1953.

McNary, Charles Linza (1874–1944). R-OR. Senate 1917–1918, 1918–1944, minority leader 1933–1944.

McNutt, Paul V. (1891–1955). Commander of the American Legion 1928; Governor of Indiana 1933–1937. U.S. High Commissioner to the Philippines 1937–1939. Prospective 1940 Democratic candidate for president until FDR announced his candidacy. First U.S. Ambassador to the Philippines 1945–1947.

Mundt, Karl Earl (1900–1974). R-SD. House 1939–1948; Senate 1948–1949, 1954–1973. Chair, House Committee on Un-American Activities that in 1948 investigated Communist infiltration into government. Chair, Senate Army-McCarthy hearing 1954.

N

Norris, George William (1861–1944). R-NB. House 1903–1913; Senate 1913–1943, Independent Republican 1937–1943.

Nye, Gerald Prentice (1892–1971). R-ND. Senate 1925–1945.

O

O'Connor, John Joseph (1885–1960). D-NY. House 1923–1939.

Owen, Robert Latham (1856–1947). D-OK. Senate 1907–1925.

P

Patman, (John William) Wright (1893–1976). D-TX. House 1929–1976.

Pepper, Claude Denson (1900–1989). D-FL. House 1963–1989; Senate 1936–1951.

Pinchot, Gifford (1865–1946). Governor of Pennsylvania 1923–1927 and 1931–1935. The first American professional forester, Pinchot was a leading conservationist and the director, 1898–1910, of what became the Forest Service of the U.S. Department of Agriculture. Performed many public offices while holding faculty rank at Yale University, 1903–1936.

Pope, James Pinekney (1884-1966). D-ID. Senate 1933–1939.

R

Rainey, Henry Thomas (1860–1934). D-IL. House 1903–1921, 1923–1934, Speaker
   1933–1934.

Randolph, A. Philip (1889–1979). Founder and President, Brotherhood of
   Sleeping Car Porters 1925–1968. First African American vice president of
   AFL-CIO, appointed in 1957. Persuaded FDR and Truman to end
   segregation in the defense industry (1941) and the armed services (1948).

Rankin, John E. (1882–1960) D-MS. House 1921–1953. Coauthor of bill to create
   the Tennessee Valley Authority.

Rayburn, Sam Taliaferro (1882–1961). D-TX. House 1913–1961, majority leader
   1937–1941, minority leader 1947–1949, 1953–1955, Speaker 1940–1961.

Richards, James Prioleau (1894–1979). D-SC. House 1933–1957.

Robinson, Joseph (1872–1937). D-AR. House 1903–1913; Senate 1913–1937,
   minority leader 1923–1933, majority leader 1933–1937.

Röhm, Ernst (1887–1934). Sturmabteilung (SA) chief of staff, arrested as part of a
   large-scale assassination operation and shot in his cell on June 30, 1934.

Roosevelt, James (1907–1991). D-CA. House 1955–1965. FDR's son.

S

Schneider, George John (1877–1939). WI. Republican (Progressive) House 1923–
   1933; Progressive 1935–1939.

Scott, Byron Nicholson (1903–1991). D-CA. House 1935–1939.

Sheppard, Morris (1875–1941). D-TX. House 1902–1913; Senate 1913–1941.

Shipstead, Henrik (1881–1960). MN. Senate Farmer-Labor 1923–1940, Republican
   1941–1947.

Shouse, Jouette (1879–1968). D-KS. Senate 1913–1915. House of Representatives
   1915–1919. President of the Liberty League 1934–1940.

Smith, Alfred E. (1873–1944). Democratic Governor of New York 1923–1928. As
   first Catholic to be nominated for president by a major party, Smith lost
   the 1928 election by a record margin to Republican Herbert Hoover.
   Initially, an intermittent ally of FDR, "Al" later was frequently critical of
   his successor as New York Governor.

Smith, Ellison DuRant ("Cotton Ed") (1866–1944). D-SC. Senate 1909–1944.

Smith, Howard Worth (1883–1976). D-VA. House 1931–1967.

Stark, Lloyd Crow (1886–1972). Democratic Governor of Missouri 1937–1941.
   Coowner and manager of Stark Brothers Nurseries. Developed (1913)
   the Stark Delicious Apple, known throughout Missouri and neighboring
   states.

T

Taft, Robert Alphonse (1889–1953). Son of president and Chief Justice of the U.S.
   Supreme Court, William Howard Taft. R-OH Senate 1938–1953. Chief
   competitor to Dwight Eisenhower for the 1952 Republican presidential
   nomination. Known as "Mr. Republican."

Teigan, Henry George (1881–1941). Farmer-Laborite-MN. House 1937–1939.

Thomas, (John William) Elmer (1876–1965). D-OK. House 1923–1927; Senate 1927–1951.

Truman, Harry S. (1884–1972). D-MO. Senate 1935–1945; U.S. vice president January 1945–April 1945; U.S. president 1945–1953; member Committee of Military Affairs, chairman of Special Committee to Investigate National Defense Program during World War II.

Tully, Grace (1900–1984). After ten years as a secretary for the Catholic church, Tully joined the staff of the Democratic National Committee in 1928 where she was assigned to assist Eleanor Roosevelt. When FDR sought the New York governorship, Tully joined the campaign staff and, except for a 1934 bout with tuberculosis remained a member of FDR's secretarial corps until his death. At the White House, she was "Number Two" until Missy LeHand's 1941 stroke elevated Tully to the top post. Tully later was secretary for U.S. Senators Lyndon Johnson and Mike Mansfield.

Tydings, Millard Evelyn (1890–1961). D-MD. House 1923–1927; Senate 1927–1951.

V

Vandenberg, Arthur H. (1884–1951). R-MI. Senate 1928–1951.

Van Nuys, Frederick (1874–1944). D-IN. Senate 1933–1944.

Vinson, Frederick Moore ("Fred") (1890–1953). D-KY. House 1924–1929, 1931–1938; U.S. Secretary of Treasury 1945–1946; Chief Justice U.S. Supreme Court 1946–1953.

W

Wallace, Henry Agard (1888–1965). D-IA. U. S. Secretary of Agriculture 1933–1940; U.S. Vice president 1941–1945; U.S. Secretary of Commerce 1945–1946.

Wearin, Otha Donner (1903–). D-IA. House 1933–1939.

Wheeler, Burton Kendall (1882–1975). D-MT. Senate 1923–1947.

Wilcox, (James) Mark (1890–1956). D-FL. House 1933–1939.

Willkie, Wendall Lewis (1892–1944). Republican candidate for president, 1940.

Withrow, Gardner Robert (1892–1964). WI. Republican House 1931–1935; Progressive 1935–1939; Republican 1949–1961.

Selected Bibliography

Abbott, Philip. *The Exemplary President: Franklin D. Roosevelt and the American Political Tradition*. Amherst: University of Massachusetts, 1990.

Abrams, Carl. *Conservative Constraints: North Carolina and the New Deal*. University: University of Mississippi, 1992.

Badger, Anthony. *New Deal: The Depression Years, 1933–1940*. New York: Hill and Wang, 1989.

Barber, James D. *Presidential Character: Predicting Performance in the White House*. 4th ed. Englewood Cliffs, NJ: Prentice-Hall, 1992.

Barber, William J. *Designs Within Disorder: Franklin D. Roosevelt, the Economists, and the Shaping of American Economic Policy, 1933–1945*. New York: Cambridge University, 1996.

Best, Gary D. *Pride, Prejudice and Politics: Roosevelt Versus Recovery, 1933–1938*. Westport, CT: Greenwood Press, 1990.

————. *The Critical Press and the New Deal: The Press Versus Presidential Power, 1933–1938*. Westport, CT: Greenwood, 1993.

Biles, Roger A. *The South and the New Deal*. Lexington: University Press of Kentucky, 1994.

Biolgi, Thomas. *Organizing the Lakota: The Political Economy of the New Deal on Pine Ridge and Rosebud Reservations*. Tucson: University of Arizona, 1992.

Black, Alida M. *Casting Her Own Shadow: Eleanor Roosevelt and the Shaping of Postwar Liberalism*. New York: Columbia University, 1996.

Black, Alida M., ed. *What I Hope to Leave Behind: The Essential Essays of Eleanor Roosevelt*. Brooklyn, NY: Carlson Publishing, 1995.

Brinkley, Alan. *The Transformation of New Deal Liberalism*. New York: Alfred A. Knopf, 1995.

Brock, William R. *Welfare, Democracy and the New Deal*. New York: Cambridge University, 1988.

Buhite, Russell D. and David W. Levy, eds. *FDR's Fireside Chats*. Norman: University of Oklahoma, 1992.

Burns, James M. *Leadership*. New York: Harper and Row, 1982.

Cannon, Brian Q. *Remaking the Agrarian Dream: New Deal Rural Resettlement in the Mountain West*. Albuquerque: University of New Mexico, 1996.

Clarke, Jeanne N. *Roosevelt's Warrior: Harold L. Ickes and the New Deal*. Baltimore: Johns Hopkins University, 1996.

Clawson, Marion. *New Deal Planning: The National Resources Planning Board*. Baltimore: Johns Hopkins University, 1981.

Cohen, Lizabeth. *Making a New Deal: Industrial Workers in Chicago, 1919–1939*. New York: Cambridge University, 1991.

Cohen, Wilbur J., ed. *The New Deal Fifty Years After: A Historical Assessment*. Austin: University of Texas, 1984.

Cook, Blanche W. *Eleanor Roosevelt*. New York: Viking Penguin, 1993.

Curtis, Sandra R. *Alice and Eleanor: A Contrast in Style and Purpose*. Bowling Green, OH: Bowling Green State University, 1994.

Dallek, Robert. *Franklin D. Roosevelt and American Foreign Policy, 1932–1945*. New York: Oxford University, 1995.

Davis, Kenneth S. *FDR: The New Deal Years, 1933–1937*. New York: Random House, 1986.

Dickinson, Matthew J. *Bitter Harvest: FDR, Presidential Power and the Growth of the Presidential Branch*. New York: Cambridge University, 1997.

Dubofsky, Melvyn, ed. *The New Deal: Conflicting Interpretations and Shifting Perspectives*. New York: Garland, 1992.

Eden, Robert T., ed. *The New Deal and Its Legacy: Critique and Reappraisal*. Westport, CT: Greenwood, 1989.

Edens, John A. *Eleanor Roosevelt: A Comprehensive Bibliography*. Westport, CT: Greenwood, 1994.

Finegold, Kenneth and Theda Skolpol. *State, Party and Policy: Industry and Agriculture in America's New Deal*. Madison: University of Wisconsin, 1995.

Freidel, Frank, *Franklin D. Roosevelt: A Rendezvous with Destiny*. New York: Little, 1990.

Goodwin, Doris K. *No Ordinary Time: Franklin and Eleanor Roosevelt. The Home Front in World War II*. New York: Simon and Schuster, 1994.

Gordon, Colin. *New Deals: Business, Labor, and Politics in America, 1920–1935*. New York: Cambridge University, 1994.

Graham, Otis L., and Megan R. Wancker, eds. *Franklin D. Roosevelt, His Life and Times: An Encyclopedic View*. New York: Macmillan, 1985.

Hawkins, Helen S. *A New Deal for the Newcomer: The Federal Transient Service*. New York: Garland, 1991.

Hawley, Ellis W. *The New Deal and the Problem of Monopoly: A Study in Economic Ambivalence*. Bronx, NY: Fordham University, 1995.

Hershan, Stella K. *The Candles She Lit: The Legacy of Eleanor Roosevelt*. Westport, CT: Greenwood, 1993.

Himmelberg, Robert F. *The New Deal and Corporate Power: Antitrust and Regulatory Policies During the Thirties and World War II*. New York: Garland, 1994.

Hodges, James A. *New Deal Policy and the Southern Cotton Textile Industry, 1933–1941*. Knoxville: University of Tennessee, 1986.

Hosen, Frederick E. *The Great Depression and the New Deal: Legislative Acts in Their Entirety (1932–1933) and Statistical Economic Data (1926–1946)*. Jefferson, NC: McFarland, 1992.

Langston, Thomas S. *Ideologues and Presidents: From the New Deal to the Reagan Revolution*. Baltimore: Johns Hopkins University, 1992.

Leader, Leonard J. *Los Angeles and the Great Depression*. New York: Garland, 1991.

Lester, DeeGee. *Roosevelt Research: Collections for the Study of Theodore, Franklin and Eleanor*. Westport, CT: Greenwood, 1992.

Leuchtenberg, William E. *In the Shadow of FDR: From Harry Truman to Bill Clinton*. Ithaca, NY: Cornell University, 1993.

Levine, Rhonda F. *Class Struggle and the New Deal: Industrial Labor, Industrial Capital and the State*. Lawrence: University of Kansas, 1988.

Lorence, James J. *Organizing the Unemployed: Community and Union Activists in the Industrial Heartland*. Albany: State University of New York, 1996.

————. *Gerald J. Boileau and the Progressive-Farmer-Labor Alliance: Politics of the New Deal*. Columbia: University of Missouri, 1994.

Lowitt, Richard. *The New Deal and the West*. Norman: University of Oklahoma, 1993.

Lyon, Edwin A. *A New Deal for Southeastern Archeology*. Tuscaloosa: University of Alabama, 1996.

Maney, Patrick J. *The Roosevelt Presence: A Bibliography of Franklin Delano Roosevelt*. New York: Twayne, 1992.

Martin-Perdue, Nancy J. and Charles L. Perdue Jr. *Talk About Trouble: A New Deal Portrait of Virginians in the Great Depression*. Chapel Hill: University of North Carolina, 1996.

Mink, Gwendolyn. *The Wages of Motherhood: Inequality in the Welfare State, 1917–1942*. Ithaca, NY: Cornell University, 1995.

Mitchell, Broadus. *The Depression Decade: From New Era Through New Deal, 1929–1941*. New York: M. E. Sharpe, 1997.

Nelson, Paula M. *The Prairie Winnows Out Its Own: The West River Country of South Dakota in the Years of Depression and Dust*. Iowa City: University of Iowa, 1996.

Nixon, Edgar B., compiler. *Franklin D. Roosevelt and Conservation, 1911–1945*. 2 vols. Washington, DC: Government Printing Office, 1957.

Nordin, Dennis. *New Deal's Black Congressman: A Life of Arthur Wergs Mitchell*. Columbia: University of Missouri, 1997.

Ohl, John K. *Hugh S. Johnson and the New Deal*. DeKalb: Northern Illinois University, 1985.

Olson, James S., ed. *Historical Dictionary of the New Deal: From Inauguration to Preparation for War*. Westport, CT: Greenwood, 1985.

Pederson, William D. *The "Barberian" Presidency*. New York: Peter Lang, 1989.

Pederson, William D. and Ann M. McLaurin. *The Rating Game in American Politics*. New York: Irvington, 1987.

Radford, Gail. *Modern Housing for America: Policy Struggles in the New Deal Era*. Chicago: University of Chicago, 1996.

Reiman, Richard A. *The New Deal and American Youth: Ideas and Ideals in a Depression Decade*. Athens: University of Georgia, 1992.

Riccards, Michael P. *The Ferocious Engine of Democracy: The American Presidency from 1789 to 1989*. Lanham, MD: Rowman and Littlefield, 1995.

Rosenhof, Theodore. *Economics in the Long Run: New Deal Theorists and Their Legacies, 1933–1993*. Chapel Hill: University of North Carolina, 1977.

Rosenbaum, Herbert D. and Elizabeth Bartelme, eds. *Franklin D. Roosevelt: The Man, the Myth, the Era, 1882–1945*. Westport, CT: Greenwood, 1987.

Rozell, Mark J. and William D. Pederson, eds. *FDR and the Modern Presidency*. Westport, CT: Praeger, 1997.

Rozwenc, Edwin C. *The New Deal: Revolution or Evolution?* Boston: D.C. Heath, 1949.

Ryan, Halford R. *Franklin Roosevelt's Rhetorical Presidency*. Westport, CT: Greenwood, 1988.

Savage, Sean J. *Roosevelt: The Party Leader, 1932–1945*. Lexington: University Press of Kentucky, 1991.

Sears, John F., ed. *Franklin D. Roosevelt and the Future of Liberalism*. Westport, CT: Greenwood, 1990.

Schayler, Michael W. *The Dread of Plenty: Agricultural Relief Activities of the Federal Government in the Middle West, 1933–1939*. Manhattan, KS: Sunflower University, 1989.

Schwarz, Jordan A. *New Dealers*. New York: Random House, 1994.

Schlesinger, Arthur M., Jr. *The Age of Roosevelt: The Politics of Upheaval*. Boston: Houghton-Mifflin Company, 1960.

Sealander, Judith. *Private Wealth and Public Life: Foundation Philanthropy and the Reshaping of American Social Policy from the Progressive Era to the New Deal*. Baltimore: Johns Hopkins University, 1977.

Sitkoff, Harvard. *Fifty Years Later: The New Deal Evaluated*. New York: Alfred A. Knopf, 1985.

Smith, Douglas L. *The New Deal in the Urban South*. Baton Rouge: Louisiana State University, 1988.

Sullivan, Patricia. *Days of Hope: Race and Democracy in the New Deal Era*. Chapel Hill: University of North Carolina, 1996.

Swain, Martha H. and Ellen S. Woodward. *New Deal Advocate for Women*. University: University of Mississippi, 1995.

Tatalovich, Raymond and Byron W. Daynes. *Presidential Power in the United States*. Monterey, CA: Brooks/Cole, 1984.

Tobey, Ronald C. *Technology as Freedom: The New Deal and the Electrical Modernization of the American Home*. Berkeley: University of California, 1996.

Tugwell, Rexford G. *In Search of Roosevelt*. Cambridge: Harvard University, 1992.

Tynes, Sheryl R. *Turning Points in Social Security: From "Cruel Hoax" to "Sacred Entitlement"*. Stanford: Stanford University, 1996.

Underhill, Robert. *FDR and Harry: Unparalleled Lives*. Westport, CT: Praeger, 1996.

Vittoz, Stanley. *New Deal Labor Policy and the American Industrial Economy.* Chapel Hill: University of North Carolina, 1987.

Ward, Geoffrey C. *Before the Trumpet: The Young Franklin Roosevelt.* New York: Smithmark, 1994.

———. *Closest Companion: A Love Story: An Account of the Remarkable Friendship of Franklin D. Roosevelt and Margaret Suckley.* Boston: Houghton Mifflin, 1995.

Watkins, Tom H. *The Great Depression: America in the 1930s.* New York: Little Brown, 1993.

Weber, Devra. *Dark Sweat, White Gold: California Farm Workers, Cotton, and the New Deal.* Berkeley: University of California, 1996.

Weed, Clyde P. *The Nemesis of Reform: The Republican Party During the New Deal.* New York: Columbia University, 1994.

Weisiger, Marsha L. *Land of Plenty: Oklahomans in the Cotton Fields of Arizona, 1933–1942.* Norman: The University Press of Oklahoma, 1995.

Weisenberger, Carol A. *Dollars and Dreams: The National Youth Administration in Texas.* New York: Peter Lang, 1994.

Weiss, Stuart L. *The President's Man: Leo Crowley and Franklin Roosevelt in Peace and War.* Carbondale: Southern Illinois University, 1996.

Whayne, Jeannie M. *A New Plantation South: Land, Labor and Federal Favor in Twentieth-Century Arkansas.* Charlottesville: University Press of Virginia, 1996.

Winfield, Betty H. *FDR and the New Media.* New York: Columbia University, 1991.

Contributors

Michael P. Barrett, J.D., M.P.A., University of Missouri at Kansas City, a former Hy Vile Scholar, Truman Foundation, is with the office of the Inspector General, U.S. Department of Health and Human Services.

Anthony Champagne, Ph.D., University of Illinois, is Professor of Government and Politics at the University of Texas at Dallas. He has published two books about Sam Rayburn and interviewed over 130 associates of Rayburn. He is currently writing a book about John Nance Garner.

Matthew Ware Coulter, Ph.D., University of North Texas, is Professor of History at Collin County Community College, Plano, Texas. His scholarly specialties are the presidency of Franklin D. Roosevelt, learning in higher education, and the 1930s East Texas oil industry.

Byron W. Daynes, Ph.D., University of Chicago, is Professor of Political Science at Brigham Young University. He has written extensively on the American presidency.

Marc Dollinger, Ph.D., University of California at Los Angeles, is Assistant Professor of History at Pasadena City College. He has conducted extensive research on American Jews.

Karl F. Johnson, Ph.D., University of Oregon, is Professor of Public Administration, Cookingham Institute of Public Affairs, University of Missouri–Kansas City. His research interests are public policy development, urban politics, and evaluation research.

Joseph Edward Lee, Ph.D., University of South Carolina, is Professor of History at Winthrop University. His research focuses on recent American history, including that of investigative reporting, published as *The New Muckrakers*, and the end of the Vietnam War, published as *White Christmas in April*.

Richard Lowitt, Ph.D., Columbia University, is Emeritus Professor of History at the University of Oklahoma. His scholarly work is primarily in the American West and recent U. S. history. His publications include the biographies, *George Norris* (1963, 1971, 1978) and *Bronson Cutting* (1992).

Stefano Luconi, Ph.D., Third University of Rome, is a postdoctoral Research Fellow in Contemporary History in the Department of History at the University of Florence. His current research is on the political mobilization of Italian Americans in Pennsylvania between the world wars.

Dennis N. Mihelich, Ph.D., Case Western Reserve University, is Associate Professor of History at Creighton University. His specialty is modern American history. His publications focus on Nebraska history and business history.

William D. Pederson, Ph.D. University of Oregon, is Professor of Political Science and Director, American Studies Program, at Louisiana State University in Shreveport. His publications are principally about the American presidency. He has organized conferences at LSU in Shreveport on specific presidents.

Arthur R. Williams, Ph.D., Cornell University, is Professor of Public Administration, Cookingham Institute of Public Affairs, Henry W. Bloch School of Business and Public Administration, University of Missouri-Kansas City. He has served as a consultant to the Philippine government and written on the Lincoln, McKinley, Taft, and Truman administrations. His particular interest is presidential decision making.

Thomas Phillip Wolf, Ph.D., Stanford University, is Professor Emeritus of Political Science and former Dean of Social Sciences at Indiana University Southeast. He serves as newsletter editor of the British Politics Group . His scholarly research has focused on the American presidency, American and British political parties, and political leadership.

Nancy Beck Young, Ph.D., University of Texas at Austin, is Associate Professor of History at McKendree College. Her primary research interest is twentieth century politics and women. She is the coauthor of *Texas, Her Texas: The Life and Times of Frances Goff*, and is completing a book on Wright Patman, about whom she has published several articles.

Index

A

Acheson, Dean, 141
Addams, Jane, 27
Adler, Selig, 28
Agricultural Adjustment Administration (AAA), 45
Allen, Robert, 20
American Jewish Committee, 38, 39, 40, 50
American Jewish Congress, 38
American Legion, 80, 85-87, 102
The American Party Battle, 122
Amlie, Thomas R., 15, 21
An American Dilemma, 137
Appeal to Reason, 16

B

B'nai B'rith, 43
B'nai B'rith Messenger, 45
Bailey, Joseph Weldon, 62
Bailey, Josiah, 149
Bailey, Stephen K., 136-138, 145-146, 152
Bankerteering, Bonuseering, Melloneering, 85
Bankhead, William, 64-65, 73, 150
Banking and Currency Committee, 90
Barbour, W. Warren, 26
Barkley, Alben, 32, 113-114
Baruch, Bernard, 30
Bast, William, 118
Beard, Charles A., 8, 122
Belgrano, Frank N., Jr., 85
Bender, George, 139
Berman, William, 152
Bernard, John Toussant, 16
Bernstein, Barton, 141
Beveridge Report, 142
Binderup, Charles G., 89
Bingham, Alfred, 17
Black, Hugo, 113
Blaine, John J., 7

N

National Broadcasting Company (NBC), 68, 82
National Conference of Jewish Social Services, 44, 50
National Council of Jewish Education, 51
National Industrial Expansion Act, 20
National Recovery Act, 126
National Recovery Administration (NRA), 45
National Resources Planning Board (NRPB), 135, 138
National Union for Social Justice, 88
Neustadt, Richard, 139
Neutrality Act (1935), 31
Neutrality Act (1941), 4, 98, 101
New Deal, 2-5, 9-10, 13-15, 17, 19-21, 27, 29-30, 39-41, 44-46, 52, 63-64, 72,
    80, 87, 98, 110, 122-123, 125-130, 135-137, 140-142, 152
The New Deal and the States, 151
Niebuhr, Reinhold, 27
Nixon, Richard M., 124, 127
Norquist, Grover, 129
Norris, George W., 7-11, 13, 72
Nye Committee, 3, 26-34
Nye, Gerald P., 3, 7, 10, 26-34

O

O'Connor, Basil, 64, 112
O'Connor, John J., 64-65, 110, 12, 118
Odum, Howard, 147
Owen, Robert L., 90

P

Paterson, Thomas, 101
Patman, Wright, 4, 79-91, 138
Patman's Appeal to Pay Veterans, 85
Patterson, James T., 149-152
Peiser, Kurt, 50
Pendergast connection, 141, 144
Pepper, Claude, 113
Phillips, Kevin, 124, 128
Pinchot, Gifford, 44
Politics, Parties, and Pressure Groups, 123
Pope, James, 26
Populism, 14
Progressive National Committee, 11
Progressive Open Forum Discussion Group, 14, 16
Progressive Party, 8, 15

Progressives, 2, 7, 13
Progressivism, 14
Prosperity Through Employment, 20
Public Law 304 (See also Employment Act [1946]), 139, 142
Public Utility Holding Act (see Utility Holding Company Act)
Purge of 1938, 4, 5, 21, 65, 108-119, 147

Q
"Quarantine the Aggressor" speech, 33-34

R
Radical Religion, 27
Rainey, Henry Thomas, 73
Randolph, A. Philip, 146
Rankin, John, 139, 150
Rauch, Basil, 123
Rauschenbusch, Walter, 27
Raushenbush, Stephen, 27
Rayburn, Sam, 4, 62-74, 79, 88, 100, 103
Reagan, Ronald, 125, 128
Reciprocal Trades Agreement Bill, 12
Reconstruction Finance Corporation, 21
Red River Project (see also Denison Dam), 66, 70
Richards, James P., 4, 98-104
Riker, William, 119
Rizzo, Frank, 124
Robinson, Joseph, 32
Rogers, Will, 27
Röhm, Ernst, 109
Roosevelt, Eleanor, 116
Roosevelt, Franklin Delano, 1-5, 7-15, 17, 19-20, 28-34, 39, 44-47, 52, 62-74, 79,
83-84, 87, 98-99, 101-103, 109-119, 122-130, 135-137, 140-141, 148-150, 153
Roosevelt, James, 64, 74, 106
Roosevelt, Theodore, 8, 141
Rosen, Ben, 42
Rosenman, Samuel, 33
Rubinow, Isaac, 38, 43, 45
Rural Electrification Administration (REA), 72
Russell, Richard, 150

S
Sapper, Harry J., 50
Savage, Sean, 114, 140
Schnattschneider, E. E., 114